Etiquette

SUNY series, Hot Topics: Contemporary Philosophy and Culture
Ron Scapp and Brian Seitz, editors

Etiquette

Reflections on Contemporary Comportment

Edited by
Ron Scapp
Brian Seitz

State University of New York Press

Published by
State University of New York Press, Albany

Printed in the United States of America

For information, address State University of New York Press,
194 Washington Avenue, Suite 305, Albany, NY 12210-2384

Production by Marilyn P. Semerad
Marketing by Fran Keneston

Library of Congress Cataloging-in-Publication Data

Etiquette : reflections on contemporary comportment / edited by Ron Scapp, Brian Seitz.
p. cm. — (SUNY series, hot topics)
Includes bibliographical references and index.
ISBN-13: 978-0-7914-6935-4 (hardcover : alk. paper)
ISBN-10: 0-7914-6935-2 (hardcover : alk. paper)
ISBN-13: 978-0-7914-6936-1 (pbk. : alk. paper)
ISBN-10: 0-7914-6936-0 (pbk. : alk. paper)
1. Etiquette. I. Scapp, Ron, 1955– II. Seitz, Brian, 1954– III. Series.

BJ1853.E85 2007
395—dc22 2006001205

10 9 8 7 6 5 4 3 2 1

In loving memory of
Michel Foucault & Immanuel Kant

Contents

INTRODUCTION

On Being Becoming

Ron Scapp and Brian Seitz

Book 1 of Marcus Aurelius's *Meditations* is a series of acknowledgements of gratitude for the specific gifts provided to the philosopher king by his family, his teachers, his friends, and even the gods themselves. As such, it could be seen as a simple literary device, a poetic conceit akin to the classical use of a dedication. Yet in this case, this particular formality embodies the rich dynamics of etiquette itself, and indicates the profound sense in which manners, mere gestures, can provide an armature for living ethically. For example, Marcus writes, "From Alexander the Platonist; not to say to anyone often or without necessity, nor write in a letter, *I am too busy*, nor in this fashion constantly plead urgent affairs as an excuse for evading the obligations entailed upon us by our relations towards those around us."[1] For Marcus, being rude, then, has an existential significance, one that implicates surfaces—in this case, *bad appearances*—within the depths of ethical complexity. In so doing, Marcus declares himself part of a renegade tradition that has dwelt within Western philosophy from its inception (what some might consider philosophy's shadow). This is the tradition that resists the temptation to baldly insist that appearance is one thing and reality another (a Platonist opens the thought here!), a tradition also inclined to equate ethics with aesthetics, living well with living beautifully and gracefully.

Etiquette, the field of multifarious prescriptions governing comportment in life's interactions, has been generally neglected by philosophers, who may be inclined to dismiss it as trivial, most specifically in contrast with ethics, which is where philosophers find the substantive issues. In its devotion to codes of behavior, etiquette may be a superficial extension of morals, but it seems far removed from serious ethical issues. Ethics is taken to be the site of life's real conflicts, while etiquette remains trapped within the shallow realm of mere appearance. Aiming toward coherence, and at least a provisional terminus, ethical inquiry offers the prospect of a comprehensive theory or stable set of principles. However, the disparate and apparently arbitrary codes of etiquette seem to confirm their inevitable relativism right on the surface, thereby circumventing hope for a serious theory from the outset, condemning analysis to endless fragmentation and indeterminate particularity. In short, while ethics offers principles, etiquette provides only precepts. This is the way the hierarchical relationship between them tends to get established. It is not our desire simply to reverse this hierarchy (an act that one might argue would only preserve it). Although we might seem to be engaged in a reversal, our ambitions are something different, since we want to upset things in order to preserve understanding, to move back in order to move ahead in exploring the outward practices that facilitate our capacity to live with each other, the practices that determine the difference between the appropriate and the offensive.

Philosophy has tended to grant absolute privilege to ethics over etiquette, placing the former alongside all of the traditional values favored by metaphysics (order, truth, rationality, mind, masculinity, depth, reality), while consigning the latter to metaphysics' familiar, divisive list of hazards and rejects (arbitrariness, mere opinion, irrationality, the body, femininity, surface, appearance). Ethics has been viewed as the principled foundation of the moral structures that pertain to life's real conflicts, leaving ethics' diminutive shadow, etiquette, to be relegated to the endlessly arbitrary sets of conventional codes that shape the superficial world of manners, a place to turn, perhaps, for advice on what to wear to a wedding or a funeral, but hardly a source for counsel on matters of life and death.

This book intends to challenge these traditional values, not in order to favor etiquette over ethics—not, as we have already said, simply to turn the tables—but to explore the various ways in which practice comes before theory, in which manners are morals, or as Mary

Wollstonecraft put it, "Manners and morals are so nearly allied that they have often been confounded."[2] To be blunt (but, we hope, not offensive), etiquette prefigures ethics, and ethics, the practice of living a good life, has always depended on the graceful relations for which etiquette provides a ticket to enter the domain of sociability.

Thus, the common starting point of all of the various elements comprising this book is a certain imperative, an insistence that etiquette must be addressed as something more than and other than just a diminutive form of ethics. An alternative, less metaphysical (less hierarchizing) reading may open up the possibility that in all of its superficiality, etiquette has substance for theoretical purchase, too, a substance worth cultivating in its own right, an enterprise that may in fact also have ramifications for ethics.

To begin with, the cosmetic codes provided by etiquette profoundly affect the functional organization of specific spheres of human activity and interactivity. Etiquette is, therefore, vital, in all senses of this powerful word. Simply consider the significance of greetings. The style in which one says "hello," in any language, may initiate patterns of inclusion and exclusion, distance and intimacy, as we negotiate all of the names we have for each other, whether names of respect or of flattery, names of love and of optimistic expectations, hospitable names, the names by which we address our hosts, names of disdain or derision, even the insults we hurl at those who have offended us. Consider, too, the ramifications of a faux pas, such as the awkward forgetting of someone's name. What tends to get dismissed as mere manners shapes the contours and borders of particular domains of existence, and cannot be skimmed off the surface by theory without falsifying the nature of the life in question.

This book considers the possibility that ethics relies on etiquette in ways previously ignored or underestimated by most philosophy. But one might ask whether such a consideration is really likely to make much headway. For us, this sort of move would only be a transitional maneuver, a transition that might lead to a new understanding of not only etiquette but also of the experience of ethics. The general assumption of the contents of this volume is that etiquette matters.

"Tact is a brief and modest word," writes Alphonso Lingis, "but it designates the right way to speak or to be silent before our adolescent child in his anguish and before the excitement of two people in the nursing home who have fallen in love."[3] The chapters in this book aim to engage anguish and love on this side of the hypothetical, as the collective contents of the volume categorically constitute an exercise in eidetic variation on what Foucault thought of as the art of living well.

What does "living well" mean in this context? Contemplate the following familiar images, breaches, conflicts, imperatives, and notes of generosity and rudeness, all of which seem unavoidably to refer, oddly enough, to something like a universal. What makes you take offense? Some things do.

Automobile protocol, for instance, is not just about vehicular formalities. Consider the moment when lanes must merge. Consider what it means to "take turns" here, and the way people respond to jerks who rudely cut in line (maybe you are one of these jerks). The breach constituting "cutting in line" here has little to do with morality, but everything to do with patience and generosity, and therefore with a common understanding of what needs to be done, or, more precisely, should be done. Driving etiquette expresses the sense in which we can work together, because we must in order to make progress.

But rude behavior can be ameliorated: things set straight. The phrases "excuse me" or "I'm sorry" can compensate immediately for inadvertent clumsiness or negligence; timing, too, then is crucial, since apologies delayed are often apologies not genuinely offered . . . nor accepted.

When is it okay to eat in public? Picnic, okay. But in a bus or a subway it is always bad manners, bound to elicit glares of various forms—including jealousy—even though it is otherwise normally rude to stare (but then, of course, staring is quite different from glaring). Here, bad form is bad aesthetic; eating in the wrong situation is simply ugly. Appropriate or acceptable behavior clearly contrasts with a juridically conceived understanding of right and wrong. In short, in this situation, it is impolite to eat when others cannot.

And what about sexual etiquette? For instance, keeping track of when, where, with whom, and how many times is surely not an ethical question. That it matters, however, is a positive indication of the significance of etiquette, which in this case has to do with taking care of the other and the way the other feels, taking care, too, of oneself.

So somewhere between aesthetics and ethics is the philosophically significant domain of etiquette, which links the two, and ensures that the line between them is often difficult to discern. And this ambiguity may be more important to some cultures than to others. For example,

William Fenton writes, "There is a principle that students of the Iroquois must inevitably learn: the way a thing is done is often more important than the issue at stake."[4] Who says what, in what order? On some occasions, such protocol makes all of the difference. Who gets served first and last? Men? Women? Children? These are questions that really matter, sometimes maybe even more than proper moral issues, as Thorstein Veblen intimated when he wrote, "A breach of faith may be condoned, but a breach of decorum can not. 'Manners maketh man.' "[5]

Of course, there is also the utter indeterminacy and disorientation of those moments lost beyond meaning precisely because etiquette can find no purchase, moments when the architectonic of cordiality, civility, and consideration are rendered inoperative, that is, when people just don't care. It is perhaps only at times of such absence, of such lack, that etiquette is understood in its full social and political, that is to say, material merit (just like Heidegger's broken hammer).

Some, therefore, might want to consider etiquette as ritual—ritual that binds, ritual that heals, ritual that sustains human interactions locally and globally. Tempting as this thought may be, we want to resist the desire to restrict etiquette to a question of formulaic or enforced codes. As Aristotle understood, good habits—and thus good manners—are gestures of grace beyond measure rather than of conformity to law as such, something truly fine. The practice of etiquette is not, finally, about mere compliance to external rules or static imperatives.

As the chapters in this volume suggest, etiquette is about the execution and performance of those opportunities for consideration of the other, whether stranger or friend, that emerge in everyday lived experience. Etiquette duly acknowledges the existence and necessity of boundaries while negotiating, respectfully traversing, and even transforming the conditions that allow one to become presentable, and thus allow one to extend oneself to the world, as we extend ourselves to you.

Notes

1. Marcus Aurelius, *Meditations*, ed. and trans. C. R. Haines (Cambridge: Harvard University Press, 1994), p. 11.

2. Mary Wollstonecraft, *Vindication of the Rights of Woman* (New York: Norton, 1988), p. 4.

3. Alphonso Lingis, *The Imperative* (Bloomington: Indiana University Press, 1998), p. 2.

4. William N. Fenton, *The Great Law and the Longhouse: A Political History of the Iroquois Confederacy* (Norman: University of Oklahoma Press, 1998), p. 493.

5. Thorstein Veblen, *The Theory of the Leisure Class* (New York: Dover, 1994), p. 42.

CHAPTER ONE

Aristotle's Aesthetiquette

NICKOLAS PAPPAS

Aristotelian Virtues of Sociability

The virtues of social intercourse that Aristotle surveys in *Nicomachean Ethics* IV.6–8 come close to capturing that mix of finesse and seriousness that characterize etiquette.

When Aristotle identifies "friendliness" (he admits that term is misleading) as the mean between obsequiousness and churlishness (*Nicomachean Ethics* [*EN*] 1126b10ff.), he has named one of the principles of polite behavior that modern moralism would mark off as not fully ethical. Moralists will let you be churlish, and they probably won't even object to your obsequy if it is not strategically fraudulent. They would call these matters of personality and not of character.

In the same part of the *Ethics* Aristotle speaks of "truthfulness"—again this is a virtue with no ordinary name (1127a14)—as the mean between boastfulness and false modesty. There is less to this virtue than meets the eye: "We are not speaking of the one who is true to his word about contracts, nor in things pertaining to justice or injustice (this would belong to another virtue), but of the man who is honest both in word and in living when it makes no difference, [simply] because he is that kind of person" (1127a32ff). As "friendliness" fell short of friendship by dint of its failure to contain affection (*EN* 1126b21ff.), truthfulness amounts to only one dimension of full honesty, given that it makes no difference, nothing is at stake (*mêden diapherei*).

The third field of social behavior is amusement, fun (*diagôgê, EN* IV.8). Entertainment is a natural part of life, says Aristotle (1127b34). People amuse themselves and each other: the buffoon too much, doing anything for a laugh; the boor, who refuses to be amused, too little; the man of ready wit to just the right degree. That third type of man makes proper jokes, responding nimbly to a risible situation but remaining tactful about it, and laughs only at the jokes that are worth laughing at.

Aristotelian Etiquette?

Somewhat as "magnificence" does (that mean between vulgarity and stinginess with respect to spending money, *EN* IV.2), friendliness and a ready wit and truthfulness about oneself stand apart from the major virtues.

You honor these virtues on the assumption that you want to mingle with company, which is not a thing Aristotle would say about justice or temperance. Moreover, friendliness and ready wit are matters of pleasure, occupying places in between pleasing too much and not pleasing enough. This is the pleasure of human company, which is to say that sociability is pursued for its own sake. In this respect the domain of social intercourse is again the domain of etiquette. Social virtues hardly have any purpose or significance above and beyond the mutual pleasure found in social intercourse, except for suggesting what someone's character is like (1127b2ff., 1128a17ff.). But that's what you would also say about etiquette.

Aristotle plays down the virtues of social intercourse. For instance, though he warns that many states of character have no name (*EN* 1107b2, 1107b29, 1108a5, 1115b25, 1119a10), it is normally an excess or deficiency of some motivation that lacks a name, not the mean. But in the social domain two of the three virtues treated are nameless, as if one rarely had occasion to praise those traits. These seem to be smaller virtues, as etiquette is thought of as smaller in stature than ethics.

When it comes to amusement, Aristotle nearly apologizes for including the subject in his moral theory. He begins with a reminder that life includes rest as well as activity (1127b34) and concludes with the same plea for the subject's inclusion (1128b3). Later in the *Ethics* (X.6) he will sound less tolerant, frowning away the suggestion that happiness might be a matter of fun (1176b8–1177a11). He was willing to talk about leisure and entertainment, but only as long as they stayed in their place.

Etiquette without Rules

Aristotle does not offer the specific advice you might associate with etiquette. *EN* IV.6–8 never mention nuances of protocol, carefully evacuated rituals like the exchange of the question "How do you do?" and its answer ("How do *you* do?") upon introduction. What kind of etiquette can he talk about without rules that guide courteous intentions to concrete acts of courtesy?

This worry is misplaced. Aristotle's virtue theory as a whole, with a few remarkable exceptions, also lacks such rules. Aristotle will specify the difference between the courage of a citizen-soldier, a professional soldier, and a drunk (III.8), but not the exact times that it is better to fight than run, nor the difference between real and apparent dangers. One ought to get angry on the right occasions, at the right people, and to the right degree, but Aristotle offers no formula for identifying these right moves and denies that anyone can (IV.5). His ethics is a moral psychology, not a catechism; likewise his etiquette.

Comedy and the Social Virtues

Aristotle's etiquette leads him into literary criticism. He drops a judgment about comic genres into his discussion of tactful jokes: "The joking of an acculturated man differs from that of the unacculturated. One can see this in old and new comedies: to the authors of the former the funny thing was obscenity, but to the authors of the latter it is innuendo that is funnier" (*EN* IV.8 1128a20–24). One comic genre improves on another by exhibiting more propriety.

This *Ethics* passage squares with fuller accounts of comedy's evolution that Aristotle gives elsewhere. The *Poetics*, for one, locates the origin of comedy in the invective or lampoon, out of which comic drama grew in the direction of something "greater and more respectable," very much as tragedy grew from epic (*Poetics* 1449a1ff.).

And it is possible to spell out what made comedy respectable. Richard Janko has argued persuasively that the medieval Greek manuscript known as the *Tractatus Coislinianus* (*TC*) is a condensation of the lost second book of the *Poetics*, on comedy.[1] And the *Tractatus* distinguishes comedy from abuse—marking comedy off as superior by reason of this difference—as a genre that suggests the laughable qualities of people instead of naming them.[2]

In other words, comedy in general improves on abuse, as the *Ethics* says that recent comedy improves on its older form, that is, as the tactful wit improves on the buffoon. The evolution of comedy, which for Aristotle means its progress toward a perfected state (see *Poetics* 1449a15 on the progress of tragedy and *Politics* 1252b32 on natural growth in general), consists in an improvement in its manners from raillery to dig.

The *Tractatus Coislinianus* too speaks of older and newer comedies, and brings the *Ethics* to mind when it does: "[The kinds] of comedy are (a) old, which goes to excess in the laughable; (b) new, which abandons this, and inclines toward the grand; and (c) middle, which is mixed from both" (*TC* 18).[3] It does not matter precisely what the *Tractatus* means by "old comedy" (almost certainly not what that phrase means today), as long as old comedy is the same thing here as in *EN* IV.8, namely the genre abandoned to the dustbin of literary history for its rudeness.

The Etiquette of Comedy

In another sense all comedy, old and new, has rudeness for its subject.

The *Poetics* says that comedy's characters are worse than real human beings and a fortiori worse than comedy's spectators (1448a17)—not worse with respect to every trait, but only in those ways that make the characters funny. What is laughable, says Aristotle, is the kind of ugliness that causes no pain (1449a32–35), which is to say minor moral failure.

The *Tractatus Coislinianus* explains comic ugliness. The characters that comedy depicts are the buffoon, the ironist, and the braggart (*TC* 12). Notice that these are all traits that *EN* II.7 has called excessive: irony for its untruthful understatement and the brag for its untruthful exaggeration, buffoonery in its intemperate pursuit of the pleasure of amusement (1108a21–24). They are the vices characteristic of social intercourse (etiquette), which in the first place confirms the relative unimportance of that domain from a moralistic perspective (since you can fail at such virtues without becoming worse than just morally ugly), and in the second place ties Aristotelian etiquette once again to critical judgments about an art form.

The point is not to make every assessment of poetry a matter of etiquette. Aristotle's overarching defense of tragedy has its roots in ethical doctrines as fundamental as his definition of happiness. The relevant question here is not the (ethical) question about whether literature as a whole has value, but the question of how to distinguish among literary works. Where in the landscape of Aristotle's moral theory is the discourse that supports such judgments?

One comment Aristotle makes, as the surviving first half of the *Poetics* draws to a close, suggests that the discourse relevant to judgments of taste will not lie within ethics proper. Surveying the accusations of inaccuracy that critics make about poetry and sometimes use in evaluating individual poems, he advises that "there is not the same correctness in poetry that there is in ethics and politics, or in any other art [*technê*]" (1460b14).

He says *politikê*, not "ethics and politics," but as a rule Aristotle uses that word to embrace all inquiry into the major matters of human life (see *EN* I.2). His point is clear: correctness in poetry is not ethical or political correctness.

The Social Virtues in Aristophanes

Aristotle cites Aristophanes as an exemplar of comic poetry (*Poetics* 1448a26–28). That's lucky for the modern reader, given that Aristophanes is the only comic playwright whose works survive. Simply turn from Aristotle's account of comedy to actual comedies and see how the account holds up.

Wasps makes a vivid case of the drama of rudeness, though several other Aristophanic comedies also do (*Acharnians*, *Peace*, *Birds*, *Thesmophoriazusae*, *Ecclesiazusae*). If *Wasps* seems particularly indecorous, that may be because of its relentless focus on social convention and its discontents.

Old Philokleon first attaches himself to the society of the Athenian jury (the only society he knows). When his son Bdelykleon shows him the oppression implicit in that attachment, Philokleon shakes off jury duty without regret or nostalgia. But now he is untameable: he goes on to escape the contrivance of a home lawcourt that Bdelykleon tricks up to amuse him and then, in the last scene, an Athenian dinner party he was too vulgar for.

The mock trial at home, with kitchen utensils substituting for the apparatus of the court, combines the characteristics of the dinner party and jury duty in an oneirically associative link that highlights the artificiality of all convention.[4] Bdelykleon lays out the mock court with elaborate stage management, all the props listed (805–820) as they get listed in other Aristophanic scenes of dramatic impersonation (see *Acharnians* 415–479; *Thesmophoriazusae* 213–262). So Philokleon manages to escape the social strictures of law, home, and theater all at once.

When the home trial fails, Bdelykleon makes a last effort to rehabilitate his dad. He will take Philokleon to a banquet, he says; but the old man obviously has no idea how to behave. So Bdelykleon spends a scene changing his father's wardrobe, supplying *mots* for Philokleon to tell over dinner, and initiating him into table manners (1122–1264). He shows Philokleon how to lounge at the table (1211ff.) and takes him step by step through the dinner—"We eat, we wash, we pour libations" (1217)—like a director coaxing a performance out of someone so unseduced by theater he will not even pretend to be holding a wine bowl (1218).

The next scene opens with a crowd chasing Philokleon out of the symposium. He has gotten drunk and insulted the other guests (1299–1334). Now he staggers drunk and lecherous through the streets, finally turning his exuberant choler against the young sons of Carcinus, who have tried to make careers as tragedians (1474–1537). The man who would rather insult his host than behave at a banquet is not apt to respect the conventions of drama either. Like most of Aristophanes' successful heroes, Philokleon comes to equate the glittering falsehoods in dramatic performance with the niceties of all social intercourse, and shrugs off dramatic and social roles together when they hamper the expression of his earthiest motives. Theater depends on a social agreement, in the interests of mutual pleasure, that comedy refuses to honor.

The Rudeness in Aristophanic Comedy

Buffoonish, churlish, and braggadocian, Philokleon mocks all the virtues of social intercourse. Like most (male) Aristophanic heroes, he curses and belches his way out of society and feels no shame about it.

So Aristotle would seem to have described Attic comedy. But he has not gone far enough, for comedy's characters are not only rude but winningly rude.

The rudeness in Aristophanic comedy does not lie just outside the play's world as it does in the New Comedy of Menander and his successors (the first examples of which were produced after Aristotle's death), where it is a source of humor that the characters cross into but return from in time for the comedy's resolution. Rudeness is indeed a source of humor in Old Comedy: part of its pleasure, as the *Tractatus* recognizes, derives from our ability to ridicule the characters (*TC* 6, 8). But this function of comic rudeness requires that a play reaffirm the virtues it has been violating, and Old Comedy refuses that move. Laughter at an Old Comedy is rude.

The question is simple. If comedy takes as its subject that which is laughable, and if what is laughable turns out to be what violates etiquette, then comedy's subject is and only ought to be rudeness. And how can judgments grounded in etiquette tolerate systemic rudeness?

Urbane comedies give a satisfying answer: the audience laughs from an elevated position (the laughter is exclusively laughter of ridicule) and thereby puts the rudeness in its place. Comic catharsis calibrates ridicule as tragic catharsis calibrates pity and fear. The norms of social intercourse are saved.

But Aristophanic comedy is not urbane. Rudeness emblematizes happiness, while politeness comes off as hypocritical and effeminate. The hero's progress out of stultifying convention into rude truth gets depicted as a transition from superannuation, disease, and death, into rejuvenation; often enough as well, when cultic imagery threads through the plots, from Dionysian fragmentation to the resurrection of the vegetation god.

Discourtesy is not a threat for comedy to overcome but a goal for it to reach.

But in that case laughing at Old Comedy doesn't mean looking down on its characters, for when they succeed it also includes delighting in their victory. You even delight at these comedies' final explosions out of theatrical convention. Old Comedy often ends with a fatal violation of the dramatic illusion, that is, the conventions that determine what a play is; and being titillated by these violations amounts not to ridiculing them, not to seeing the comedy as a lesser being, but to guilty pleasure. You wish you had done that.

J. L. Austin observed that pretending to be rude could amount to being rude. "I was just pretending" doesn't always neutralize the rudeness; and laughing at Old Comedy doesn't always neutralize your commendation of *its* rudeness. The mere disappearance of egregious coprolalia from comedy will not undo the impropriety built into the genre.

Aesthetiquette

"Good taste" belongs in etiquette and aesthetics, what you may call the two back corners of value theory. Aristotle applauds the tact of the witty man and the growing propriety of comedy. But I have suggested that comedy as he knew it still did not mind its manners as tragedy did.

In Aristotle's terms, a good tragedy respects good taste by presenting better than average characters and plots that avoid "filthy" or "disgusting" resolutions (*Poetics* 1452b36, 1453b37, 1454a4). Seeking a mean between extremes, good tragic diction is neither prosaic nor so crowded with metaphors and dictionary finds as to be laughable, but remains measured (*Poetics* 23 passim).

The New Comedy that defined the European comic tradition began after Aristotle's death and probably felt his influence. We know that the New Comedy of Menander and Plautus avoids the discourtesies of the older genre. It reduces abuse and obscenity to nothing, makes the moral ugliness of its characters rigorously signify failings to be overcome, and insists on endings that undo the effects of rudeness—all so that the audience's laughter is sure to mean ridicule and therefore a reaffirmation of the social compact.

Thus Aristotle's aesthetiquette became truer to poetry than it was when he first spoke of ready wit in comedy. There is nothing outlandish in believing that the first New Comic playwrights read the *Poetics* or Aristotle's lost dialogue *On Poets*, which he wrote as a public work, and tried to produce works that fit his description of comedy. If comedy was better for ultimately validating the virtues of social intercourse, then they would make comedy better. So it may be that comedy became polite in order to take its place alongside tragedy and epic, and thereby made good taste a general concept of aesthetics.

Notes

1. Richard Janko, *Aristotle on Comedy* (Berkeley: University of California Press, 1985).

2. *Tractatus Coislinianus* 7. Richard Janko has edited and translated *TC* in his translations of Aristotle's *Poetics* (Indianapolis, IN: Hackett, 1987), p. 45.

3. Ibid., p. 46.

4. Thomas R. Banks, "Aristohpanes' *Wasps* and the Aristophanic Comedy of Ideas," in *The Masks of Comedy*, ed. Ann Boaden (Rock Island, IL: Augustana College Library, 1980), pp. 13–22.

CHAPTER TWO

The Art of the Dis

Hip-Hop's Battle Royale

LYNNE d JOHNSON

I grew up in a world in which talking about somebody's mama was a way of life, an everyday occurrence. For all of us, boys and girls, it was a kind of game or performance. Whether we called it "capping," "snapping," "ranking," "busting," or simply "the dozens," most of it was ridiculous, surreal humor bearing very little resemblance to reality. . . . More than anything, it was an effort to master the absurd metaphor, an art form intended to entertain rather than damage.

—Robin D. G. Kelley, *Yo' Mama's Disfunktional! Fighting the Culture Wars in Urban America*

Name callin' hasn't fallen into what I'm runnin'/ I wouldn't dis another sister unless she had it comin'.

—Queen Latifah, "Name Callin' "

In hip-hop music, more specifically in the rapping aspect of the musical genre, there exists a cultural performance practice referred to as "dissing," meaning to disrespect, ridicule, or insult, that is the progeny of African vernacular traditions. After Africans were transported to the Americas, these oral traditions later evolved into signifying, toasting, and playing the dozens. When a rapper (hereafter referred to as an "MC," as in master of ceremonies or mic controller) disses another MC, and the other MC responds in live performance, on mix tape, or on commercial recording, this practice is called a "battle." In battling there are very few rules. In fact, as with any other competition, the goal is to defeat your opponent. The winner of a rap battle garners the reputation of a skillful lyricist and also boosts his street or authentic "real" rap credibility. Yet, while in hip-hop music's early days, battling was practiced and performed in jest—for entertainment purposes—today's rhyme battles have brought about much controversy and departed from their original social and cultural contexts. This is where any questions about the role etiquette plays within hip-hop, specifically the rap battle, can be raised. While the rap battle has its place in a rich African American cultural history, in the 1990s it resulted in a bicoastal war that brought about the death of two of the music's most popular and most profitable rappers. And today, in a scenario similar to the battle royal that Ralph Ellison describes in his *Invisible Man*, the rhyme battle is being utilized as a marketing tool to churn out significant profit for the music recording industry.

Rhyme Battle's Roots

The MC's rhetorical skills can be traced back to Esu-Elegbara, the divine messenger and trickster figure found in Nigerian Yoruba culture. Samuel A. Floyd, in his read of Henry Louis Gates's *The Signifying Monkey: A Theory of African American Literary Criticism*, states:

> The inspiration for Gates' hermeneutics, as developed in *The Signifying Monkey*, is Esu-Elegbara, the mythical African "classical figure of mediation who is interpreter of the culture," "guardian of the crossroads," "master of style," and connector of "the grammar of divination with its rhetorical structures." Esu, one of the African pantheons of gods, is also a trickster figure. His African-American descendant—his "cousin," so to speak—is the Signifying Monkey, a symbol of antimediation in black vernacular culture in the United States. Both of these tricksters—Esu and the Signifying Monkey—provide keys to the interpretation of black vernacular culture.[1]

Signifying, as it is discussed here, becomes a way of interpreting the MC's role in the continuum of African vernacular cultural traditions. Floyd writes, "Signifyin(g) is a way of saying one thing and meaning another, it is a reinterpretation, a metaphor for the revision of previous texts and figures, it is tropological thought, repetition with difference, the obscuring of meaning—all to achieve or reverse power, to improve situations, and to achieve pleasing results for the signifier. For in Signifyin(g), the emphasis is on the signifier, not the signified. In African American music, musical figures Signify by commenting on other musical figures, on themselves, on performances of other music, on other performances of the same piece, and on completely new works of music."[2]

Clearly, rapping, as performed by an MC, is a direct descendant of this vernacular tradition. It can be heard in MCs boasting, dissing, and heavy use of pop cultural references. In "Rapper's Delight," recorded by the Sugarhill Gang in 1979 and said to be the start of the commercialization of hip-hop music, Big Bank Hank boasted:

Well I was coming home late one dark afternoon
A reporter stopped me for an interview
She said she's heard stories and she's heard fables
That I'm vicious on the mike and the turntables
This young reporter I did adore
So I rocked a vicious rhyme like I never did before
She said damn fly guy I'm in love with you
The Casanova legend must have been true.

When Grandmaster Melle Mel and the Furious Five released "Step Off" in 1984, we heard a prime example of dis rap. In the song, Keith Cowboy rapped:

Well, I'm Keith Cowboy and you're my cow
So what you MCs gonna do now?
It's gonna be a slaughter and here's my plan
You won't even get bread and water, my man
Gonna put you on the racks like a pair of slacks
With another wack rapper tied to your back
And if you wanna hang yourself out to dry
It's the beautiful round up in the sky.

I'm the carry out kid when my trigger's in cock
I'll be carryin' out bodies stiff as a rock
Carryin' out a million dollars in my pockets and hand
But I carry out orders from no man
'Cause anything you wanna do, I already did
You used to see me rock the house when you was a kid
But in my MC school, my class is packed
And tricks are for kids so I left your ass back.

In terms of the utilization of popular culture references, the MC duo of Das Efx took the practice to exaggerated heights. In the song "Jussummen" on the 1992 album *Dead Serious*, you can hear insanely humorous lyrics, wrought with pop cultural references such as:

When I'm proper, I doobity dibble dabble wit my winnings
I drop a Def Jam as if my name was Russell Simmons
I'm funky, spunky, I clock bread like Wonder
I'll jump and flex, make you think I'm Jane Fonda
I shiggity slam Rito, I'm laid back like Tito
I good gots nuff wisdom like Mama Montigo, amigo
Se Vente, yes I can samba
I'm known like Geraldo, shishi karamba
The jibbity jibba jammage, always with the hippity houser
I got crazy smarts like that kid Doogie Howser.

Sugarhill Gang, Grandmaster Melle Mel and The Furious Five, and Das Efx all exhibit and exemplify that rap is a continuum of African oral traditions. Robin D. G. Kelley, in *Yo' Mama's Disfunktional: Fighting the Culture Wars in Urban America*, looks at signifying's cousin, the dozens, and further explains its significance in rap music: "The goal of the dozens and related verbal games is deceptively simple: to get a laugh. The pleasure of the dozens is not the viciousness of the insult, but the humor, the creative pun, the outrageous metaphor."[3]

Playfulness and storytelling are central to rap music. In signifying, MCs often sample (as in the technical-production aspect of hip-hop music wherein a producer samples a drum track, bass line, or entire rhythm from a previously recorded song) others' lives and stories. The playfulness of rapping can be heard in the wit and egotistical boasting of the MC's text. Kelley writes, "But what counts more than the story is the "storytelling"—an emcee's verbal facility on the mic, the creative and often hilarious use of puns, metaphors, similes, not to mention the ability to kick some serious slang (or what we might call linguistic inventiveness). As microphone fiend Rakim might put it, the function of Hip-hop is to "move the crowd."[4] Tricia Rose explores the art of storytelling and battle rap further: "Narrative originality is lodged in creating new stories, and these stories are associated with the rapper. However, rapper's rhymes are clearly influenced by, if not a direct outgrowth of, the African-American toast tradition. The dozen-playing bravado of toasts such as the Signifying Monkey is brilliantly captured in Kool Moe Dee's "How Ya Like Me Now." Furthermore, in keeping with oral forms, unique introduction of materials takes on greater significance in the live performance."[5]

It is in this context—that of signifying and playing the dozens—that the art of the dis, or more appropriately battle rapping, must be understood and examined. Rapping is about aesthetics, style, and keeping it real. The realism in this case, for the MC, is about representing locale and staying true to the culture or even the MC's roots. In order for an MC to be deemed authentic, the text must reflect what is held to be true—and often the most popular cultural practices—of African American urban life. At one time, within rap music, it was partying; at another time it was about delivering a message, then it was sexual boasting and misogyny; and at other times, it was the portrayal of hardcore gangster and pimp culture. Even Black Nationalism and the acquisition and flossing (showing off) of material wealth (referred to as "bling bling") have been the content and culture of rap lyrics. Overall, from its early days and even up until the present time, when MCs are more concerned with getting paid, rapping is still about having fun. MCs rap because they enjoy it and because it has a playful quality, as well as providing both physical and psychic pleasures. MCs play with lyrics to outperform their peers and competitors, and in many cases to outsell them or outrank them on the *Billboard* charts. It is from this perspective that rhyme battling is to be explored.

A Battle Rap Primer

> There's an old hip-hop adage that goes back to battles in the park: Once given a mike, an MC won't voluntarily relinquish it until he has rocked the crowd.
>
> —Nelson George, *Hip Hop America*

Back in the early days of hip-hop music, before the genre was pressed to vinyl or reached its current commercial success, it was enjoyed on the streets of New York. Initially in outdoor public spaces, such as city parks, schoolyards, and block parties, and then later at community centers and clubs, DJs and MC crews would battle over turf or to determine who had the best crew. The battle was always a crowd-drawing and crowd-pleasing event: "Every Bronx youth who ever witnessed an MC control the crowd has dreamed of basking in those frenzied cheers of approval as well. But competition was stiff, and reputations were built on the charred remains of 'sucker MCs' who were reduced to dust with scathing disses (insults)."[6]

Often MCs would write rhymes specifically for the event, or in many other cases, they would freestyle, improvising on the spot, to lyrically slaughter their competitors:

> One of the first battles to really get people's attention took place on December 30, 1981, between Harlem's Kool Moe Dee and the Bronx's Busy Bee Star Ski (whose name was obviously 'borrowed' from fellow DJ/MC Luvbug Starski). Busy Bee opened the proceedings with his usual crowd-pleasing routine, but when Kool Moe Dee responded with rhymes written especially for this event, he not only put Busy Bee in his place, he set a new standard: "Now to bite a nigga's name is some low-down shit/ If you was money, man, you'd be counterfeit. . . . Between me and you who do you think they'll choose?/ Well, if you think it's you/ I got bad news." Moe Dee reigned supreme that night—but hip-hop hadn't seen anything yet.[7]

The battle between Kool Moe Dee and Busy Bee set a precedent, and soon all rap battles would follow that blueprint. With Kool Moe Dee as the leader of the old-school rap era, new-school rappers would later set their rhyming intentions upon dethroning him, and at least one MC, LL Cool J, would prevail (to be discussed later).

Perhaps one of the most visually appealing commercial depictions of a rhyme battle can be viewed in the film *8 Mile*, directed by Curtis Hanson, starring the white rapper Eminem. The tale, which loosely imitates the MC's real-life rise to stellar rap status, is about a working-class trailer-park white male who overcomes a host of obstacles that will change his life forever. Inasmuch as the film illustrates the cultural assimilation of Eminem into this black cultural performance space, at its heart, the film is also about battle rapping. In the opening sequence of the film, Jimmy Smith (aka "Rabbit"), the character that Eminem portrays, is seen backstage, nervous. Rightfully so, since Rabbit is a white male—at a Detroit club, attended by an all-black audience—who is positioned to enter a rap competition against a cast of all black male MCs. Upon his first attempt, he chokes when he comes on the stage. By the end of the film, after confronting the personal demons he faces throughout the film, he is able to take center stage and compete masterfully. As described by Elvis Mitchell in his *New York Times* review of the film, "Rabbit's main competitors—Papa Doc (Anthony Mackie) and his Leaders of the Free World squad—often dismiss him as "Elvis," a white boy appropriating black culture. But when Rabbit starts hollering or rapping, he does indeed give off the explosion of vitality that Presley had while singing in his early movies. (Here, he becomes the real Slim Shady.)"[8] It is at this moment, when Eminem wins the battle, that we think about race's contextual place in rap music, and its place within this black cultural tradition:

> Eminem is authentic. He has talent. But though his music is embraced by black radio stations and African-American youths, blacks remain sensitive about the way black culture has so often been appropriated and exploited at their expense. Rabbit artfully undercuts racist verbal attacks by confronting race before his tormentors can. It works for him. The movie, however, merely ignores the incendiary subject at its heart. The way it's told imparts a Tarzan-King-of-the-Jungle air. It's hard not to see this as being about a white interloper proving his superiority, beating the black man at the black man's game.[9]

The question, at this juncture, is whether in this black vernacular culture there is room, or whether it is even appropriate, for a white man to be titled king of rap. Much like his character in the film, Eminem came up through the ranks of hip-hop battling other MCs. It is what earned him his authenticity. But is he an interloper in this game? It would seem so. In a battle against Raymond "Benzino" Scott, cofounder and visionary of Source Enterprises and CEO of Surrender

Records, the race question is addressed. Benzino, in an MTV online article, "compares Em to racist figures ('You're the rap David Duke, you're the rap Hitler. . . . I'm the rap Malcolm [X], the rap Martin [Luther King]')."[10] Benzino took his attack further in the February 2003 issue of *The Source*, in a five-page interview and "an accompanying cartoon poster that depicts Scott holding a gory trophy: the decapitated head of Eminem."[11] Is it proper etiquette for a white man to reach platinum-selling status while beating out the black man at his own game? When race becomes the issue does it change the nature of the game? Racial issues aside, *8 Mile* depicts the spontaneity and adrenaline rush encountered in rap battles, as well as its inventive lyrical manifestations. While in real life, Eminem may always be viewed as suspect by the African American hip-hop listening audience, and especially hip-hop's staunchest advocates and critics, he has mastered the true artistry of battling.

When the Game Changed

Since the days of Kool Moe Dee vs. Busy Bee Star Ski, there have been numerous battles that gained public attention. In 1988, it was the battle of the boroughs when KRS-One of the Bronx's Boogie Down Productions went head to head with Queens MC Shan of the Juice Crew. This battle was significant in that each borough wanted to claim its home turf as the true birthplace of hip-hop.[12] In a sidebar to an article entitled "The Bridge is Over: Are Today's Musical Mudslingers Looking for Fame . . . or Trouble?" (2000) written by Aliya S. King in *The Source*, the MC Shan vs. KRS-One battle is listed under the heading, "What's Beef? Some of Hip-hop's More Infamous Battles." Other battles listed include Tupac vs. Biggie (Notorious B.I.G.), LL Cool J vs. Cannibus, and Cormega vs. Nature.

The Tupac vs. Biggie battle is one in which etiquette is also addressed. In 1996 and 1997, Pac and Big were murdered within six months of one another. If not a direct result of the beef they had, and bicoastal war that sprung up in response to their beef, it was definitely an indirect result. Once friends—they even rapped together in a live freestyle, which can be found recorded on *Funkmaster Flex & Big Kap The Tunnel* (Def Jam 1999)—the MCs soon turned enemies. Pac blamed

Big for his being set up and shot outside a New York recording studio, and the battle followed. The battle divided the hip-hop community in an East Coast vs. West Coast war, and more specifically in a Bad Boy Entertainment vs. Death Row Records beef. Following Pac's disses of Big on record, East Coast MCs put on their armor and started slaying West Coast MCs, and vice versa. The urban and hip-hop presses, it has been reported, were held responsible for fueling the beef by giving it copious amounts of ink to boost newsstand sales. The East Coast vs. West Coast war got so out of hand that even Louis Farrakhan's Nation of Islam called for a Hip-hop Day of Atonement in 1996 to squash the beef.[13]

The East Coast vs. West Coast beef was beyond a typical rhyme battle. It greatly contributed to an era of negativity, in both rhyme lyrics and in physical action for the hip-hop community. Not only were Pac and BIG gunned down, but MCs released songs viciously and personally attacking MCs on the opposite coast. Eventually the beef was resolved (at least East Coast and West Coast MCs began collaborating again), though Sean "Puffy" Combs, the leader of Bad Boy, and Suge Night, the leader of Death Row, are still not on speaking terms. And to this day no one has been captured for the murder of either Tupac or the Notorious Big. But the murders are still claimed to be the result of this bicoastal war.

And still tragedies persist. As reported in *The Source*, the magazine of hip-hop music, culture and politics, MC 50 Cent was shot in front of his grandparents' home in Queens. The attack was only two weeks after he was allegedly stabbed at a recording studio. Although it is not the official word, rumors throughout the music industry suggest that another MC and perhaps even a label executive are behind both assaults.[14] In many circles it is believed that 50 Cent was stabbed in an altercation with the multi-platinum-selling, gravelly-voiced rapper, Ja Rule. As far as rap battles go, 50 Cent has reportedly taken the credit for the recent proliferation of dis records. On his 2000 "Can I Live," he claims, "Since 'How to Rob,' a lot of niggas been naming names/ Monkey see, monkey do/ I done changed the game."[15] Interestingly enough, 50 Cent was recently signed to Eminem's Shady label with an advance of one million dollars.

While in the past, hip-hop artists never took their wars on wax seriously, present-day rap contradicts this notion. Hip-hop impresario and mogul Russell Simmons invited two battling MCs—Beanie Sigel and Jadakiss—to squash their beef because it was getting out of hand.[16] In the most controversial recent spate of rhyme battles, enter Jay-Z and Nas, of Brooklyn and Queens MCs, respectively. Dissing often got personal as the MCs played out their rivalry on disc, on freestyles, and in live performances. When New York urban-format radio station Hot 97 played Nas's "Stillmatic," label representatives for Jay-Z went to the station, asking that it stop instigating beef between the artists. Jay-Z displayed a photo of Nas's Queens MC peer, Prodigy, in a dance outfit on the big screen at a Summer Jam concert.[17] And Nas wanted to lynch an effigy of Jay-Z on the stage at the 2002 Summer Jam, but Hot 97 officials (sponsors of the event) stepped in, telling Nas he could do anything he wanted verbally, but no props or videos would be allowed.[18] Nas later waged his war, now an attack against both Jay-Z and Hot 97, on competing New York City hip-hop and urban-format radio stations.

In other ways, the focus of rap battles changed as hip-hop became more commercially viable. The confrontation went from battling over turf and vying for the title of rap king, to battling over market share. Murray Forman, in *The 'Hood Comes First: Race, Space, and Place in Rap and Hip-Hop*, analyzes the shifting focus of the battle as he discusses the war between new-school rapper LL Cool J and old-school rapper Kool Moe Dee in 1988: "The older, established artists were challenged by up-and-coming talent displaying different skills from those of their predecessors. This was played out most prominently in the ongoing public battle between the old-school artist Kool Moe Dee, who co-founded the pioneering Treacherous Three (and who appeared in a cameo role in the 1984 film *Beat Street*), and LL Cool J, who personified the arrogant self-confidence of the mid-1980s new school. The issue sparking the combat was simple in principle: who is the baddest, freshest, deffest rapper in the business?"[19]

Forman further argues, "The spatial context for Kool Moe Dee and LL Cool J's battle, waged on wax over the course of several releases and on several occasions in front of live audiences in concert settings, was, at its core, also directly influenced by rap's commercial popularity."[20] Describing one of today's commercial rap battles, Douglas Century wrote in "Two of Rap's Hottest Return to the Dis," which appeared in the *New York Times* on January 6, 2002, "In a season when real-life war in Afghanistan has made much of the violence in the entertainment industry seem like quaint posturing, hip-hop—a musical genre struggling to remain relevant—has returned to its roots with an old-fashioned, insult-laden feud. Past rap battles, not coincidentally, have been excellent for CD sales. Now, two young, up-from-the-housing-projects African-American multimillionaires—once fast friends, now bitter rivals—each acclaimed as among the most talented rappers of all time, are trading put-downs and below-the-belt innuendo."[21]

In this era when rap battling has become the vehicle by which an artist gains market share, Ellison's "Battle Royal" becomes the classic case study. In the first chapter of *Invisible Man*, Ellison describes the battle royal. The story's narrator is invited to give a speech in front of the town's leading white citizens. Before giving his speech, he is to partake in a battle royal to be fought by some of his schoolmates as entertainment. First the boys are made to watch a nude white woman dance, with the American flag tattooed on her belly as if saying, "This is what being white in America can offer you." Yet the boys are yelled at and told not to look at her, being denied what America has to offer. Later, blindfolded, the boys are thrown into the ring and pummel one another. The crowd of privileged white men is in frenzy, enjoying this portrayal of black-on-black crime. The winners of the battle, the narrator being one, are awarded money, but they have to pick it up from the rug where it has been thrown. After it is all over, the narrator is allowed to give his speech about humility being the key to progress. For that he is awarded a scholarship to the state college for Negroes.[22]

The significance of Ellison's battle royal for today's rap battles is that as rap has moved out of a local space, to a global one, it has become a proliferating commercial commodity. And though the music is, by and large, created by black artists with black execs behind them,[23] the recording industry and the distribution vehicles via which rap music becomes a global commercial product is still primarily a white male's game. Like Ellison's winners in the battle royal, reigning MCs are rewarded for the black-on-black crime they perpetrate on recordings. MCs are shown all the materialistic goodness that America can offer them, but once they no longer reign supreme they are stripped of their platinum-selling and living status. Yet no artist ever makes anywhere near the zenithal amounts that hip-hop earns the recording industry. In this era of bling-bling rap, the culture remains fascinated by threats and insults. John Leland, in his *New York Times* article "In Rap Industry, Rivalries as Marketing Tool," explores the business of rhyme battles.

Here rhyme battles are no longer simply about the cultural art form, but more about selling records. Leland reports, " 'Companies make out well,' said Bert Padell, an account manager whose clients include Madonna, Run-DMC and others. 'Managers make out well.' Mr. Padell said it was common for a performer with an album generating $17 million in sales to wind up with as little as $70,000 before taxes. When the performers feel compelled to use that money in competitive flossing, or showing off, tempers can flare."[24]

Leland's article highlights that top MCs and executives, including Jay-Z, Nas, Snoop Doggy Dog, Eminem, and Jermaine Dupri, have all advanced their careers through battles. Much of the talk is inflammatory, and all of it is disseminated and promoted through record companies. For the artists, and ultimately the record labels, the feuds create low-cost publicity. And while much of the beef is promotional, due to previous events (such as the murders of Tupac and Big, and shooting of 50 Cent) MCs often fear for their lives, carrying around weapons, wearing bullet-proof clothing, and outfitting their vehicles with bullet-proof enhancements. In fact, as reported by the Associated Press, 50 Cent, the Queens-based rapper and protégé of recently slain hip-hop veteran Jam Master Jay (of Run DMC), was arrested on weapons charges after two guns were found in his car on the morning of December 31, 2002. Nowadays, even hip-hop magazines have stepped into the battle arena, with biting dis editorials in competing publications *The Source* and *XXL*. Taking the fray over the top, *The Source*, in the same issue in which Eminem was pictorially dissed, depicts the editor of *XXL* "being crushed by a hulking monster wearing a Source T-shirt. Beneath the image is the warning 'Respect the architect or get broken.' "[25] There is no doubt that the rap battle has come a long way from its roots in African oral culture or its African American roots in signifying and playing the dozens. It has also been firmly uprooted from its own playful roots of simply inciting an uproarious response from the crowd at an opponent's expense.

Yet hip-hop beefs have become even more popular than the rap artists themselves. Utilizing the draw of the hip-hop beef, the over-the-top version of the hip-hop battle, Quincy "QD III" Jones III produced *Beef*, a definitive look into the deep and harsh world of high-profile beefs told by the artists themselves. Released in September of 2003, the documentary focuses on the following lyrical battles: 50 Cent vs. Ja

Rule, Jay-Z vs. Nas, Tupac vs. Biggie, Common vs. Westside Connection, Ice Cube vs. NWA, KRS-One vs. Nelly, and Ice-T vs. LL Cool J. Much attention is given to the 50 Cent vs. Ja Rule clash, in that it has created a lot of controversy in the past couple of years and also because much of what has been battled on mix tapes and label releases has also played itself out in the streets. "I was really close to Tupac," says QD III in an interview at a screening of *Beef* at the Magic Johnson movie theater in Harlem. "I worked on albums with him and he was going to marry my sister. His death really touched us. When he passed away it made me want to investigate these situations further. Beefs are compelling to the audience, and we used that draw to teach a lesson that these guys are human. We also explore the topic in a way that upcoming artists can see what not to do."

It is within this framework that a standard, a code of behavior—etiquette—is addressed and questioned. How an African vernacular cultural practice came from its inception on America's shores as an art form, a form of entertainment (without being commodified), and as an interpreter of the culture, to its newfound space could be the result of a lack of moral codes. Yet by no means does this argument suggest that all MCs have lost their connection to the cultural tradition from which rap descended, nor to its initial purpose of moving the crowd. There is still symbolic creativity within the music—Outkast, Common, Talib Kweli, The Roots, and others in their artistic company contribute to this fact. For them, rap is an art form—a vehicle for sharing a story—which is based in a love of words and music, where the business of the industry and negativity take a backseat. Likewise, other platforms still exist—battles and freestyle competitions—in which underground and upcoming MCs engage in lyrical warfare simply for the fun of it or to earn or maintain street cred. In our oversaturated age of reality television, rap battles certainly make for great fodder. One need look no further than the wildly popular youth-oriented program *Interscope Presents 'The Next Episode'* that appears on the Showtime cable network. The show follows the trials and triumphs of undiscovered rappers from across America struggling to become the country's top MC. Rappers from Atlanta, Los Angeles, Detroit, Philadelphia, and New York battle for the top honor. Interestingly enough, a set of rules is applied in this particular competition, unlike what plays out on mix tapes, especially those hosted by DJ Kay Slay, the Drama King. While rap's dis may today be full of drama—attributed to its highly publicized controversy and violence—it is still ultimately responsible for providing much pleasure for both its creators and listeners.

Notes

1. Samuel A. Floyd Jr., *The Power of Black Music: Interpreting Its History from Africa to the United States* (New York: Oxford University Press, 1995), p. 7.
2. Ibid., p. 95.
3. Robin D. G. Kelley, *Yo' Mama's Disfunktional! Fighting the Culture Wars in Urban America* (Boston: Beacon Press, 1997), p. 34.
4. Ibid., pp. 37–38.
5. Tricia Rose, *Black Noise: Rap Music and Culture in Contemporary America.* (Hanover, NH: University Press of New England, 1994), p. 86.
6. S. H. Fernando Jr., *The New Beats: Exploring the Music, Culture, and Attitudes of Hip-Hop* (New York: Doubleday, 1994), p. 256.
7. Shani Saxon, "Battle Rhymes," in *The VIBE History of Hip Hop* (New York: Three Rivers Press, 1999), p. 84.
8. Elvis Mitchell, "White Hot: From Rap to Riches," *New York Times*, November 8, 2002.
9. Eric Harrison, "Hip-Hop '8 Mile' Doesn't Quite go the Full Distance," *Houston Chronicle*, November 8, 2002.
10. Shaheem Reid, "Benzino Calls Eminem 'The Rap Hitler,' Says There's No Beef," MTV.com News, December 5, 2002.
11. Geoff Boucher, "Rapping out Battle Lines," *Los Angeles Times*, January 17, 2003.
12. Saxon, "Battle Rhymes," p. 84.
13. Marcus Errico, "Nation of Islam Plans a 'Hip-Hop Day of Atonement,'" *E! Online*, September 17, 1996.
14. Aliya S. King, "The Bridge Is Over: Are Today's Musical Mudslingers Looking for Fame or Trouble?" *The Source*, August 2000.
15. Akiba Solomon, "Ego Trippin': Are Inflated Domes the Cause of All These Rap Wars?" *The Source*, September 2002.
16. Kim Osorio, "Confronting Controversy: Should Hip-Hop's Recent War of Words Be Cause for Alarm?" *The Source*, November 2001.
17. Ibid.
18. Jon Caramanica, "Destroyed," *Village Voice*, July 17–23, 2002.
19. Murray Forman, *The 'Hood Comes First: Race, Space, and Place in Rap and Hip-Hop.* (Middletown, CT: Wesleyan University Press, 2002), p. 166.
20. Ibid, p.167.

21. Douglas Century, "Two of Rap's Hottest Return to the Dis," *New York Times*, January 6, 2002.

22. Ralph Ellison, *Invisible Man* (New York: Random House, 1993).

23. Amol Sarva, "White Star, Black Galaxy," Salon.com, November 20, 2002.

24. John Leland, "In Rap Industry, Rivalries as Marketing Tool," *New York Times*, November 3, 2002.

25. Lola Ogunnaike, "War of the Words at Hip-Hop Magazines," *New York Times*, January 29, 2003.

CHAPTER THREE

Gay Etiquette

A Brief Consideration

JEFF WEINSTEIN

"Age before beauty."

"Pearls before swine."

Whatever the truth of its origin, this telling exchange has become apocryphal, at least in a New York sort of way. Here's my version:

Writer and other-deprecating wit Dorothy Parker walks toward the entrance of one or another gilded Manhattan skyscraper. At the same time, equally barbed author Claire Boothe Brokaw—before she was Luce, before she penned *The Women*—approaches the same entry. You can hear heels click, then stop.

Were I polite, I would presume that you, worldly reader, know just which smart-suited figure said what to the other and, to cap the frosty encounter, swept first through the door, victorious.

But nowadays, even a generous commentator must choose realism and spell out anything that carries the merest whiff of historical specificity. College degrees are awarded in these United States to students who have no idea who Marilyn Monroe or Rock Hudson were, and departments of major metropolitan newspapers are led by editors who think Stonewall is a brand of jams. Whom, as etiquette-challenged Joan Crawford is said to have said, is kidding whom?

A useful writer can no longer assume anything. Actually, he or she never could: not history, not language, not culture, not gender, and certainly not rules of etiquette, broken or intact. Nothing, least of all the many faces and crimes of Crawford (she was a film star), may ever be taken for granted.

In the parable above, she of the too-simple etiquette insult, the conservative mean spirit, is "Claire"; "Dorothy" is the master of reversal, embodiment of the agile urbane. The moral of the story? If forced to select, one would obviously choose to be a friend of Dorothy.

Politeness might also have led me to assume that rules of etiquette, however they trickled down, up, or sideways from the teapots of London or fountains of Fontainebleau, would continue to serve their superficial purposes until those purposes no longer served their underlying purpose: to promote the survival of the status quo.

I was reminded in an etiquette-book introduction that good manners go back at least as far as AD 700, when *Beowulf*'s Queen Wealtheow, "mindful of etiquette," passed the goblet first to the king, then to the court's courtiers, and lastly to herself—at which point, Machiavellian moderns might imagine, she didn't need to partake because her poisoned mead would have done its job.[1]

May I at least suppose that readers of this volume already understand that etiquette, a kind of cultural hairnet, exists to keep its flyaway subjects in their places? Cunningly, the origin of etiquette's rules, sometimes even their very presence, is hidden or erased, and, if all goes well, so is etiquette's mechanism of control, which taps deeper springs of social behavior, such as the need to be able to dine in public without being gored in one's back.

For reasons I am certain authors to the right and left of me have already listed, the social etiquette with which we in this nation have been most familiar for the past one hundred years is dying. (The official or governmental form of etiquette, consolidated in protocol, still holds on.) In the process of decomposing, however, the wrinkled relic is trying artfully to adapt, somehow understanding that even Internetted, shape-shifting citizens of the world require some kind of comforting limits beyond those urged by purchase power, religion, law, or the splendid popular narratives of the moment.

Just look at the books. By the way, if you have any doubt that etiquette as we may have known it is on its last stockinged legs, recall that Emily Post and Amy Vanderbilt, the Fanny Farmer and Julia Child of etiquette, spread their rules of engagement mostly via thick, biblical tomes. Where's yours? Hiding under that now collectible stack of *Talk* magazines and crusty pile of McDonald's ketchup packets?

Since the 1960s, the scant titles on the post-Post etiquette shelf have been aimed specifically at the nouveau niche. When an African American middle class grew large enough to constitute a major market, out came the manners books with advice about how to distinguish between and respond to intended versus unintended racism—an etiquette for "us." When it became acceptable to admit that you pick up or are picked up by people at weddings and funerals—etiquette central—and go home and have sex with them, then suddenly appeared *Rules for the One-Night Stand*, also known as *Who Buys the Condom?*

[Oh, maybe the silly queen is *finally* getting to gay.]

Hold your horses. All I wish to indicate is that once social etiquette fractions and particulates, it begins to lose its raison d'être, which is to provide a way for every diner at civilization's table to be higher or lower than someone else. In other words, if the ostensible universality of etiquette is questioned, its hipbone cracks. What good is a dancing card if you can't rise from the chair?

Oh, I know, *quelle surprise*. But I would like to suggest a way to use the old dame before she disintegrates completely, to "play" etiquette in order to change the rules of the game. The logic is simple, and I can compare it to the logic of the African American jewelry designer who not so long ago produced startling and beautiful portrait cameos—that most prudent of feminine decorations—but in reverse, coal-black figures on milky white ground. All the old-school, "how lovely" cameo responses are evoked ("Has that been in your family long?"), but the stifling and often snobbish history of the original is negated, slammed, in one quick glance. Has that been in your slave family long? This brooch intervention is achieved, by the way, without denying the underlying art and appeal of the cameo form itself. In fact, separating this polite jewelry, this piece of solidified etiquette, from its mummified past invests both the old jewel and its remade sister with at least a shadow of current vitality.

Can you and I do the same with behavior?

Let me tell a gay, peripatetic story, not about etiquette exactly, but about rules of social behavior so far buried as to be invisible, except in certain test-tube circumstances—like the main street of Provincetown, Massachusetts.

Provincetown, the fingertip of the crooked arm that is Cape Cod, has for centuries been an outpost, a haven for pirates and artists, a classic land's end. It has also long been a gay resort, which for years meant a place where gay men and lesbians could visit and safely cluster, gather on the windy beaches, play in bars, and in most cases feel like the warp, if not the weft, of the social fabric that clothes an unusual American town.

During the summer season, the main drag, called Commercial Street, is full of folks both gay and not strolling back and forth past T-shirt shops and ancient shingled homes: a typical resort promenade. On this stroll, you soon notice that the sidewalks of Commercial Street are extremely narrow, allowing not more than two, maybe three if skinny, persons abreast, which circumstance befits the artery's age and appeal.

So, predictably, Commercial Street sidewalk rules developed, as firm as if they were chiseled in granite:

- When a single person of either gender comes upon a couple of any sort, the single can squeak by without forcing the couple to disengage.
- Groups of three almost always split up when faced with even so much as an unleashed dog.
- When a male-female couple comes upon a male-female couple, each disengages, and the mates pass in single file, although whether the male or female of a duo goes first is unpredictable.
- When a same-sex couple comes upon a same-sex couple, male-male or female-female in either direction, the same rule of polite disengagement applies.
- However, when a same-sex couple of either gender comes upon a male-female pair, the mixed couple does not disengage, and the same sex couple must choose to separate and edge by one by one, or stay coupled and be forced into the street.

I haven't gathered sufficient data about transgender or transsexual encounters from which to generalize.

After years of mindless obedience, this writer decided to try an experiment. I convinced my placid partner—male—to hold fast when faced with a male-female obstacle on the main street of New England's gay mecca. Flip-flops, not clicking heels, provide the sound track this time—and here they come, vanilla cones in hand. I grab his hand. The two social dyads approach, cross that etiquette-drawn line and come face to face. They must stop. We must stop. We do not budge.

Rarely does life provide so vivid an opportunity to watch as thoughtless behavior is sparked into puzzlement. "What is the matter?" their crinkled eyes and furrowed foreheads say. "Why is this happening?"

We stand still, pedestrian antagonists, for five seconds, ten seconds, fifteen seconds. From their points of view, choices are limited. Wait until the two fellows wake up and move around us. Split up and pass them. Stay together and walk into the street.

Without a word between them or to us, they divide. We take their cue a short but gratifying instant afterward, and divide as well. Bread and butter, gay bread and butter.

⁂ ⁂ ⁂

This patient partner of mine told me recently that someone he met at a party asked him, after he mentioned me in passing, which was "the one who cooked." The question, memorably rude in itself as well as superbly ignorant of contemporary domestic life, was indirect and probably considered polite—a polite way of asking who is butch and who fem, who top and who bottom, who husband and who wife.

Neither of us. Our chef's name is Wolfgang.

Laminating older rules of etiquette onto situations that will rot their foundation can yield priceless results. Just look what happens when a hoary etiquette volume tries to update its authority and powder the wrinkle of gay.

The following examples are from the "gay couples" category of the fiftieth anniversary edition of the serially "updated" *Amy Vanderbilt Complete Book of Etiquette* (2002). Gay singles had not yet been folded into the batter, except in this generic advice:

When Referring to Homosexuals:

"Male homosexuals are known by the word 'gay.' No other reference is ever used in conversation. [That's *Mr.* Faggot to you.] Women homosexuals prefer to be called lesbians to distinguish themselves from gay men. [Otherwise we'd never be sure.]"[2]

Alternative Families:

"Instead of referring to one of the partners as 'husband' or 'wife,' you use the word 'companion.' The politically correct term for children of such liaisons is simply 'child.' "

"It's up to a gay couple to decide what names they want their child to call them."[3]

Birth Announcements:

"In the case of a lesbian couple, both women are credited on the announcement, even though one woman actually gave birth."[4]

Introductions:

"When a heterosexual or homosexual couple living together go out socially, they may want to get across the point that they are romantically involved and not available to others. [Or they may not.] The way they handle this is to say, 'I'd like you to meet my companion, Bill Wooster.' This is a term that corresponds to 'This is my wife' or 'This is my husband.' "[5]

Kimberly, I'd like you meet my slave, Jerry.

The old corset of etiquette is simply too inelastic to conceal the lumps and edges of any crucial social change—the full acknowledgement, for example, of same-sex love. This is why no matter how hard they try to reflect "up-to-date concerns," etiquette's hegemonic rules will warp into grim funhouse humor. You want to fit in, do the right thing? Here's how to frame a belated bereavement note to Matthew Shepard's immediate family. Learn the correct way to suggest that there is no danger of infection when dividing the material estate of your bachelor uncle who has passed away from AIDS. Be puzzled no longer over which stepparent is responsible for providing the photograph of the fugitive gay teen to the local paper or milk carton (and should a self-addressed and stamped envelope be included)?

To the gay men and lesbians among you, I suggest you use these dwindling rules to your advantage, facing down anyone who will not share your path (it goes without saying that such paths be well trafficked and lit). If and when you choose to marry, let me assure you that post-Vanderbilt propriety will take second place to the unsettling fact that you and your beloved stand at the alternative altar in hard won, resistant, possibly joyful union.

And finally, dear reader, don't forget that "coming out"—still listed under "Debut"—plus all that it entails is always impeccably correct.

Notes

1. Tucker, Nancy and Nancy Dunnan, *Amy Vanderbilt Complete Book of Etiquette 50th Anniversary Edition* (New York, Doubleday: 1995), p. xi.

2. Ibid., p. 696.
3. Ibid., p. 22.
4. Ibid., p. 10.
5. Ibid., p. 687.

CHAPTER FOUR

The Breathing Breach of Etiquette

KENNETH J. SALTMAN

There are bodybuilders and there are hardcore body-builders. Most bodybuilders lift weights before or after a workday segmented by regular Tupperware feedings on proper quantities of protein, complex carbohydrates, and supplements. For most hardcore bodybuilders pumping iron is a full-time job, maybe even a religion: the gym, feedings, supplements, steroids, the gym, sleeping, tanning, shaving, the gym. Only the elite of the hardcore, the most pious of the body-building cult, collect pay from the likes of Joe Weider or Robert Kennedy for posing in the pages of the muscle mags—*Flex, Muscle & Fitness, Ironman.* The rest deal steroids which provide both an income and a free source of the most expensive tool of the trade. Some work as bouncers when the gym is closed. Some sell their ass. None let work, family, friends, or other nuisances interfere with the growth of the body to superhuman proportions. They do not identify with you and your car payment, you and your mortgage, you and the growth of your stock portfolio, you and the growth of your prestige among your colleagues and in your field. Your chest is a joke. Your ass an affront. You are some kind of monstrosity walking around like a decapitated chicken but you are going in circles with your lats cut off, trapezius excised, and deltoids amputated. To the hardcore bodybuilder the chicken is far better off.

Hardcore bodybuilders identify with Gods, animals, machines, and money. And this is what they become.

Hardcore bodybuilders do not identify primarily as consumers, workers, family members, religious followers, or citizens. Yet, it is hardly the case that hardcore bodybuilders are outside of capitalist social relations. In the legitimate economy they buy gym memberships, supplements, magazines, sportswear, and cures for steroid-induced baldness, impotence, and high blood pressure. In the illicit economy they buy steroids by the barrel. However, while they do consume commodities and services specifically marketed to them in a niche economy, do hardcore bodybuilders follow the proper codes of behavior, social norms, and etiquette that assure the necessary regular, stable, and predictable consumption and production patterns and social groupings of individuals in the present form of capitalist economy? The untempered individualism, the antisocial tendencies characterizing the market and hardcore bodybuilding's performance of it are best exemplified by the greatest ever of the fold, Arnold Schwartzenegger: "Whatever I thought might hold me back, I avoided. I crossed girls off my list—except as tools for my sexual needs. I eliminated my parents too."[1]

Schwartzenegger, and perhaps more properly Joe Weider's media empire (he currently publishes *Muscle & Fitness* and *Flex*, both of which advertise Weider supplements), pioneered the extremity of the sport of bodybuilding not merely by inventing new exercises and nutritional regimens but by transforming barbell culture from what was once associated with "health and Christian living" from the days of Bob Hoffman's York Barbell Company, to a hyperindividualistic, image-oriented, and highly competitive sport geared toward ever bigger competitors. And there could be only one winner. One Mr. Olympia judged by size. The Weider/Schwartzenegger era of hardcore male bodybuilding was monotheistic. There could be only One God and He had to be the biggest.[2]

Hardcore bodybuilding has its own rules, its own etiquette, and these have principally to do with building a more massively muscular lean body than anybody else. It is about being the biggest and the best. Hardcore bodybuilders will destroy not only their personal relationships but their health as well. Stacking steroids, they gladly trade kidneys and livers for an inch on the tricep, swap hair and normal testicle and clitoris size for an inch on the latissimus dorsi. The prime principle of hardcore bodybuilding is the same as that of capitalism: growth at any cost. And bodybuilders transform the body into a showcase of this principle. They are walking anatomy lessons—every muscle, tendon, and artery on display. They are what Jean Baudrillard in *Fatal Strategies* means by obscene—they reveal the workings of power: "All structures turned inside out and exhibited, all operations rendered visible. In America this goes all the way from the bewildering network of aerial telephone and electric wires (the whole system is on the surface) to the concrete multiplication of all the bodily function in the home, the litany of ingredients on the tiniest can of food, the exhibition of income or I.Q., and includes harassment by signals, the obsession with displaying the innards of power, the equivalent of the mad desire to locate the critical function in the lobes of the brain."[3]

With the revelation of a vast network of veins, the exposure of every muscle striation, the bodybuilder is a moving, breathing anatomy lesson with each part of the physique exploded for easy reading. Bodybuilding is the only sport in which the product of the athlete's labor has no object outside of himself or herself. Whereas a basketball player trains the body to perform for activities within a game, the bodybuilder's labor remains invested in the body. The body becomes both the catalyst of production and the product of one's labor. Not only is the body the site and end of labor, but each part of the body is continuously reproduced with the specialization of labor, an endless series of repetitions designed specifically to increase mass and better reveal the workings of the product. Bodybuilding incorporates mass production and reproduction into the body itself. Hardcore bodybuilders are perhaps the purest expression of capitalism. They do not identify with the use of capital. They identify as capital. Hardcore bodybuilders display the virtues of competition, discipline, accumulation, and self-sacrifice on their flesh. Capitalism builds them. In the words of perennial Mr. Olympia contender Shawn Ray, "I am a commodity."[4]

Despite its seeming compatibility with capitalism, in the 1990s hardcore bodybuilding became less acceptable in popular culture, medicine, and law. As fewer enormously muscular characters appeared in films except as villains, psychologists evolved the term "anamorphism" to describe the drive for size as a mental illness akin to the eating disorders anorexia nervosa and bulemia. At the same time a movement swept the growing prison industry to eliminate bodybuilding from lockups across the nation.

Why would not hardcore bodybuilders be ideal models for all to follow in a culture in which the highest faith is to the market? What is it about the blatant revelation of the workings of the body as capital that makes the hardcore bodybuilder freakish and obscene? What makes the hardcore bodybuilder an enfleshed lapse in etiquette, like a conversation at a restaurant in which one conversant casually mentions over pâté, chopped liver, black bean dip, or a hot fudge sundae that he happens to be suffering from a bout of explosive diarrhea and the other diner inevitably responds with "That was more information than I needed"? Likewise, the hardcore bodybuilder is more information than you needed. The verbal reference to explosive diarrhea at the table might ruin one's enjoyment of the deliciously turgid brown dip precisely by closely mirroring it and thereby breaking down the symbolic barrier that one has erected between the exemplary appetizing food and excrement, the most symbolically prohibited item one might imagine consuming. The gustatory excess of such an edible indulgence as fudge brings the eater to the boundary of a prohibition. The fat and sugar and cocoa is not all that makes that chocolate seductive to the diner educated in the vices of calories and cholesterol. U.S. consumer culture is organized by an ambivalent dictate on the one hand to hedonistically consume and on the other to ascetically resist consumption. The prohibition that is attached to excessive consumption of chocolate or chopped liver or any other food has as its limit the ultimate indulgence, the ultimate prohibition, the ultimate excess, excrescense in its pure form, shit.

Likewise, what makes the hardcore bodybuilder "more information than we needed, thanks," or what make this an obscene body is just how close this body comes to the simultaneously desired and disavowed limit of the excessive body. The hardcore bodybuilder as embodied excess is the limit of the idealized body in contemporary U.S. consumer culture. Through drugs, diet, and exercise regimen this is a disciplined body that has accumulated as much muscle as biologically possible while simultaneously reducing body fat to a level that is, as well, at the biological minimum. The hardcore bodybuilder embodies the above-stated ambivalence of hedonistic consumption (excessive consumption needed to accumulate this muscle) and acetic denial (the denial of excess calories from fat and carbohydrates, the denial of sodium, and so on). This is a hard body hard disciplined for consumption.

Yet what makes the hardcore bodybuilder obscene, a breathing breach of etiquette, is the fact that this is a body that is so much at the limit of the social ideals of the body that it threatens to break down the barrier between the human body and the nonhuman body, breach the boundary between the living body and the dissected cadaver. This monstrous body threatens to take on a life of its own. An article in *Muscle & Fitness* titled "Monster Mash: The Sequel" reads:

> The strength of Frankenstein, the size of King Kong: This sequel has it all, in five muscle-building formulas. You know what happens in sequels, right? No matter how gruesome the final scene of the first movie, no matter how much mayhem and destruction, no matter that it seemed the villain was shot, hanged, burned or otherwise fatally wounded, somehow he rises from the grave to plunder and pillage a new crop of terrified teens. In this Muscle-fied sequel, our super-sized rouges are back—despite the vein-popping, muscle-crunching, will-testing trials they endured in Part I—and ready to descend into the dungeon, known to outsiders as the gym. Yet they aren't on the hunt with a blade and a lust for vengeance. They're definitely out to maim, however, through a rather insidious tactic: full-bore weight training. The plot twist? The type of pain our miscreants prescribe will make you stronger and bigger, perhaps a monster yourself. Dare to enter, and perhaps accomplish what many sequel "good-guys" can't: survive for Part III. . . . No. 1: Wake your triceps from the dead. This full-on assault will make all three triceps' heads pop out of your skin, wriggling and writhing as they take on a life of their own.[5]

As this and countless other advertisements and articles make clear, hardcore bodybuilders aspire to monstrosity, to breaking down the borders of the body, losing control of the insides of the body, which come out to the surface wriggling and writhing as they take on a life of their own. This, the most regimented, disciplined, and controlled body found in our culture, the disciplined body par excellence, is a body that defies control. This skin so thin reveals the workings of arteries, the twitching of fiber, the interstices between tendon, meat, and bone. This body is meat. This body is you.

So while the hardcore bodybuilder does not identify with you and your car payment, you and your mortgage, you and the growth of your stock portfolio, you and the growth of your prestige among your colleagues and in your field, you identify with him and his finite flesh, and perhaps what is most monstrous to you about the hardcore bodybuilder is that in the body of the hardcore bodybuilder you see yourself, a more honest version of yourself: you and your car payment, you and your mortgage, you and the growth of your stock portfolio, you and the growth of your prestige among your colleagues and in your field. That is you, baby. Metastatic, an enfleshed crisis of overproduction. Those are your values. That is what they look like carved in human flesh. You see in the pulsing pounds of inflated flesh that it is you who are the breathing breach of etiquette.

Notes

1. Schwartzenegger, Arnold and Douglas Kent Hall, *The Education of a Bodybuilder* (New York: Fireside, 1977), p. 28.

2. As many authors, such as Leslie Haywood, Susan Bordo, Joanna Frueh, and I have discussed, within bodybuilding struggles over gender and sex take place. See, for example, my "Men with Breasts" (*Journal of the Philosophy of Sport*, Vol. 25, #1, December, 1998, pp. 48–60), in which I reveal the extent to which gender and sex break down as male bodies transform into female bodies as the hypermasculine form unravels at its limit. Simultaneously, female bodies transform into male bodies. As I argue in that article, the phenomenon of bodybuiding offers glimpses into the extent to which such discursive constructs as gender and sex are forcibly maintained and yet in their seeming strongest incarnations offer critical readings of how discourse structures bodies. Here I intentionally refer to the hardcore bodybuilder as "he" because in the Weider era of bodybuilding (which we are still in) the hardcore bodybuilder is male. There have been periods in which female hardcore bodybuilding has taken center stage, only to get beaten back. Most recently, the Ms. Olympia contest was delinked from Mr. Olympia, and Mr. Olympia was linked with the Ms. Fitness, contest which celebrates the sleek model body rather than the powerfully muscular body. The early battle between feminized and hardcore female bodies can be seen in the film *Pumping Iron II*. What has yet to be adequately explored in the literature is the relationship between the struggles over gender and sex in bodybuilding and the struggles over labor which play out on the body. Most literature on gender and sex in bodybuilding celebrates the "subversive" tendencies of these big bodies for challenging gender norms. I contend, however, that these alternative body forms quickly become commodified in niche markets and, like body art, hardly threaten to overturn power relations. Perhaps the clearest evidence of this is that in Las Vegas female hardcore bodybuilders can be special ordered to hotel rooms with such options

as "big clit." Female hardcore bodybuilders also sell Altoid mints and commodified academic work as in the "Picturing the Modern Amazon" exhibit in New York City in 2000. The question that has yet to be answered about hardcore bodybuilding is how it could subvert dominant power relations: patriarchy, labor/capital, white supremacy, and so on. My own suspicion is that like other forms of transgression, this one may not only do nothing to challenge power relations but may more effectively keep power relations in place. The consumption of transgression in the rise of extreme sports, suvs, violent action films, and so forth, relates to the decline of actual transgression—acts that threaten the social order. That is, the fantasy of transgression seems to actually replace transgression. The question remains whether transgression is possible any longer as a progressive political stance, and if not, whether the guise of subcultural radicality now in fact does little more than function as the ultimate ideological tactic.

3. Baudrillard, Jean, *Fatal Strategies* (New York: Semiotext(e), 1990), p. 29.

4. Quoted in Lipsyte, Robert, "Extreme is in the Eye of the Beholder," *New York Times*, October 11, 1998, p. A13.

5. *Muscle & Fitness*, September, 2001, p. 110.

CHAPTER FIVE

The Etiquette of Adoption

Michael D. Colberg

As a society we use etiquette to help create a set of expectations. We like to know what to expect and we like to understand the meaning behind people's actions. Are we being treated fairly? Are we being treated with respect? Are we at risk? When used for the highest good, etiquette is meant to convey respect and caring. When used in a more banal way, etiquette allows people to hide behind normalized behaviors or rituals in order to avoid expressing certain truths or unpleasant feelings. Although etiquette is intended, I believe, to make the world a more pleasant and comfortable place in which to live, there are times when we pay a high price for making comfort a priority.

Understanding the role that etiquette plays in adoption helps us to understand the complex nature of the word itself. The word "etiquette," which comes from the French word *etiquette* or "ticket," can be defined as "the conduct or procedure required by good breeding or prescribed by authority to be observed in social or official life." Put another way, etiquette is a set of behaviors that reflect established norms meant to facilitate social interaction. Think of etiquette as outlining a set of behaviors which, if followed, gain us a ticket enabling us to move forward smoothly.

How does this apply to adoption? There are many forms of adoption, each having its own unique set of characteristics and challenges.

For purposes of this discussion, I am going to talk about the private placement of infants as it is currently being practiced in the United States. Many people think of adoption as the transfer of parental rights from one parent or set of parents (the birthparents) to another parent or set of parents (the adoptive parents). A great deal of effort is expended to make this transfer move forward as smoothly as possible. The problem is that this definition of adoption fails to take into account the impact that this move out of one family and into another has upon the adopted person and both the birth and adoptive parents. There is a lot more to adoption than the transfer of physical custody and parental rights.

Adoption is a lifelong set of relationships that begin with the removal of a child from one family and the placement of that child into another family. This transfer has lifelong implications for the child and both the birth and adoptive parents. The meaning of this move, from one family to another, will be understood differently at each stage of the family's development. When this is understood, a deeper form of etiquette is followed, one that is fueled by respect and caring for adoptees and their long-term needs. The groundwork is laid to understand that an adopted person faces long-term challenges that are in addition to and different from those faced by children who were not adopted.

Adopted people have to make sense of their history and reconcile and integrate those pieces of themselves that come from their biological background with those that come from their adoptive family. When this is not understood, adoptees and their adoptive and birth parents are put at a disadvantage. A form of etiquette that makes comfort in the moment is prioritized. This increases the probability that these additional tasks will not be acknowledged and that adoptees will grow up behaving as if they were born into the adoptive family. At times when adoptees wrestle with those pieces of themselves that come from their biological heritage, we may fail to understand that this is normal developmental growth and think that something has gone wrong.

How do parents conduct themselves in ways that take into account their families' short- and long-term needs? How can they use etiquette to guide and support their parenting? In order to understand the role that etiquette plays, we must ask, facilitate social interaction for whom, and over what period of time? Are we considering the needs of the adoptive and biological parents alone, or are we including the needs of the adopted person as well? Are we merely facilitating the ease of social interaction between the two sets of parents surrounding the period of transfer of legal and physical custody of the child, or are we attempting to set a course of relationship that facilitates interaction between triad members over the long term?

The answers to these questions will provide a context for the rest of our discussion. The role that etiquette plays in adoption depends on how adoption is viewed and what the ultimate goal of the social interactions among the adult parties actually is. If the goal is to make the placement of a child into an adoptive home go as smoothly as possible, one kind of etiquette is practiced. Preadoptive parents and pregnant women or couples will do everything they can to make sure that they do not offend each other. By doing this, they will tend to focus on the present. They want the adoption to happen, and they want it to happen quickly. Both parties will present themselves as being totally resolved in their desire to move forward and, if there are any hard questions (Have you been drinking or doing drugs during your pregnancy? Will you still want to adopt if my baby is born with a serious birth defect?), they either go unasked or are asked by the agency worker or attorney. Everything is done with an eye on whether it affects the comfort of the other, and perhaps the surety of the adoption plan. Etiquette dictates that everyone look toward the adoptive placement as an end point.

When the goal lies elsewhere, when it lies with an awareness of the long-term nature of adoption, discussions can take a more direct, difficult, and rewarding turn. A different form of etiquette underlies the interactions when the goal is to convey respect and caring for all of the people involved, even the unborn child. It is not possible to build this kind of relationship with just anyone. Everyone has people with whom they can and cannot relate. Therefore it is very possible that the adoption process may take longer if one is looking to build a relationship that contains a deeper level of respect than that offered by merely being polite and acting in a way designed to avoid conflict. Both preadoptive parents and pregnant women and couples need to search until they feel that they have found someone with whom they connect. Normally, people need time and must invest energy to get to know each other. Pregnant women and couples have time pressure—a baby will be born. Likewise, the preadoptive parents have typically been trying to create a family for quite a while before they turn to adoption. They too are feeling pressure to move quickly. They cannot afford the luxury of taking the time it usually takes to get to know someone. They have to jump in and begin to form a serious relationship right away. A different sort of etiquette exists in these situations.

Preadoptive parents and birthparents often confuse intensity with intimacy. In situations where people have the time to get to know each other, they have the possibility of being polite and slowly deciding whether or not to develop a relationship. If they choose to form a relationship, over time they begin to sense whether they are being shown respect and caring and they come to trust in and depend on what is being communicated. Trust is one of the foundations upon which intimacy is built. In preadoptive situations, people do not have a great deal of time. They are sharing an intense experience and yet they are strangers. Often, people fall back on the kind of etiquette that is, in many ways, similar to that shown a foreign dignitary during a state visit. We need that individual in order to accomplish our goals. The stakes are high. We have a short time to create an understanding and use our behavior to send signals. We are polite and careful. We are out to make a good impression. Our government follows a very carefully choreographed protocol during the visit in order to send the appropriate signals.

The same patterns exist in many preadoptive relationships. In the end, people have used "the conduct or procedure required by good breeding or prescribed by authority to be observed in social or official life" in order to send a message. In the end they don't know each other any better and they have not developed the kind of relationship where caring and respect are relevant. The goal is to create an adoption. However, we do ourselves and the children a disservice when the focus is on becoming parents rather than being parents. When parents' goal is to be the best parents they can be, they learn enough about adoption to take into account both their present needs and the needs and challenges that they and their child will face in the future.

Adopted children have many developmental challenges that are unique to their having been adopted. They need to make sense of what it means to have been born into one family, placed out of that family, and then moved into another family. They have parts of themselves that come from their biological background and parts that come from the family that raises them. Think "nature" and "nurture." The goal of an adopted person, as I see it, is to be able to find value in all of those pieces of heritage—at the same time. This task is made a great deal easier when adoptees grow up knowing that deep respect and caring exist between their adoptive and biological parents. They have integration of identities modeled for them through their experience of the feelings that their two sets of parents have for each other. Remember, adoption is supposed to be about what is in the best interest of the child. We do well when we create an etiquette that includes the child's long-term needs. When we do not, when we are guided solely by the kind of etiquette that limits our actions to making sure that the two sets of parents are comfortable during the placement period, we set the stage for later living as if adoption plays a minor historical role and does not set the stage for a series of important developmental challenges. Keeping the child's needs in mind leads us to conduct ourselves in ways designed to help the child become whole. It is through the development of a real relationship that the participants follow this deeper etiquette, one designed to help adoptees grow up feeling good about who they are in all senses.

How do we do this? How do we create this deep level of relationship in a short time? We cannot. What we can do is be very honest in expressing our intention to create a relationship that meets the child's long-term needs. Each set of parents will have something to offer the child that only they can provide. The adoptive parents are parenting the child and are responsible for all that that entails. The birthparents are the only ones who can let children know that although they have been placed for adoption, they have not been rejected, are not forgotten, and are a loved and included member of the biological family as well. People show each other respect and caring by having the courage to discuss differences or uncertainties that emerge when these truths are faced and integrated over time. It is hard to expose your insecurities and vulnerabilities to another, especially someone you do not know and whose acceptance you need. Generally, if the match is a good one, it is this exposure and a shared vulnerability that leads to building trust. All parties understand that they are being shown respect and caring and they understand that it is important that they reciprocate. The process that this entails forms the foundation for a relationship that will develop over time.

Preadoptive parents and pregnant women and couples need to understand that the relationship that they are building will exist for the rest of their lives. Even if they never see each other again, they will not forget the connection that they have and they will continue to occupy a permanent place in each other's psyches. The relationship will, for the adoptive parents, inform and flavor how they think about their child and the way that they teach their child about the child's background. If this lifelong nature of adoption is understood from the beginning, then people begin to place a deeper level of importance on how they conduct their preadoptive experience and they follow a form of etiquette that truly honors the purpose behind the word.

It is also true that honest discussion creates an opportunity to look into the future. The placement period is one moment in time. Interestingly, although adoption is supposed to be about the welfare of a child, during the preplacement period (in infant adoption) there is no child. The child has no present needs that must be considered. When people are being polite, they tend to limit their view, they don't look too closely. Adoption etiquette, as it is often understood, encourages preadoptive couples and pregnant women and couples to limit their focus to the pregnancy. They do not focus too much on what will come later. Their concerns lie in the present. The pregnant woman or couple wants to make a plan that addresses their untimely pregnancy. The preadoptive parents want to become parents as quickly as possible. Little thought is given to what it will mean for the pregnant woman or couple to become a biological mother or father but not parents and little thought is given to what actually being a parent is all about.

When preadoptive parents and the pregnant woman or couple begin to discuss who they are and what their goals for the child are in a more real way, they are provided with an opportunity to realize that the baby that they are talking about will become a toddler, a child, an adolescent, and then an adult. Along the way, adoptees will have different needs and although they cannot at this moment in time represent themselves in the discussions about their future, the pregnant woman or couple and preadoptive parents can take the time to learn about the long-term nature of adoption and the needs of adopted persons throughout their lifetimes.

Adoption etiquette as it is most often practiced works against addressing long-term needs. Private adoption often has a certain rhythm to it. Preadoptive parents contact an attorney or agency who will help guide them through the steps that are necessary to prepare for an adoption. Usually the clear goal is to become parents through adoption—as quickly as possible. Likewise, pregnant women or couples who are considering placing a child for adoption find their way to a private agency or attorney or put themselves directly in touch with preadoptive parents and go from there. Their goal is to find a solution to their current situation. They are about to give birth to a baby they do not feel it right to keep and parent. This they must do in a timely manner. So there is a complementarity of needs. One set of adults longs to become parents and another is making an adoption plan. This complementarity sets the stage for their initial interaction and often forms the basis for what comes after.

Often there is some form of contact between the woman or couple who is going to have the baby and the preadoptive parents. Sometimes this contact is conducted through intermediaries and sometimes there is direct contact between the preadoptive parents and the pregnant woman or couple. Sometimes it is through the exchange of letters or phone calls and sometimes it is in person. The attorneys or private agencies involved have the responsibility of guiding this relationship as it continues toward the goal that everyone has subscribed to: the transfer of a child out of one family and into another. The professionals who guide this relationship have a responsibility that ends just as the adoption begins. Their focus is limited to the needs of the preadoptive parents and the pregnant woman or couple up to the placement. They cannot have much awareness of what the child's needs will be in the future and therefore cannot take those needs into account.

Situations in which polite interaction is the goal differ in significant ways from situations in which people are reaching for a deeper form of etiquette—for ways of getting to a place where their interactions are filled with care and respect. When people are trying to be polite, they tend not to question things that they are told or asked to do. They forget their needs and behave in ways designed to please authority figures. This desire to appear as attractive potential parents tends to place the attorney or agency in the driver's seat. The participants worry that the professionals will reject them if they ask too many questions or express ambivalence. Being afraid to ask certain questions of the adoption professionals can be hidden in being polite. Couples tend to minimize any differences of opinion that they may have. They tend to remain silent about their doubts and fears about being adoptive parents.

The entire discussion tends to limit itself to becoming rather than being adoptive parents.

Pregnant women and couples often feel an enormous amount of stress. They may feel some shame about being in a situation where they will have to place a baby for adoption. They want this period in their lives to be over. They are no longer experiencing the present but are trying to reach for a time when this experience is behind them. They are often easily led down a path that works against learning about and questioning their own long-term needs, their confusion about parenting or placing their child for adoption or their understanding of what it means to be a birthparent. They are often allowed to believe that their "problem" will be solved once the baby is placed with adoptive parents. One of the ways that this urgency is communicated is that pregnant women or couples allow themselves to be referred to as "birthparents" even before there is a baby. They are asked to behave as though their decision is final even before they have given birth. Nobody explains to them that adoptive placement does not end their relationship with the child or with the adoptive parents. That will continue, whether in fact or fantasy, for the rest of their lives. The truth is that birthparents are changed by their experience and have their own ongoing developmental challenges to address.

When the baby is born, the complementarity of needs ends. The preadoptive parents wonder whether the adoption will actually take place and the pregnant woman or couple need to decide whether to parent or place the child for adoption. This can make for some anxiety and confusion during the hospital stay following the delivery. This is the period of time during which people may have an inkling that the relationship that they have built based on superficial politeness and established adoption etiquette may not have given them all of the security that they now need in order to feel comfortable with the other set of parents.

Once a decision has been made to move forward with an adoption plan, physical custody of the baby is given to the preadoptive parents, who are now called the adoptive parents. Sometimes arrangements are made with the biological family to remain in contact and sometimes they are not. Whatever the arrangements are, people cling to them. The adoptive parents realize that they are not yet the legal parents of the child and they do whatever they need to do to convey to the birthparents that they have made the right decision and that the baby is now in the right place. The birthparents are encouraged to move on with their lives. Haven't they longed for a time when all of this would be behind them? If the adoptive and birthparents have based their relationship on the more superficial form of etiquette, they may feel embarrassed about some of the feelings that now emerge. No longer are their needs complementary. The adoptive parents want to create their identity as a family and the birthparents need to come to some understanding of what it means to have given birth and not be parenting. Each set of parents is experiencing feelings that are not polite. They are feeling the intensity of the feelings that come with an adoption. If the foundation has not been built which allows them to acknowledge these feelings, they tend to pull away from each other.

In situations where a real relationship has begun, it is possible to acknowledge the present needs and realize that they are just that—needs of the moment. Both new adoptive parents and new birthparents have to address challenges that do not include the other. Each must adjust to their new identity. If people have done the deep work that real etiquette demands, they have developed a relationship which allows them to trust in the intentions of the others. They know that as needs change, their counterpart will be available to renegotiate their participation based upon what is in the best interest of the child. As the child's needs change, the adults, who have built a relationship based on the long-term, will feel free to be in contact with each other, each feeling willing and able to do their part in helping to make the child feel whole.

As the years pass the adoptive parents realize that their interest lies not, as it was in the beginning, in becoming parents, but rather in being the best parents that they can be. The birthparents realize that placing a child for adoption did not end their relationship to that child nor their concern for that child. It becomes apparent that the child has needs, and depending upon which form of etiquette guided their earlier relationship, they either have or have not built a foundation which makes it easier to facilitate their child's well-being.

The relationship that it is most important to honor is the children's relationship with themselves. That is the relationship that we want to make easy. We therefore need to act in a child-centered way. We should ask ourselves, is what we are doing, when viewed through a child-centered lens, making it easier for children to value all of who they are—at the same time? If the point is to help children become whole, can we afford to limit ourselves to following rules of etiquette where priority is placed on the adults' comfort, or do we need to reach further? Do we need to practice a form of etiquette whose underlying purpose it is to ease children's relationships with themselves, a respectful relationship which models for children the integration of the pieces of themselves that come from both birth and adoption? Parents are acting for the highest good and are practicing the highest form of etiquette when they honor the truth and think about the long-term ease of relationship regardless of whether, in that moment, it is awkward. They are providing their children with a "ticket" toward a fulfilling future.

CHAPTER SIX

Impolitics

Toward A Resistant Comportment

TRENT H. HAMANN

impolitic / a. LI6. [f. IM-2 + POLITIC a.] Not politic; not according to good policy; inexpedient.

—*The New Shorter Oxford English Dictionary*

There's a difference between a thug and a rebel.

—Rapper Chuck D., lecture at Shoreline Community College, Shoreline, WA, February 10, 2000

Power is tolerable only on condition that it mask a substantial part of itself. Its success is proportional to its ability to hide its own mechanisms.

—Michel Foucault, *The History of Sexuality*

The Little Ethics

In the middle of the eighteenth century, etiquette *(la petite éthique)* was unveiled in Lord Chesterfield's letters to his son as a new form of propriety that was clearly different from its historical antecedents, courtesy and civility. Whereas courtesy had been an economy of behaviors radiating from the central figure of the Christian God and civility was focused around the European sovereign, etiquette allowed new and diverse practices of propriety to become multiply defined by various distinct aristocratic groups. In addition, despite coming to be known as "the little ethics," etiquette thoroughly disengaged the norms of propriety from their former foundation in religion and morality. The new secular forms of propriety began to exhibit the apparently more trivial characteristics of class convention and fashion. Today, the multicentered practices of propriety are even more fragmented and contextualized than in Chesterfield's day, having come to be associated with such diverse concerns as social mobility, international business, the proper rituals and comportment at weddings and wakes, legal and diplomatic protocol, dining behavior, and Internet "netiquette." Beginning with its birth in the 1700s, etiquette hasn't so much demanded that one always be one's proper self, as courtesy and civility once did. Rather, propriety today requires that one have many proper selves at one's disposal in order to perform them whenever and wherever deemed appropriate. In what sense, then, can any of these selves be considered "proper"?

By way of beginning to investigate this question and its possible ethical and political implications, I turn to the work of Michel Foucault. I want to suggest that etiquette or the modern discourses and practices of propriety might usefully be described in terms of what Foucault calls "governmentality," that is, the complex nexus of (1) the social strategies used for governing populations and (2) the associated tactics deployed by individuals as techniques of self-governance and subjectivization. Any analysis of governmentality must recognize the role played by individual techniques of the self in fulfilling the implicit strategic goals established for the sake of governing a population and maintaining certain relations of power. In this case, the norms of comportment prescribed by etiquette might be viewed as playing a vital tactical role at the more visible end of this bipolar structure of governmentality, the other end being the strategies of social governance that, as Foucault suggests, often remain surreptitious and silent.[1] This would suggest that the apparent "everydayness" of good etiquette might operate as a form of subterfuge that allows behavioral norms and prescriptions to function as an explicit form of socially sanctioned self-governance. In other words, the exigencies of propriety are able to perform their subjectivizing work upon individuals in so subtle and effective a manner precisely because, among other reasons, they appear to be both less serious than the imperatives of morality and less stable than the kinds of epistemic prescriptions made by the social sciences. Because etiquette (1) is adopted as "mere" performance; (2) appears value neutral due to its lost ties to morality; and (3) is sometimes as fickle as the trends of fashion, it isn't hard to see why most philosophers have not appreciated it as a worthy object of study. Nevertheless, beginning with its inception in the middle of the eighteenth century, etiquette has carried out the decisive social and political tasks that have continuously been refined and elaborated by every historical form of propriety. That is, etiquette continues to operate as an important set of techniques through which individuals actively participate in the social constitution of themselves as subjects living within complex relations of power—what Foucault calls "technologies of the self" or "ethics."[2]

For a brief example of this fundamental role played by etiquette, consider the last chapter of the 1969 edition of *Emily Post's Etiquette.*[3] Here we discover a number of guidelines for creating a "happy marriage" that, in fact, can be critically recognized as reproducing some of the gender-based inequalities that have traditionally characterized heterosexual marriage in the West. Of particular note is Post's claim that "for some reason, it seems that the bride generally has to make more effort to achieve a successful marriage than the bridegroom."[4] Within this single remark we might begin to recognize the significant capacities and formal characteristics that make etiquette worth paying attention to. Because the rules of proper behavior are prescribed by Post as simply being "the thing to do," no reason or rationale is required for them and none is offered, thus helping to preserve their apparently value neutral and everyday character. The rules of comportment simply are what they are "for some reason," a reason that is presumably unknown even to a popularly recognized expert like Post. Nevertheless, the binding force of these rules must apply to all who would normally be expected to appropriate them as the maxims of their own behaviors, in this case any newly married couple in late 1960s America.[5]

The imperative force of etiquette need not remain a mystery to us. Perhaps what was possible in 1969 is not so today—the long list of prescriptions for the new bride accompanied by a more meager set of advice for the groom is itself immediately suspicious. We can no longer read such passages from Post without recognizing these "neutral" behavioral guidelines as a set of tactical rules used to enact, embody, and reproduce some of the sexist gender norms that have been strategic for institutionalized heterosexuality in postwar America. The absence of the need for an explicit rationale here has two primary functions. First, it operates as a mask for the hidden connections between what is prescribed and the unmarked social strategies that depend on the active participation of those subjects conditioned by them. In light of this function we see that it is absolutely crucial for etiquette to appear autonomous and arbitrary if not trivial. Second, it produces the effect of causing the actions of those who do refuse the prescriptions of etiquette to appear arbitrary and unfounded. Such individuals necessarily come across as merely willful, petty, immature, stricken with bad taste—anything but resistant to the strategic forces that often covertly determine how we fashion ourselves as subjects.[6] To even consider questioning contemporary etiquette is already to risk disappropriating oneself from the coherent domain of propriety, thereby rendering oneself as either inappropriate, incoherent, or some combination of the two.

The Différend: Manners in Dispute

> It is always possible one could speak the truth in a void; one would only be in the true, however, if one obeyed the rules of some discursive "policy" which would have to be reactivated every time one spoke.
>
> —Michel Foucault, "The Discourse on Language"

In his letters to his son, wherein he coined the word "etiquette," Lord Chesterfield emphasized again and again the fact that the actual substance of the behaviors of genteel company matters not at all if one's sole purpose is simply to belong to that company. What is important is that one manage to appropriate the form and formality of those behaviors, no matter what they are:

> Take the tone of the company that you are in, and do not pretend to give it; be serious, gay, or even trifling, as you find the present humour of the company; this is an attention due from every individual to the majority.

> Remember that there is a local propriety to be observed in all companies; and that what is extremely proper in one company, may be, and often is, highly improper in another.[7]

Lord Chesterfield's prescriptions suggest the possibility that the imperative force of etiquette is a form of panoptic power reproduced through the continuous observation of the rules that constitute a given company.[8] The appropriate rules of behavior are those that one observes in a company in order to appropriate them for oneself. One then observes those rules in one's own practice in order that one's comportment be observed and judged favorably by the company. The objective is to belong to, or be appropriated by, the group through a process wherein each individual is both observer and observed in relation to every other individual. In this sense etiquette operates more like a language, a semiotics, or a code.[9] What each code conveys in its specifics will vary from context to context; however, Lord Chesterfield implies that this is of secondary concern if indeed it is of any concern at all. What this semiotics of propriety signifies in general is nothing but a purely formal, one might even say "categorical," willingness to be appropriated, a will to belong within the exclusionary borders defined by the group.[10] As the sociologist Jorge Arditi has put it, "Manners becomes a language, a formal property through which a group takes shape."[11] Because they are ostensibly autonomous and defined internally, the codes or regimens of any given genre of comportment resist being held accountable to anything or anyone outside their proper domain. Consequently, one can never properly demand such accountability. To have a recognizable voice, to speak the proper behavioral language within a given genre of comportment, one must already belong to it, in which case one would probably not make the inappropriate demand that it legitimate itself in the first place.

Of course, one can certainly traverse multiple genres of propriety, but the various regimens that produce the specific activities that distinguish one genre from another prevent particular behaviors from being properly transferred or translated across genres. I have adopted Lyotard's terminology here because it proves helpful for understanding particular behaviors or manners in terms of relations of power. As to the impossibility of properly translating specific behaviors across genres of comportment, he has explained in his book *The Differend: Phrases In Dispute*, that "a universal rule of judgment between heterogeneous genres is lacking in general."[12] But the problem I wish to address is not that of the incongruity between different genres of comportment, an incongruity that, after all, most of us manage to embody quite nicely every day. Rather, I wish to address the differend that occurs between propriety and impropriety. Lyotard writes in his preface, "As distinguished from a litigation, a differend [différend] would be a case of conflict, between (at least) two parties, that cannot be equitably resolved for lack of a rule of judgment applicable to both arguments. One side's legitimacy does not imply the other's lack of legitimacy. However, applying a single rule of judgment to both in order to settle their differend as though it were merely a litigation would wrong (at least) one of them (and both of them if neither side admits this rule)."[13]

Here the two parties are propriety on the one hand, and that which hopes to question, to challenge, and perhaps refuse it on the other. Of course, in this case, one side's legitimacy certainly does imply the other's lack of legitimacy. As I've already proposed, even to question propriety is to consign oneself to the realm of the inappropriate precisely because propriety applies "a single rule of judgment" to all behaviors it recognizes as proper to its genre. That which is deemed inappropriate must either become appropriate(d) or be rendered silent. Impropriety is by its very nature impolitic, illegitimate, and ill begotten under the hyperpanoptic gaze of propriety and thereby has no authority to make proper judgments of its own.[14]

Chuck D., former member of the rap group Public Enemy, may perhaps have been right when he claimed that "there's a difference between a thug and a rebel," but there has never been a rebel who wasn't summarily judged to be a thug by the regime against which he or she rebelled. The 1969 housewife who might have refused to be the designated unpaid domestic laborer within the marriage partnership would likely have been perceived by her husband, her family, her friends, her neighbors, and perhaps even herself as an improper wife. In fact she would have been improper insofar as her refusal would have been impolitic, that is, inexpedient, imprudent, and injudicious in relation to the functional partnership she had contractually agreed to with her husband (who we may assume was performing his own proper roles as laborer and wage earner in the public realm, and minor sovereign in the private domicile). However, we should recognize that perhaps it isn't the legal parameters of such contractual relationships that determine the types of subjectivation produced within them so much as the imperatives of propriety and the sanctions one risks being subjected to if one chooses to resist them. Just as every rebel is judged a thug or criminal, those who are impolitic are deemed merely impolite, uncivil, and rude if not psychologically dysfunctional. Indeed we can imagine this housewife having become frustrated due to her plaint being silenced and rendered illegitimate in advance by what she herself recognized as appropriate. We can also imagine her one evening smashing the dirty dinner dishes to the kitchen floor.

On December 1, 1955, when Rosa Parks refused to give up her seat to a white man on a Montgomery, Alabama, bus, she was breaking the local laws of segregation. Interestingly, when she was arrested by the police and subsequently fined fourteen dollars, the specific charge brought against her for remaining seated was "disorderly conduct." Certainly she broke the law, but what is more significant is that she defied long-standing customary behaviors. In the moment when she refused to move, it wasn't the letter of the law that became an issue for the passengers on the bus. It was the discomfort produced by an impolitic challenge to custom, behavior, and the unwritten rules of proper orderly comportment. What appears to us today as the cruel stupidity of the law in 1955 can only make the slightest bit of sense if we consider what was taken for granted as the everyday orderly conduct between the races. These forms of comportment constituted a complex network of behaviors that not only conformed to the written law, but also reinforced and reproduced the unmarked strategies of racist white supremacy. Had there been no revocation of the laws of segregation, perhaps the name of Rosa Parks might be as little recognized today as that of Claudelle Colbert, who previously had also been arrested for refusing to give up her seat on a Montgomery bus. But to overemphasize the rule of law at the cost of ignoring the rules of propriety is to miss the significance of the impolitic actions of Claudelle Colbert as well as Rosa Parks and the many others whose actions precipitated the Montgomery bus boycott—a great impolitic event. To focus on the law is also to not grasp the imperative forces at work on the nameless white man and others like him who demanded a seat. We can assume that it wasn't principally a desire to put the law to good use that motivated his behavior. Rather, it may have been his sense of his own being, specifically his sense of propriety and racial entitlement in being a white man subject to his own judgments and the judgmental gaze of the other white passengers on the bus. It is telling that following the legal revocation of segregation it took much longer for such racist habits of comportment to even begin to change.

The Frailty of Propriety

> A certain fragility has been discovered in the very bedrock of existence—even, and perhaps above all, in those aspects of it that are most familiar, most solid and most intimately related to our bodies and to our everyday behavior.
>
> —Michel Foucault, "Two Lectures"

Why speak of a comportment of resistance in terms of impolitics? Why an emphasis on what is not in accord with good policy, what is inexpedient, unwise, not prudent, and injudicious? I do so primarily because impolitics is a refusal of what is politic—the individualizing tactics of self-governance that often lend support to whatever is instrumental for the smooth operation of social strategies of domination. A resistant comportment can be understood as a semiotics of power generated from within a different behavioral genre. Its possibilities are recognizable within the minutiae of self-forming activities produced in daily activity and its meanings are evident in the social strategies they resist. The resistance of a hypothetical housewife in the 1960s or an African American woman on a Montgomery bus in the 1950s constituted new tactics that not only disrupted their own subjectivation, but also placed a compelling ethical demand on others around them. The husband in his domicile and the white passengers on the bus were faced with the choice of either dismissing these demands as groundless improprieties or acknowledging them as imperatives calling for a response. What kind of response and responsibility would that be? In the anthology *Angry Women*, bell hooks has quoted Thich Nhat Hanh as saying that "understanding comes through our capacity to empty out the self and identify with that person whom we normally make the Other. In other words, the moment we are willing to give up our own ego and draw in the being and presence of someone else, we're no longer 'Other-ing' them, because we are saying that there's no space they inhabit that cannot be a space we connect with."[15]

Ironically, we've already seen this process of "emptying out" and "identifying with the Other" in Lord Chesterfield's paradoxical formulations that suggest one must always become one's proper self. To properly come into one's own, one must first be appropriated by others; that is, one must recognize that one is always already other to one's self in the endless processes of subjectivation. This paradoxical instability and frailty of the proper self and its politics is precisely what makes possible its own continuous undoing, be it understood as an impolitic resistance, a new creative form of self-governance, or perhaps even the requisite vulnerability of a loving identification with others.

Notes

1. For a more detailed analysis see my article "Modern Etiquette and Foucault's Ethical Technologies," *International Studies in Philosophy*, 32, no. 1 (2000).

2. Michel Foucault, *Technologies of the Self*, ed. Luther H. Martin, Huck Gutman, and Patrick H. Hutton (Amherst: University of Massachusetts Press, 1988).

3. *Emily Post's Etiquette*, ed. Elizabeth L. Post (New York: Funk & Wagnalls, 1969), pp. 703–711.

4. Ibid., p. 706.

5. While it certainly can be argued that readers of etiquette books and manuals have traditionally been relatively privileged individuals within society, there are rules of comportment—written or not—that apply to any social group. The idea that propriety functions as a means of policing the borders of social groups is discussed below.

6. For an excellent analysis of the privilege of invisibility characteristic of dominant social strategies, particularly those of heterosexuality, see David M. Halperin, *Saint Foucault* (New York: Oxford University Press, 1995).

7. Lord Chesterfield, *Letters*, ed. David Roberts (New York: Oxford University Press, 1992), pp. 57–58.

8. Chesterfield's use of the word "company" is certainly instructive insofar as it implies for us a group of individuals gathered together as well as a commercial business, a body of soldiers, a group of actors, and so on. "Company" suggests not only personal accompaniment, but economic and class

commerce, strategic power, and public performance, all of which I would argue are closely related to etiquette and the demands of politic behavior.

9. For an analysis of codes as a formation of power, following Foucault, see Gilles Deleuze's "Postscript on Control Societies" in *Negotiations*, trans. Martin Joughin (New York: Columbia University Press, 1995), pp. 177–182.

10. Of course, one of my main objectives here is to suggest that it is very likely a fallacy to consider any behavior a pure formality separable from its substance and its matter. It is doubtful that formality can ever be *pure* and unsullied by matter.

11. Jorge Arditi, *A Genealogy of Manne* (Chicago: University of Chicago Press, 1998), p. 211.

12. Jean François Lyotard, *The Differend: Phrases in Dispute*, trans. Georges Van Den Abbeele (Minneapolis: University of Minnesota Press), p. xi.

13. Ibid.

14. Concerning the issue of illegitimacy and that which is ill begotten, it may be of some interest to consider the possibility that Lord Chesterfield's own enduring anxiety over the propriety of his male progeny may have had to do with the fact that his son Philip was a bastard.

15. bell hooks, interviewed in *Angry Women*, ed. Andrea Juno and V. Vale (San Francisco: Re/Search Publications, 1991), p. 83.

CHAPTER SEVEN

Coldness and Civility

ALISON LEIGH BROWN

Which rule of etiquette is violated when we eavesdrop? Which novel of manners persists without an internal self-analysis? Which foundational philosophical principle underlies each act of courtesy? Who gets to ask these questions? What is a customer? What is an audience? What is a potential audience? Is it rude to write for the potential reader at the expense of that one here, listening to every word, caring about minor events? Who is this editor who listens to these women writing a life for the edification of others . . . ?

Editor's Preface to *A Curious Correspondence*, by C. W. Meridith, Literature and Self-Awareness, College La Mer

It is an astonishing feature of our age that the novel is accorded both undue and no respect. Unduly as the cash cow for future films, novels are property. Not respected as a commercial project. To elevate them to theoretical treatises involves an endless string of absurdities. Novels show us what is human, what is historical, what holds our cultures together. They show us how to behave—which fork to use. To relegate them to theory erases their humanity. Everywhere one finds the ridiculous practice of making the classics into film—and how badly these are done, the basic coldness of great novels sentimentalized beyond recognition. Not only is the novel lost, but also the power of what makes a movie a movie is buried under too much meaning. Following in spite of themselves the gender politics of the movie, women and men become unrecognizable as creatures commanding any interest beyond celluloid excitement. Movies are embodied; novels are cerebral. Austen's novels can be, and have been, translated into film with none of the humor, none of the strength, captured or portrayed. Women without agency in these novels become mere objects of romance. That is, the delicately crafted tension circumscribed by their lack of agency is buried or erased. A coldness found in fictional heroes is turned to a syrupy devotion to men. These men are changed from strategizing robots to sappy devotees of the female form.

Myself, I am devoted to the novel. I spend hours a week reading as fast as I can. When I was asked to compile the correspondence between Chantal Berger and Marianne Post I balked. The history of this sorry affair is well known. The *Chronicle of Higher Education* ran the front-page story on their treachery. Letters concerning the events were printed for months. *Harper's* had the roundtable on the state of the academy in which this tale was the central example of all that is bad there. After much soul searching I decided that I would take on the task. There is good to be found in any story and lessons to be learned. What is instructive in the letters is an unconscious awareness that the university itself is largely responsible for the paucity of meaning attached to the novel. University life can be vicious and idiotic. There seems to be little question that this is the case. Turf is cautiously guarded; personalities become the focus of every dispute; grown-ups spend their time fighting over pitiful amounts of money and empty honors. Honors that they deride, win or lose. From these halls, from those subjects, it is not surprising that the grandeur of the novel cannot be appreciated. What is worst in these letters is the intelligence of the correspondents. One could easily decide that there is something of worth in these missives. I reprint them here not to show intellects at work. One could deduce that these nihilistic letters exhibit something noble and good—that even in the pursuit of personal relations, academics are working, working, working. But this can no longer be seen as work if the academy is to survive. Work must be redescribed as it once was. Finding the good and the beautiful and the true in the artifacts of culture has to be returned to intellectual life. I do not print these with any aim to hold these awful women up as exemplars of the pursuit of knowledge. Instead I print them for their subtexts. They exhibit a moral bankruptcy, which many readers may not recognize exists to the extent that it does. Facility with words has long had a power that obscures treachery and pettiness. It is forgivable that we fall prey to its force. I urge the reader to stand firm against the seeming logic of their words. To keep my conscience clear I had to write these short prefatory remarks. I beg the reader to remember at all times that I reprint these as a cautionary tale. My goal is to alert the public concerning the true nature of the university system. It is the public, after all, that is the moral and financial support of the university system. Because of these times, I cannot echo the noble intentions of the editor of *Les Liaisons Dangereuses.* That editor writes, "I think, at any rate, that it is rendering a service to public morals to reveal the methods employed by those who are wicked in corrupting those who are good, and I believe that these letters may effectively contribute something to this end." There is no one in this bathetic chronicle who is capable of corruption—all parties being always already hopelessly beyond redemption. Not everyone in the world, however, falls into this classification. Some of us are able to escape the clutches of vanity and shortsightedness. Some of us maintain a love for all that is noble in literature. To you I offer these letters as testimony and proof that something is rotten in the ivory halls: there is no ground, no governing principle. There is little time for those of us who have remained firm against the growing chaos to reclaim the glories of the written word and of the human soul. We find ourselves in an age with a dead god, a dead state, a dying sense of civility and value. But there is some time and there is some grounding. Let us act decisively. No less than civilization is at stake.

Excerpt from *A Curious Correspondence*
Letter #1
Marianne to Chantal

My dear Chantal,

Forgive me for the long time it has taken me to get back to you. You raise so many issues, all of which interest me immensely, as you surely know, and none of which allows an easy answer. As you also know, I am hard at work on the new novel, which practice leaves me scant opportunity for thinking or conversing. But to recount the details of my workaday life would be unforgivably boring. Loving you, I spare you the details of my coffee making, pencil sharpening, pacing, etc. I write in part selfishly. You raise so many interesting points in your last letter, many of which I need to work out to have a thematically interesting novel. To do justice to your intensely theoretical letter would take twenty pages at least. Consequently, I will address just one of the issues you raise. I cut short my theoretical responses because I want to share with you some very interesting gossip. Theory first.

What I am working on in the novel is complex. One of my characters is finding increasingly that she is incapable of love. She is loved but she cannot love in return. As she examines the details of her life for clues to this sorry state she realizes that she is not unique in this regard. There is a sense in which not being capable of love is part of the human condition. This depresses her very much. She thinks about this new state of affairs—not only is she incapable of active loving, she is terribly depressed. It strikes her that her reaction to depression is shameful. Hers is not a biologically based sadness. Instead, it is justifiable sorrow in the face of actual loss. Since contingent in this way, she decides that she should be able to will herself out of her deep sadness. Right now I am working on the manner in which she finds the strength to get out of her predicament. My problem is turning this to action. No one wants to read a novel wherein the character is merely introspective. What novel would work wherein the hero solves her problem by solving a philosophical problem? I have to find a plot line that shows her working through this depression in a way that is interesting but which nevertheless illuminates the philosophical insights she has. (I know that this is not impossible: look at Nabokov! Dostoevski!) The other problem is purely theoretical. The issue at stake is, what is it about every era that seems to its writers as too, too depressing? There are so many answers but it is difficult to find one that is not repeated endlessly throughout history—at least Western history. I think that the answer lies in recent theorists reacting to the great wars by spending their time analyzing something which should be left unthought: the basic emptiness at the core of human consciousness. Why can't we just acknowledge this and move on? This is the problem on which I am working. Since in my novel, it is tied up with love, I will spend my time responding to the things you write to me about love.

Of course, this is painful to me. I'll never understand why you can't reciprocate my love for you. We both know enough to know that sexuality is fluid. (Remember your essay on Austen and Dickinson wherein that is your theme. What a great essay that was. I loved watching you give it. Was it in San Antonio? Was the name of the conference "Requeering the Canon: Sapphic Desire and Spinster Poets?" It was fun in the early nineties wasn't it?) Still, everything you said was right. Sexuality is fluid so you constantly frustrate me. I think that we know each other too well to be in love and that thought depresses me beyond anything which stands in the category of making me depressed. Maybe if when we'd first met I had not needed so desperately to be your friend then things could have been better. In any case, I content myself with knowing that we are irrevocably friends.

How verbose I become under certain circumstances. I'm sorry for the sorry aside about "us." I know it bothers you. I know you will not respond to it. I know that I promised to never bring it up again. So, I'll turn to your theoretical musings on love. At least that way I can write to you about love and not break my vow of silence.

You are concerned, it seems, that Spinoza is all wrong about love. You cite Proposition XXXIII of the third book, which I will recopy for your benefit. There should be at least some clarity of thought in what will surely be one of my more rambling missives and we'll let the lens grinder provide, eh? He, Spinoza, writes, as cited to me last month, "When we love a thing similar to ourselves we endeavor, as far as we can, to bring about that it should love us in return." The proposition immediately following that one reads, "The greater the emotion with which we conceive a loved object to be affected toward us, the greater will be our complacency."[1] The worry you are experiencing is basically something like this. If Spinoza is right in both propositions, which he has a good chance of being, the always on-target set of sweetnesses that he is, then it appears we have the following sadnesses. First, after spending energy and heartache getting some other to love us, the achievement of our aim ends in dissolution of the motivating love we had enjoyed with pleasure in the first case. Second, there is an odd tying up of successfully achieved pleasure with complacency. That is, when we get what we want, we are bored. Finally, there are devastating consequences in the text for love in general: if one finds commitment and reciprocal loving, then surely that love must wane; on the other hand, if fear and uncertainty are kept alive, the result, as subsequent propositions make clear enough, is hatred or jealousy.

Hoping that I have accurately represented you, let me address these issues together because unlike yourself, I find it impossible to disjoin these three points. Try as I might, any definitions I come up with for the central terms reduce to the same basic set of concepts, and this assimilation of like to like is only exacerbated by the fact that there is crucial overlay of appearance taking precedent over reality. It is telling that the only word in the five or six pages you reference from Spinoza, on which you fail to discourse, is "similar." I will return to this omission.

Allow me another aside? You are dying to get to the gossip I am sure and I recognize the tedium of this particular letter. Still, I must inform you that I recall sitting on a beach with you, which beach I cannot recall but it was certainly a Pacific one, both of us having recently reread the Austen novels. You were irritated at the focus on marriage while I found the focus endearing but misguided. We both opined that it would be wonderful to have had a novel based on the less domestically inclined Jane. You will recall the entire conversation, I am sure, since it ended badly, in a fight. I indicated to you that it was important to remember that marriage was rather the thing at the time. To read the novels against any other backdrop seemed so beside the point. Take *Mansfield Park*. The impoverished and indebted Fanny must marry. She has no other options. The man she chooses, he who she schemes to obtain, is sufficiently similar to herself that one is made quite ill. What a pair they are! So self-righteous! So pompous! So unable to enjoy themselves in play! It is so interesting that the event that seals their love is their coming together against the theatre. I love the scene where he decides that in order to protect the morals of the assembled houseguests, he must be in the play. He is so polite! It slays me! Poor Fanny doesn't know how to think about this. She cannot participate in such lavsciousness and if Edmund does, then he is violating all the principles he has taught her. But he must be right because he is not only a good man, but also a potential man of the cloth. In their discussion of this matter they fall in love for the first time. That they don't know this is all the more delicious. Edmund and Fanny united in the evils of the world. United against the frivolity of dresses and curls. One can assume that in the case of that particular pairing Spinoza is dead on target with the whole love thing. She must make Edmund love her; she must possess him. He is her mirror image, her soul mate; more's the pity for both of them. Additionally, one can be sure that complacency permeated the happy scene at the end, which again I retype for your convenience. (I am certain that your study looks much as it always has done—finding any given novel would take you the better part of a morning. I can picture you wandering among your stacks, coffee cup in hand, eyes that unfocused way which quickly turns to a sort of quiet rage when you realize that you have spent several hours looking for something which you know so well without seeing that you need not have bothered looking. I save you from that now because I love you. I really do, you know, and feel not the slightest complacency in either my love for you or in anything like certainty in your love for me, all the while knowing that the intensity of your emotion for me is quite strong, and etc. Besides which, we are not so similar you and I, although we are sufficiently like that we might converse as equals and etc. Christ I'm in love with you. Can I take back my promise to not talk about this? I know your answer will be silence. You are so principled.)

So dear Jane writes about the eventual coming together of Edmund and Fanny. Perhaps we too shall come together in spite of ourselves and external enticements.

> With so much true merit and true love, and no want of fortune or friends, the happiness of the married cousins must appear as secure as earthly happiness can be.—Equally formed for domestic life, and attached to country pleasures, their home was the home of affection and comfort; and to complete the picture of good, the acquisition of Mansfield living by the death of Dr. Grant, occurred just after they had been married long enough to want an increase of income, and feel their distance from the paternal abode an inconvenience.
>
> On that event they removed to Mansfield, and the parsonage there, which under each of its two former owners, Fanny had never been able to approach but with some painful sensation of restraint or alarm, soon grew as dear to her heart, and as thoroughly perfect in her eyes, as everything else, within the view and patronage of Mansfield Park, had long been.[2]

The key word here is "appear." Like our blessed one, St. Jane understands that the eye of the beholder is the only one that counts.

Perceiving that we are loved, held in intensity of emotion, is as good as it gets. Fanny's eyes behold perfection in particulars but also in "every thing else," the poor dear, and complacency is so thick in this scene that the happiness resulting from true merit and love appears to the reader as thin, or, at least, less than robust. Our Edmund would have been much happier with the evil Miss Crawford, and much less complacent. Then we would have the entire love/hate thing to keep things in motion. Miss Crawford is so much more . . . fun! She gets all the good lines. She gets to be funny and charming. Fanny. The scenes in her home of origin are so typical of her brand of tedium. Trying to whip some manners into her pathetic siblings, overcoming the shame she feels for her father but only partially, refusing to see any nobility in her continuously sacrificing mother. If Fanny had failed in her attempt to snare simple Edmund, she would have been able to always keep him as that thing which she could not have, occasioning her mind with fodder for the years left her. She could have sat in her pathetic, dark, damp, and odoriferous urban home commiserating on the impossible chains of the proletariat. Both happier. Both more interesting.

All of which brings me to the word "similar." Loving the alien need not have the same results (of either a fading or waning or the sorry state of jealousy and hatred.) That is, maybe Fanny could have found excitement with Mr. Crawford. She could have made of him a project. She could always be consulting with her brother-in-law, Edmund, about how to tame the animal advances of randy Mr. Crawford. She could dish with Edmund about the lack of seriousness in his evil wife and their eyes would continue to speak volumes of desire each to each. Complacency could not be the result of those particular pairings. And this is also why we know that Austen is not about marriage. Any reader necessarily imagines the other ending. Same to same is boring. We can converse on this matter more if you wish—I await your reply, which I will scan quickly for a change in heart! I don't want to write more here, now, until I know if we are on the same playing field.

Basically the problem you see in Spinoza and consequently in life, is that one's achievement of love is negated by itself. This is related more generally to the notion that pleasure achieved is a kind of satisfaction that turns to complacency. Such a sad state of affairs is only marginally better than that other possibility—the increasingly fierce jealousy or hatred caused by continued uncertainty. Well, that is rather mushy, I know. Bear with me. I will supply you with three responses detailing why you are wrong that love negates itself and that pleasure, once achieved, is dissipated.

First, there is no possibility of the certainty Spinoza references. In other words, it is merely a feature of an architectonic which is true enough in a trivial way but which we have no fear of attaining. One can achieve this in novels only if immediately on attaining one's goal the novel is over—*Mansfield Park* again, or if the aim, once achieved, is shown to have been duplicitous, *Les Liaisons Dangereuses*. So even in fiction, it is recognized that certainty of that kind is illusory, meant to tie up loose ends or to reveal treachery. The lines in the Vincomte de Valmont's letter to the Marquise are the best in the literature for this point. He has attained the prudish de Tourvel. He is astonished that she is less than prudish in love and after making predictable points along those lines, poor sod, he reasserts his ability to be distanced from this strategic seduction: "It is not the charm of love either: for if I did at times, beside this astonishing woman, experience sensations of weakness which resembled that pusillanimous passion, I was always able to conquer them and to reassert my principles."[3] That de Tourvel loves him is clear in some sappy sort of way. That he will not, that he cannot be a real person, is equally clear. So there is a mutually satisfying achievement of pleasure saved from complacency by the fact of denying the certainty. This is necessary only for one of the pair. Astonishing, non? The vicious Valmont notes, "The access of pleasure I experienced in the moment of triumph, and which I still feel, is nothing but the delicious sensation of glory. I encourage myself in this belief because it spares me the humiliation of thinking that I might in any way have been dependant on the very salve I had subjected to my will; that I might not find in myself alone everything I require for my happiness."[4]

He enclosed for the Marquise's and his continued amusement at the prude's expense de Tourvel's outpouring of love and devotion. Such behavior, as we both know, is no caricature of excessive evil. How many times have we laughed at our conquests, especially earnest ones? That we, and by "we" I denote all breathers, that we still fight for certainty in love is something I think I can explain. It is my belief that there is a core coldness to each of us that asserts and reasserts itself as a kind of certainty about death. This certainty is awesome and untenable. Thus, Heidegger, for example. He never ceases in his discoursing on our being-toward-death. Subsequent and contemporary philosophers and theorists continue in this vein, pointing over and over again to this space that has no meaning in spite of its universality. There is nothing to say really about this ache in each of us. If we are in theoretical mode we explain this feeling as somehow historically contingent. The horrors of capitalism produce an alienation from our species being which must be overturned by the overthrow of capitalism. Then we'll be happy. We'll have the certainty of objective, proletarian science. Or, the clash between increased technology and civilization overlays our instincts toward love and aggression sufficiently that we must work very hard at not feeling alone and mean. Or, we are cold and brutish, requiring all sorts of codes to keep us from killing and raping each other. As if. My insight is that there is a root coldness because we only really are in concert with others. In those moments where we feel alone, where we recognize death and lovelessness, we search for the wrong kinds of certainty. We spin theories—or make quilts! We should, you know, just get on with the matters at hand. There are points at which theorizing becomes beside the point. The awful thing for us right now is that we know too much. "The world is too much with us; late and soon/ Getting and spending, we lay waste our powers"—you know that sort of thing.[5] This horrid obsessing about the wrong things. What we should concern ourselves over has to do with the overlays we create. I will not believe that we create them as reaction formation or revolutionary activity only. I want to believe in a world where we overlay our existence with words and actions because those activities are intrinsically valuable and beautiful. The other explanations underline over and over again a narcissistic belief that we are pointless. The fact is that there is no way to theorize ourselves out of death. We do, by which I mean that we try. But how puny our efforts, how much power we waste in this endeavor. And we do it increasingly as the overlays go all to hell. If we would focus on the overlays and let go the fears of the blind thoughts' vitality and power, the world would be different: strange and beautiful and full of uncertain love. (On which more later on the phone if you feel so inclined. God, I miss you Chantal. Are you still wearing your hair black? Do you still smell the same way? I went to buy your perfume the other day and realized that this too was an obsession of the sort that is impossible to meet, and restrained myself. Are you proud of me? Do you love me? No! Of course not.) The point of all of this is that there are things for which there are no names, no definitions, the most important one of which being that we are alone and dying. This means nothing however and requires no discoursing. But it does imply something, namely, that certainty is a ridiculous standard toward which to strive. Since that certainty is not possible, one need not fear complacency of the kind Spinoza references. Even Fanny and Edmund look at each other over their tepid, weak tea and wonder, who is that person? What am I doing in "our" parlor? Why is our tea so bad? So darling, don't worry about love. You will never need fear that your fierceness be negated just because you love well. (And further, but not unrelated—I cannot keep myself to brevity where you are concerned—the overlays are interesting and lovely. They escape negation by their messiness. On which more later.)

Second, you must be wrong about love's self-negation and pleasure's exhausting itself because of your implicit understanding that fear and desire operate in some sort of opposing manner. We have made an art of terrifying ourselves over our desires. I mean really, Chantal, look at how we eat in this country and how guilty we feel about it. Look at the way we talk about abortion. Look at how we vilify women for expressing any sort of sexual desire whatsoever. There is a reason for our foibles in this regard. Earlier I wrote about coldness. Desire in general is related to our attempts to shield ourselves from our basic meanness, our stinginess, our inability to forget death, the frantic worries over things which even as we worry about them we know to have no meaning. Sometimes I think that what we write about as the human condition (I know we are so careful to relegate everything to historical and societal constructions, but really we believe ourselves to be writing truths about humans; you know I am speaking the truth here, I cannot lie to you about anything), what we are really doing is amplifying the facts of our profession. Perhaps nonacademics do not worry about the same sorts of things with the same fierceness. Perhaps we are not really like humans at all. (Forgive me; I am in a bluish mood.) To resume, desire becomes the positive thing which might overcome fear, the negative one, and the dialectic is off and running, making both states of being negations. Look what happens when persons decide to refuse to converse on this emptiness.

> Now and then Rogozhin would suddenly begin to mutter, loudly, harshly, incoherently; he would cry out and begin laughing; the prince reached out his trembling hand then, and softly touched

> his head, his hair, and began stroking him and stroking his cheeks—he could do nothing more! He started to tremble again, and again his legs seemed to be failing him. Some completely new sensation oppressed his heart with infinite anguish. Meanwhile it had become quite light; at last he lay down on the cushions, as though completely powerless in despair, and laid his face against Rogozhin's pale motionless face; tears flowed from his eyes onto Rogozhin's cheeks, but perhaps he did not notice his own tears and was not at all aware of them.[6]

What need have we, Chantal, of going on and on about this coldness, which neither the prince nor Rogozhin blame on anyone else. Or anything else. Are we better than they? Surely not. Now one cannot overlook the fact that they have a narrator to explicate their feelings for us. But we are not muted for not being characters in a masterful novel. In "real" life we have the evidence of, the fact of our bodies to express these things. Looking at someone through the eyes is sometimes all that is required to communicate on this issue. It is always beside the point to go further with this. But we do and we say all sorts of superfluous things. Among these we "believe" simultaneously that desire is bad and fear is good, and desire is good and fear is bad. We're knotted over with our perhaps valiant efforts to evade that which should not be spoken in any case. So, your fears over and desire for love need not be in opposition in the ways you suggest. (I know, I know that you are trying to make sense of Spinoza. You know I can't help but personalize the theoretical. It is in my blood.)

Finally, jealousy and hatred are realities. My final reason for suggesting (arguing?) that you are wrong has to do with another set of realities that we try to avoid with ridiculous result. Let me tell you a story. Assume a man and a woman. The woman has told the man that she is jealous of the time he spends with his family. (Maybe it is Edmund and all this complacency has sent him into the arms of another. Let's call her "Mistress." Mistress is tired of all those children and of Fanny in particular. Instead of reassuring her of his love, or, better, of explaining the situation to her by saying, "I love Fanny and I love you. I cannot leave Fanny for you. It would destroy her life if he begins to discourse on the irrationality of her position, etc." Let's say that instead of doing the reassuring lover thing, he says to her that she is sorely mistaken in being jealous. Jealousy, he might say, results from an imperfect understanding of our love. We love each other; this much is clear. The certainty, the attainment of our connection is such that these exterior concerns are beneath us. Therefore, what you are experiencing as jealousy is illusory. It cannot really exist. There is no rational place for it. Mistress will be enraged beyond speech. She may strike our Edmund with her little white fists, grabbing at his hair, attempting to make a mark on his face. "Let her see that," she might be thinking. All real discussions of jealousy and hatred must begin with the assumption that they exist and persist. In real cases where jealousy arises, the lover and the beloved must acknowledge the facticity of jealousy and hatred. Explaining them away "for" someone is immoral because necessarily false. Spinoza knows this. He knows and we should likewise know that these states of being cannot be transcended. As such, we are foolish, or so I believe, if we assume that it is possible for two persons to achieve complacency with respect to each other. Look at us! Our tension is palpable. We can hardly sit in the same room without manifestations of both jealousy and hatred and we love each other like sisters. This last point is best expressed by that philosopher you love to hate, Deleuze.

Here, I think he could be very instructive to you. He knows that there are at least two kinds of thinking, each of which is important and only one of which is philosophy. The one that is philosophy is that which thinks and analyzes concepts. The other is that which navigates the world. Let us not make the mistake of thinking that Spinoza didn't know this. His discourse on love is not intended, I think, to be a discourse on how to love. Rather, thinking on love this way will have the effect of making us better lovers. There is a world of difference here that you will readily grasp.

But enough philosophy. I am very interested in your response. Please be quicker in responding to me than I was in responding to you. I have, as noted, terrific gossip of an especially intriguing nature. Once I have told you my gossip, you will need to perform at least one action in response to my startling news. As you know I have troubles with this confessional age. One of the delightful features of our friendship, to me at least, is your immaculate respect for privacy. And as you know, it is practically impossible for me to respect others' privacy all the while jealously guarding my own. It is inconsistent. It is immoral. What can I do? I won't confess but I draw endlessly the private thoughts of others. My whole body invites them to say what they otherwise would not, could not say. I often think that this cannot be helped given the absolute banality of this age and this time.[7] In any case let me cut to the chase. Kathy is up for early tenure at Cleveland. That college deserves better, as we both know. I simply cannot abide that she should achieve a coup against the likes of which none of us can compete. Here is the story.

As you know, gratitude is not the most obvious feature blossoming forth from this woman we nurtured through graduate school. I'll never forget the first time we saw her, sitting under that tree, reading Kristeva, in French, and crying. (Already at work making maudlin mechanistic cruelty. She's made rather a profession of it, don't you think?) She was all wiping away her tears when she saw us, taking quick, short drags off those awful menthol cigarettes. Do you remember our initial disdain? I think we took her to P. D. Fronts or someplace like that for coffee and told her all the things she had to do to get ready for early comps. She sat so sweet and girl-like as if she wasn't listening. The pose she affected was along the lines, I am here to learn; I will take the weary comprehensive exams since I must to pursue this pure dream I have of knowing and explicating truth. Christ, what a dreadful combination of naïf and shrew that one is. I can't imagine how she lives with her bathetic self.) Anyway, it was so strange to see her at the meetings last year and to realize that I had grown to really like her. Even her worst feature, this tension between consummate scholar and manipulative careerist, struck me as endearing and quaint. I practically fell all over myself flattering her. And then to find what she had done to you. You poor darling!

The story is this. I was out to dinner with a bunch of people from the lit theory section and we were discussing the upcoming meetings. All of us are on the program, some of us twice, so that was a cool thing for Mall State. Our Lacanian turned to me asking what Kathy had done for me with respect to getting on the program. It was then I realized that she was on the program committee and had not even called to invite me to read. So I called around and found out that she had not done anything for you either. I could live with that—even though we practically wrote her dissertation, you know? (I won't even mention the fact that she was elected to the committee on committees and not only failed to make a committee for us—it would help us in our quest for

Full of course and she knows that—she also failed to construct a committee relating to gender in any respect whatsoever, no matter how far one stretches the functions of the pathetic little groupings she devised.) But that on top of these abuses, the way she took away your graduate students is more than I can let go. Cleveland is just not good enough to justify luring away the students you had brought to dissertating stage. I hope I'm not upsetting you by telling you the story about the program. I know this is not the best time for you. But I think we could lick our wounds in a very attractive way. We could give her back a little of that which she dishes out and we could do it in such a way that we would have the deniability she has with respect to her student snatching and her program snubbing. In short, it would be quite easy to turn around her tenure. We should get something out of being associate profs, don't you think? There are few enough perks for that achievement: lifelong employment indeed! Academic freedom, hah! I'll call you with details if you seem remotely interested in sabotaging the little prima donna. Let me know as soon as possible, won't you? All work, no play is making me tiresome and catty. I think that a project such as this is exactly what I need to fight my growing malaise and my sorrow over having lost the possibility of winning you.

I remain your dear and loving and ever faithful,

Marianne.

Mille bises. xxxoooxoxox

Letter #2
Chantal to Marianne

Dear Marianne,

It is quite astonishing the ways in which you (willfully) misinterpret the things I write to you and that I say to you. I am quite sure that I have never discoursed with you concerning Jane Austen on any beach. The only conversation of this kind that we have had together was in a bar in Atlantic City. Do you remember? (We were there for the Association of Psychoanalytic Theory for the Elimination of Violence in Fiction conference and you read the paper on Wanda von Masoch to wide acclaim. I loved the outfit you wore. Incidentally, darling, you should have kept your hair that way. My hair is still black but quite short and I've had three peels.) To resume, we were in a bar, not on a beach, and the conversation about Jane Austen in no way reflected unwillingness on my part to address the issue of marriage as a backdrop to those contrite texts. What I had remarked was that I was tired of doing literature in general. That I was bored with a sort of hot obsession with property assignations in the period I've chosen for my concentration. So your comments on Austen and "her" Edmund and Fanny mystify me and fail to delight me. I have nothing to say on those matters. I do wish that you would try to remember what we have talked about. It is quite annihilating to be chided for comments I have not made. Enough of that. (And darling, I miss you too. It is unbearable to me that you are there at Mall and here am I at Mississippi. Did we ever imagine in graduate school that we would not be able to continue our morning coffees and evening cocktails? It is astonishing to me that I can work at all without your constant stimulation. Astonishing too the funny ways you need to categorize things. Let's stop talking: "Don't talk of love, show me" and so forth. Your romance thing is just getting old, dearest one. I have never encouraged this and I am beginning to feel a trifle *stalked*.)

Moving on to other points in your not so scintillating letter. My letter was not so much about Spinoza as it was about a whole host of other writers on whom I was working at the time of that letter.[8] Still, I do remember referencing him, however tangentially. I know, however, your great fondness for him and know that if I mention him, I risk your going on and on about Spinoza this and Spinoza that, so the risk is mine and the pleasure is, as usual, all yours.

But before responding to your pedantry let me dive in first to the gossip and the more personal comments you make. First, my little cabbage, I have gossip of my own. You left a message on my machine a few days ago informing me that Ryan had received tenure and that I should send flowers or something. You are uncivil in some respects, ma chère. Marianne. Professor Post. Of course I had already sent a tenure gift to Ryan. But being the busy little thing that I am, I would like to tell you the gossip to which I refer in the antepenultimate sentence from this one. Corey is Ryan's new boyfriend. He is lovely to look at and amazingly smart. I want to marry him. (Just joking! You deserve this for your comments on Austinian matrimony.) This is gossip in the true sense. Because all our gossip is practical in nature and because we are the best team, I beg your assistance in following out the natural trajectory of this delightful set of stories. (You know about

Michael and Ryan's breakup so I won't add any of the new details here—you're sure to be able to invent better ones on your own in any case. I don't know if you've talked to Ryan about Corey. Trust me that there is not one thing I could tell you that you couldn't anticipate. Very predictable.) I am demanding, indeed, your help at achieving a very particular and simple aim. So I think we have plotting to do. Ryan was quite mean to Michael. Remember he left him right after the contract fell through and didn't wait even two weeks before moving dishy little Corey in. I think that we should find someone Corey cannot resist and send him his way. It is just the right shade of mean and it will not be our fault if Corey falls for our lure. So we will be quite blameless, we can avenge our Michael, and we can exact covert revenge on Ryan. So are you in? I'll call you with details. Will you help me?

Did you believe that I was serious, Marianne? Had you chosen the man? If you believed that I wanted to do something like that you are more lost in a fantasy world than is healthy, darling. I think you are oversteeped in your novels of manners. You must read for more than plot and you must remember the humor with which they were, if not written, read. (Although I am perhaps not being totally fair. I am thinking of course of Jane Austen's total disdain for Laclos and Richardson coupled with her inability to not love them and reference them.[9] But from that position, she recognized that they were indeed novels, dear, pieces of fiction about the end of civilization as some particular groups knew it. I mean look, there she is bridging the vulgarity of the eighteenth century and the fussiness of the nineteenth reading these mannered novels descriptive of other cusps. You cite the Idiot at me and that too, it strikes me, is a novel of manners, although I realize I am in the minority position writing that down, committing it to print. It seems to me that you assimilate the characters into your consciousness as some sort of exemplars of model behavior, but darling, surely you notice the moral bankruptcy of these men and women.)

Second parenthetical. It is interesting to me that the novels you choose to reference are so sanctioned. You never refer to anything that is not a classic. For the points you made throughout your last much too long last letter—Marianne, sweetness and light, you must write shorter letters to me, I am a very busy woman—Genet's *Funeral Rites* would have been much more appropriate. I know that before I begin you will be thinking that there is no certain love there. Jean is dead. How can there be love when the beloved is dead? You miss the point even though you recognize the primacy of language. In a late scene between Erik and Riton, Riton says to Erik that he loves him more than he had before. The lover, the narrator, comments, "No tenderness could have been expressed, for as their love was not recognized by the world, they could not feel its natural effects."[10] This oddly gentle person, facing, after all, a much more definitive end of the world than the one we face, has certainty in love at every turn.

> I loved those tough kids who didn't give a damm about the blighted hopes of a nation, whose distress in the heart of everyone, as soon as he spoke about it, merged systematically with the most beloved being of flesh and blood. And the armed youngsters were perhaps thrilled at moving in the halo of shame with which their treason surrounded them, but there was enough grace in their gazes and gestures for them to seem indifferent to it. I was happy to see France terrorized by children in arms, but even more so because they were crooks and little rats. Had I been young, I would have joined the Militia.[11]

Now here is the thing. It is impossible to deny love in these passages, even certain love. There is no complacency in these livings. There is no attempt at metatheorizing this core coldness to which you refer. There is the systematically aesthetic overlay through practices of huge refinement and ethic. Who can forget the scenes where the lovers so tenderly prepare each other for any bodily act, even one ending in death? Who can deny that it is love with which the executioner showers his young love? We can make these allowances. We can weep at the vulnerability and strength of their codes. Why then is it so hard to be generous to Edmund and Fanny? Is it that their war is at a remove? Is it that their overlays are boring? Where do you get a position from which to judge one overlay more boring than another? One can imagine that eventually Erik and Riton tire of their forced brutality. That even the phantastic overlay of the Führer becomes mundane and repetitious. So choose better examples, my sweet darling. I think that you are right that I demand silence on some things. Sometimes, when you are feeling charitable you ascribe a respect to privacy to these acts on my part and go so far as to say that these are the qualities that cause you to love me most. You might want to reflect on this seeming contradiction. You have a blind spot too, my dove. You cannot see the beauty of the bourgeois. Enough of this. I fear I have not been clear. One more attempt before closing off this discussion. You are right that I am afraid of love. You, sweet pet, are afraid of bodies. The novels you are forever citing have no bodies or closed off bodies or caricatures of bodies. Try reading the many novels where bodies are born. One last cite? You'll allow it? "But Jean will live through me. I shall lend him my body. Through me he will act, will think. Through my eyes he will see the stars, the scarves of women and their breasts. I am taking on a very grave role. A soul is in purgatory and I am offering it my body. . . . A sleeping soul hopes for a body; may the one that the actor assumes for an evening be beautiful."[12]

As I was saying, you are overinvested in the wrong parts of your work. Your job is to take some distance from these descriptions of typical situations and judge them morally. In that space of contemplation you are meant to say to yourself, "There but for the Grace of God go I," and improve the life you live accordingly. Instead, you let these characters run slipshod over your consciousness. They at once make you disgusted with the current state of affairs and sure of your right to then behave as them since you too find yourself at yet one other fin de sciècle. But context does matter. Finding love and meaning at the in-between of wars, in the actual making of incorporated war machines, is not extensionally equivalent to having to grovel for tenure. It just isn't. And we do a worse job of it. Give it up, girl. Find some intensity outside of your textual enclosing. Make a trip somewhere. Express yourself. You're allowing yourself to get stirred up in most disturbing ways. You are allowing yourself to see hurting Kathy in the same light as Valmont chasing after a sense of being alive when the subject position that he knows can no longer exist. He knows that the game is up. There is no more French aristocracy. There will be nothing left for him to do but die. Really. There is absolutely no hope for him. Nowhere to go. You could, you know, leave the academic mess. There are no chains here. You could garret yourself somewhere and write a novel from a body that is alternately ravaged and cherished on a regular basis. You are not so stuck as you think. Pauvrecite! Are you serious? Join our massive intellectual power to hurt pathetic little Kathy over tenure? Chantal, you must know that I spend my days and nights working so hard for my students to get tenure-track jobs. This is what I do when I am not writing on my current paper. (Sweetheart, you would die to read it but it is two drafts away from that. It is a comment on the bitchiness underlying the civility in Austen's middle-period novels. I am having ever so much fun with it and think it will be a perfect conference paper for the Literature and Civility conference—I've covered both bases, don't you think? Then I can send it out, where I don't know. Finally, it will be a good chapter for the book I'm working on too. So three birds with one stone, eh?)

In any case, of course I will not help in sabotaging Kathy's career. You are not mistaken in your assessment of her; she is an insipid, humorless little thing, but so what? The academy needs such creatures to function. Who else would do all that committee work? So enough of your petty meanness. Really darling you must move down here where manners abound. I fear that I do not believe in American culture. We are worlds apart from south to north. If we were to sabotage dear Kathy we would have to do an encoded silent body discourse with each other on the subject, do our worst work, and never reference it again. You are losing your touch there in the Midwest. No offense intended if these comments have set you fuming. By the time you receive this we will have chatted on the phone and I can tell you in person, as it were, my incontrovertible refusal to participate in such shenanigans.

In your letter you ask forgiveness for your most recent attempts to manipulate me. Darling. If you had read my penultimate letter you would recall that this is not the way in which you should talk to me. You will recall my whole forgiveness/forgetting riff. (In this context, one might say, for instance, "Forget Kathy.") If you wish to engage me in this sort of discourse you would do better to give me reasons to forget what you had said. But don't do me the incivility of begging my forgiveness. To forgive is always uncivil. The assumptions of forgiveness involve all sorts of inequalities and presumed states of grace, or lack thereof, which seem a little out of place from our theological perspectives. I mean, darling, do you suppose that an atheist can forgive another? How exactly would that make sense? No, dear heart, what we must do as a fast and true friend is forget the injustices we have inflicted on each other. I can say no more on this subject. But on other subjects I can converse at length, as you know all too well. And I am holding you to your vow of silence by refusing to comment further.

Please honor my request—and your acquiescence. At least show some self-respect if you find yourself unable to respect me. So begging you to forget the more boring details, I will turn to the substantive content of your infuriating missive.

As noted, I did not write to you about Spinoza and I am both puzzled and annoyed by your lengthy lecture to me on your bizarre reconstruction of his quaint notions on love. Particularly hilarious is your comment that I am not really analyzing Spinoza on love, but coming to terms with my own inability to love. Oh Marianne, how we see each other in the other's mote. (Do I have this bit of New Testament material correct? I was raised to be a little heathen, as you know; still, I try to make the occasional allusion to show that I am not entirely without education.) I do believe that love negates itself on its completion. (What Spinoza has to say on the matter I am sure I do not know. I haven't read Spinoza since my undergraduate days, when the big question was "Hegel ou Spinoza"? This hardly seems the question that concerns you.) I additionally believe that pleasure exhausts itself. Your response to those beliefs you say I attribute to Spinoza however bear some response simply because they are so perverse that I find myself intrigued in spite of everything.

First you say that there is no possibility of certainty and therefore even if it is structurally the case that love negates itself, it could not because one could never be certain that one was in love. Did I get you right? What you say is insane, you know. You needn't lecture me on Deleuze. I've had my fill of that defenestrator. So your point is (and you mustn't attribute this idiocy to him, it is so rude) that love can be conceptually negated on its conceptual completion but no one ever really knows that love has been accomplished so the conceptual thing, while helpful, isn't really "true" in particulars. (On this reread my musings on *our* St. Genet.)

First may I be the first to congratulate you on remaining the only unadulterated Hegelian alive who counts herself Deleuzian. Does this come about because you have done so much work on the incoherency of the concept "alienation of affection"? What you cite as Deleuzian is merely straight Hegelianism. You are so cute—your entry into texts is frightfully willful. Sometimes I wonder if you paid someone to take your comps. (Sorry, darling!) (I do hate that you are so rich.) But more seriously, of course there is "real" or "concrete" or "particular" love in "real" etc. life. One knows that one is in love. Imagine saying to your current beloved (Is there one, sweetest Marianne? I shall die of jealousy if the answer is yes and will feel genuine sorrow for you if the answer is no. See how torn I am for you?)—What was I saying before that aside? Ah yes, imagine saying to your current beloved, "I believe that I love you." There is no purchase in such musings. One must say only, "I adore you. I love you. I have never been more certain of anything in my life." Now you may be sufficiently without ardor that you say these things expediently, in which case shame on you. Worse, you may believe that when people say such things what they mean is, "I am saying these things to stave off death. I am in fact lying because I do not know now, nor shall I ever know that I love you in fact." In which case double shame. Here I am taking down two with one blow again. Your arguments are all mushed. We should have done our course of study in philosophy. Clearly.

I can hear your retort. "What I meant, darling," you'd say, "was only that one can never be sure that one is loved." This is quite different, perhaps true, but clearly beside the point. The issue is one's amour propre. Without loving oneself, and one can be quite sure unless one loves oneself, one can love no one else, one has no knowledge of anything. Sorry to be trite. The point is only that the core of any knowledge is self-love. Importantly, however, one can know that one loves another and in that moment, the love is somewhat diffused. In real space and time. I love you absolutely. Therefore, I must turn my attention to other unmet desires. These desires may include keeping you. They may include giving into you, they may involve talking with you at length about those things I would not broach with any other. In these activities one is once again alive. So the negation is weak but exists nevertheless. Have I made myself clear on this point?

The reason for your confusion here can be traced to your recent meanness. You have really turned into an incredible bitch and I am not sure that the bitchiness is of the charming sort: you know that bitchiness to which one aspires after watching one's mother drink gin all afternoon with beautiful, manicured women dishing it good. I think that you feel empty because you don't know what you're doing and rather than figuring out what is wrong with you, you translate that emptiness onto humanity as a whole. But who's the bitch now?

Your second discussion, that on fear and desire, is quite unremarkable. Of course what you say here is right. The insanity lies in your feeling the need to say it. Indeed, I am of the opinion, that is, I believe, that you mention it only because you wanted to inject misanamphibian comments in an effort to elliptically hurt my feelings.

In your ranting about fear and desire, you talk about what you call coldness and its overlay of civility. I agree with you that civility is an overlay, but I must question your ontological category of coldness. Say more if you wish. I do not understand you. It sounds like ranting to me. You can infer from what I've already written that I think you are suffering from an identity crisis. You look around the halls where you profess on the great works of literature from the desk where you write thereon and you think, "Is this what I worked and work and will work for?" You slay me with your personal questions. Sorry to change the subject so abruptly, but I felt I was perhaps overstepping my bounds. Some answers to your questions regarding my body. I am wearing the same perfume. It is pointless here, however, where every corner brings some new heaven of olfactory sensation. The entire world from this vantage point is nature's perfume decanter. I effuse but you must come and visit in the spring. Nothing smells so good as Mississippi. And that's the truth.

You note in passing that jealousy and hatred are real. I think we are in a very strange profession, you and I. Of course they are real. How does that affect the line of argument you have falsely attributed to me? (I can't believe I am trying to argue against you using a position I never held nor thought worth holding. You have such power over me.)

Final note: You are wrong about *Mansfield Park*. Edmund and Fanny love each other. It is a sweet book. Fanny rises above what she is given and Edmund makes of the fiasco that ends up being his life something calm and beautiful. That they do not share your aesthetic does not mean that they cannot be happy. Complacency is not the worst thing in the world. And I am not sure that this is what they achieve. Fanny is a little bit of a bitch to be sure, but the big bitch here is Austen herself. Austen is completely self-aware and finds delight in creating characters that are not. This makes a distance between the smart-as-a-whip narrator and the plodding characters. What a delight it is to read through this chasm. And there is no complacency to be found between the love she has for her writing and the success she has in achieving pleasure with respect to it. It is interesting then that she is so vicious about the mores that make her tone possible. How she hates the culture that informed her perfect language. There is something perhaps awry in the culture, but there is nothing necessarily sinister about Edmund and Fanny.

With respect to the odd selection from Dostoevski I can only say that whatever Fyodor meant, the lesson to me is that breaking down of civility is worse than becoming an idiot.

I have a wonderful new student. She is ruthlessly polite, quite smart, moderately well read, caffeine laden and darting. We are working on her speaking style that is still too excitable. She exclaims over Irigaray and finds it hard to find fault with someone she reveres. I am doing my best to point out the worst in Irigaray's work so that Carinessa (that is her name, her parents must be crazy) can adopt a more sophisticated distance from authors she loves. I am absolutely committed to getting her hired. It is more important to me this year than finishing the book. (This chapter will be done, it might be enough to send out with a prospectus but I don't even care. How much better to have a live work out and about spreading good words about my brilliance and replicating my work. Carinessa will be my greatest product to date. It is terribly exciting to have, finally, a really good student. I wish you could find somebody.)

Oh my, it is time to go eat dinner. I am finding that if I make a dinner appointment for every night, my work goes much better the next day. The conversations of the night before give a rhythm to my writing it would not otherwise have. Tonight I sup with the darling Corey and the adulterous Ryan. I called and invited Michael just to be mean; that is, I was hoping he would say yes and then I could watch Ryan watching the extent of his loss played over and over again. But Michael said no and who can blame him for that? We are going to a Chinese place that is quite good. I am bringing Terri and Jennifer. I invited Carinessa but she is too shy to eat with the great Ryan. (She says to me, to me having just come from receiving tenure, I know you know these things but it is galling beyond measure to have her all gaga over Ryan when I have the better record. She says to me, "Oh I couldn't possibly swallow a morsel in his presence." I thought she was going to say "He's so awesome," or some other American phrase I would mangle, but not completely, given my acculturation and etc.) When I wake tomorrow morning I'll work out vigorously, going over the things Ryan has said and noting without a little cattiness the way he has to change his vocabulary to talk to the adorable Corey. Then I will turn to my treatise on civility with great happiness, marred only by your lack of being here. I love you and miss you and wish we could finagle jobs in the same state, hell, since it is a fantasy, in the same town. Well enough for now. Ta ta, ciao, good-bye, adieu,

Love and a million little kisses, your adoring,

Chantal.

P.S. Made you laugh, made you stare, made you think you weren't aware. (Sorry, can't help myself.) Of course I'm in. Help me get a job for Carinessa and I'll do whatever you require to stall little Kathy's stellar ascent. Can you wait? Love you so much. You fantasticate the world and all that is in it.

Notes

1. Benedict de Spinoza, *The Ethics*, trans. R. H. M. Elwes (New York: Dover, 1883), Proposition XXXIV.

2. Jane Austen, *Mansfield Park* (New York: Bantam, 1983), p. 386.

3. Choderlos de Laclos, *Les Liaisons Dangereuses*, trans. P. W. K. Stone (London: Penguin Classics, 1961), letter 125.

4. Laclos, letter 125.

5. It is unclear whether Professor Post understands these lines from Wordsworth. I cannot fathom what they have to do with epistemology.—Ed.

6. Fyodor Dostoevsky, *The Idiot*, trans. David Magarshack (New York: Penguin Classics, 1977).

Dostoevsky, p. 628.

7. Our correspondents are academics, as you may have gathered from the tone thus far, the many unnecessary references to text, and the general sense of malaise occasioning the missives. (I too am academic. An academic. I have been given the task of compiling these sorry letters to hasten what my editors call an increased understanding of the decline of civility not just in institutions of higher learning but also in the society at large.) The purpose of this note is to lessen any alarm he or she might be feeling at the heightened sense of cynicism therein. They inhabit a space of accidie the likes of which I believe are not found in other areas of the cultural arena.—Ed.

8. The correspondence between the two esteemed professors was begun shortly after they finished graduate school. I have the entire correspondence at my disposal but it is not a stretch, indeed there is nothing hyperbolic at all in saying that the correspondence is a veritable mountain. One would need volumes to contain it. I have Marianne's letters in two three-drawer file cabinets, so one can imagine the difficulty one would have in editing the collec-

tion down to manageable (and publishable) length. In any case I chose just one of the schemes these two have concocted to include in the current collection.—Ed.

9. Because I am reading Anthony Grafton's amusing and informative *The Footnote: A Curious History* (Cambridge: Harvard University Press, 1997), I find her reference to references sufficiently revealing that I had to go and see if she had any basis for saying what she has said about Austen here. (I had never seen such reference.) Nearly everyone who talks about Lady Susan also talks about either Laclos or Richardson or both. I can find no indication that the relationship between Austen and either of them is "disdain." The closest I can come is so tenuous that it is not really close at all. G. J. Barker-Benfield notes the use Austen makes of *Les Liaisons Dangereuses* (she "draws on it") and then a few sentences later remarks that *Sense and Sensibility* contains a criticism of societal expectations of women. So this is tenuous indeed, but it is the best that I can do. Perhaps Chantal is making a joke with Marianne.—Ed.

10. Jean Genet, *Funeral Rites*, trans. Bernard Frechtman (New York: Grove/Atlantic, 1972), p. 254.

11. Ibid., p. 78.

12. Ibid., p. 75.

CHAPTER EIGHT

Eating Dogs and Women

Abject Rules of Etiquette in 301/302

TINA CHANTER

Among the questions that will preoccupy me in this chapter are the following: Is desire structured by what the subject would outlaw? If, in order to be a subject, I must participate in cultural practices that define and codify some acts as aberrant in relation to others, by what right or authority can I identify the proper order of things? If the subject constitutes itself through processes of separation and distinction, by which one realm is distinguished from another—the improper and the unclean from the acceptable and the sanctioned—what implications does this have for the possibility of ethics? If the need to draw meaningful distinctions is part of what it means to engage in a culture, how do we challenge the ways in which culturally and politically legitimated boundaries are drawn? What are the effects of contesting the consolidation of identities that become sedimented according to authorized or legitimized demarcations? If creating boundaries, parceling out territories, designating and labeling what is mine and what is yours, separating the sacred from the profane, truth from lies, the beautiful from the grotesque, is an important part of what we do in order to live, in whose name and to what ends can traditional and discriminatory differentiations and practices be challenged? And what radicality can be claimed for whatever transformation takes place under the sign of shifting boundaries? Can anything be accomplished beyond the transference of blame from one group of subjects, collected under a particular sign, to another symbolically signified group, whose members identify themselves under an opposing sign, be it a religious, cultural, political, ethical, social, or aesthetic sign?

The meanings and effects of representation are not peripheral to the questions that mobilize my reflections. I will be concerned here, in particular, with the images that cinematic representation provides, as a medium that is capable of both reflecting and reinforcing the most hackneyed cultural stereotypes, and of undermining and destabilizing the usual ways in which a given culture articulates the boundaries between the normal and the abnormal, between what is tolerated as publicly acceptable, and what is banished as pathological.

An exercise of attempted separation, abjection operates by way of radical exclusion that nonetheless fails to completely exclude what it sets up as other. The abject is the always improperly excluded other, that which is expelled in an attempt to maintain the sanctity and integrity of the subject, but which remains constitutive of the subject even as it is ostensibly repulsed. The subject must expel what it cannot tolerate, sustain, or maintain within the boundaries of its integrity as a subject in order to constitute the clean and proper body. The discourse of abjection is one with which we have become familiar, through the work of Georges Bataille, Barbara Creed, Mary Douglas, Julia Kristeva, Judith Butler, Laura Mulvey, Hal Foster, and Rosalind Kraus, among others. Kristeva has investigated the signifying function of abjection in relation to literature, art, and film, and in doing so she has raised important and decisive questions about the mechanism of mimesis and about the cathartic potential literature has as a signifier of abjection. She has also opened up a space for rethinking the maternal and feminine associations of abjection. Even as Kristeva is to be credited with putting abjection on the agenda in provocative and inspiring ways, I want to note a certain ambivalence her writing exhibits when it comes to addressing the relation between philosophy and psychoanalysis, between politics and the individual, between the collective and the singular. This ambivalence spirals into an anxiety that might be an expression of what she must set aside in order to be able to sustain her theses about abjection. I will be concerned, then, to acknowledge what could be said to operate as a remainder of Kristeva's discourse. The gestures of exclusion that she makes in the name of exploring the strange, disturbing, but also necessary process of abjection have the effect, I will claim, of bracketing precisely the political and ethical implications of her work with which the abject confronts us. The residue, or remainder, is, as Kristeva acknowledges, ambivalent. And while I agree that such ambivalence must be maintained, rather than rendered decidable in its meaning, I am also convinced that abjection offers us a way of analyzing a tension that Kristeva systematically puts aside, evades, or remainders. This evasion, this exclusion, this—I'll say it—abjection that might be said to operate from the very center of her discourse about abjection is what interests me.

Kristeva evinces a certain anxiety about the relation of cause and effect between the speaking subject and the symbolic order, insisting that they both "follow the same logic."[1] That logic has as its goal "survival." And herein lies the problem. There is, I think, a reluctance to take on questions about the political possibilities of transgression, for how can historical and social mores come to be judged inappropriate without some acknowledgment of a gap, or fissure, or lack of fit between the symbolic order and the speaking subject? Symptoms can be read as indicative of social forces, but there is a range of questions that are surely worth asking that exceed that reading. To interpret the subject's symptom as illustrative of his or her culture leaves no room for any critical distance of the assumptions informing that culture. Such critical distance does not have to retreat into the naïveté of assuming transformation can be thorough, completely revolutionary, or unambiguously liberating. Another way of putting the problem is to couch it in terms of Kristeva's categorical acceptance of Freud's Oedipal myth as founding the social and symbolic contract. To simply say, as she does, that she takes this myth as "logically established" is to sidestep, to remainder, an array of important questions which perhaps allow her to say what she says, and to do what she does, with such brilliance, but which also sideline questions about the political effects of a symbolic system that authorizes some subjects to abject others with apparent impunity.[2] Among these questions are how and why the Oedipal model of triangulation might be inapplicable both to non-Western cultures that do not display in any straightforward way the norms imposed, enforced, and authorized by what has come to be recognized as signifying the values of Western capitalized culture. Perhaps there is a need to confront the possibility of subjects being put, or putting themselves, in disjunctive relationships to the societies in which they live.

Can the abject become a moment that must subside, but that confers a legacy whose meaning can be, if not fixed, at least interrogated? Mulvey, Foster, and Kraus have raised questions about the application of abjection to artists such as Cindy Sherman and Mike Kelly. Yet, the mechanism that dictates the necessity of expulsion remains elusive, complicated not least by its exposure of an intimate relationship between the subject's need to expunge the intolerable or unacceptable, between bodily expression of abjection in the form of vomit or excreta perhaps, and the subject's fascination for, temptation by, sometimes even obsession with precisely what it must expel, what it must become separated from, what it must place outside itself as intolerable to it.

The question for the deject, the one somehow designated by abjection, is not "What am I supposed to do?" but "Where am I supposed to be?" or "Whose logic am I supposed to follow?" There is a constant reworking of and contestation of meaning because there is an ever-present need for a confrontation with the unnameable, or with that which skirts or girds what can be known, the lining or underside of language. The one who is abject is a "tireless builder," one who must constantly begin again, from the ground up, demolishing old structures and inventing new ones, only to tear them down again, for there is a tendency never to stay put, never to settle: the deject is a stray.[3] Putting down roots would not only be too confining, it would also be to start to become who I am, to admit the possibility of definition and decision, to admit that I am already, willy-nilly, whether I like it or not, in some sense a subject, that I can take responsibility to whatever degree I am capable of for being who I have become, for becoming someone, for acknowledging that I am I. But for that I must be in relation to another who I know to be another, to a world that contains objects which can be mine. I must situate a place in which objects are located that I can name, know, and desire, I must have become a desiring subject, and this is exactly what abjection—of myself, of others, of my relation between myself and others—constantly puts into question.

301/302 is a film about two neighbors in Seoul, South Korea, both of whom find, at least initially, mutually incompatible ways in which to deal with previous trauma.[4] In a nutshell, as Barry Walters puts it, "One cooks, the other pukes. . . . Needless to say, these women have serious food issues."[5] A more sympathetic reading might observe that one takes in everything, cooking the world before she devours it, and it is still not enough, while the other takes in nothing, and it is too much. Yoon-Hee Kim (Sin-Hye Hwang) is a writer who uses her writing and her books to protect herself from the world, and Song-Hee Kang (Eun-Jin Bang) is a cook whose life revolves around nothing but food. She has an interior designer convert her apartment into a restaurant-style kitchen. Food has become her way of relating to people. She substitutes love, friendship, or anger with cooking for others, to the point of cooking her husband's pet dog (an animal who makes no demands on him, and who consequently he loves more than her) and feeding it to him. To reject her food is to reject her. By inundating her husband with elaborate food that he doesn't want and asking for his approval ("Is it good? Do you really think it is good?"), she drives him away.

After she is divorced, Song-Hee moves into apartment 301, next to Yoon-Hee, and she turns her attention and her need to have others consume her food toward her next-door neighbor. But Yoon-Hee's body refuses food: "Not only food, but everything that has to do with this world" because her "body is so full of dirty things." Song-Hee keeps on bringing her food, and Yoon-Hee keeps on throwing it out. Yoon-Hee tells her why she cannot "stuff food or men in [her] body" and why she wishes she "could disintegrate." In a flashback we learn that her stepfather, who ran a butcher shop while her mother counted the money he made and took it to the bank, raped her on a consistent basis. Her mother condoned the incestuous abuse.

Even after she has heard Yoon-Hee's story, Song-Hee still cannot understand that Yoon-Hee cannot tolerate food. She responds instead, "From now on I'll only make you tender food" and continues her efforts to force-feed her. The detective looking into Yoon-Hee's disappearance comments, "Cooking, eating, not eating, vomiting. Women are strange." Eventually, Song-Hee understands her friend and tells her, "There is nothing in this world for you to eat," and the solution they arrive at is for Song-Hee to cook and eat Yoon-Hee, whom she duly kills, chops up, and devours, in a reencactment of her stepfather's earlier metaphorical butchering of her, which is presumably meant to be cathartic, at some level, for both women.

The film presents us with the themes of rejection, trauma, death, and cannibalism. It can be read in terms of a series of moments of abjection, some of which we are introduced to through flashbacks, and some of which occur in the present, as when Yoon-Hee vomits in the face of the meal Song-Hee has meticulously prepared for her. She is, we gather, evacuating the penis of her incestuous father, which she had forced inside her as a child. The symbolism is somewhat heavy-handed, as Song-Hee sublimates her need for sex in cooking, while anorexic Yoon-Hee wants to ingest nothing from the world from which she has already taken too much (the phallic overtones of the sausage Song-Hee tries to get her to eat are a little hyperbolic, for example), but the dark humor, never far from the surface of this film, redeems it somewhat. Song-Hee brings Yoon-Hee a sausage mignon, which she cannot eat—especially sausage. Song-Hee asks her if she was raped, and Yoon-Hee retches. When Yoon-Hee hears the noise of banging coming from the next-door apartment as the interior designer works on the kitchen of apartment 301, she has a flashback to being raped as a child. A hole in the wall appears, and first single books, and then entire bookcases come crashing down, and we understand that the world of books she has constructed to protect herself since she was a child, her library, is falling in on her.

301/302 won the 1995 Grand Bell award for best film in Korea and was nominated by Korea for an Oscar for Best Foreign Film. Critics have variously identified it as a "psychological thriller," "detective story," "comedy," or as "avant-garde."[6] In its artful, lavish display of food it bears comparison with films of the ilk of Ang Lee's *Eat Drink Man Woman* (1994), Peter Greenaway's *The Cook, The Thief, His Wife, and Her Lover* (1989), Gabriel Axel's *Babette's Feast* (1987), and Alfonso Arau's *Like Water for Chocolate* (1992). The relationship of the two characters to food is in both cases an exotic one. Either food is transformed into the meaning of life, so that it comes to take the place of all other meaning, or it represents all that is threatening and violating. In the first case it is the desirable other, outside the subject, and in the second it is the threatening outside that must be kept at a distance at all costs. In neither case does food operate at the level of need and satisfaction, having become instead the epitome of desire or threat.

Replete with food loathing, vomit, corpses, and cannibalism, this film is very much concerned with the permeability of boundaries that is at the heart of Kristeva's notion of abjection. It mixes up the categories of animal and human, as when Song-Hee stuffs food into her mouth with an ardor that borders on animality, or when she cooks her husband's beloved dog Chong-Chong, having caught sight of him kissing his lover good-bye on the evening of their wedding anniversary. It mixes up waste with consumable food, as when Song-Hee discovers, by accident, her neighbor Yoon-Hee sneaking out to the trash with a bag full of the food that Song-Hee has been preparing for her over the last several days. Yoon-Hee's inability to eat is bound up with her father's sexual abuse, and the childhood guilt she bears for the death of a little girl from the neighborhood, who assumed Yoon-Hee was playing hide-and-seek when she saw her enter the meat freezer in her father's butcher's shop, when in fact Yoon-Hee was hiding from her father. The little girl enters the freezer, wanting to play hide-and-seek too, and Yoon-Hee discovers her frozen body a few hours later. Women's bodies, we understand, are of little more value than the carcasses among which they hide—commodities to be used, receptacles to contain a stepfather's excess sperm, expendable bodies, laboring bodies for the production of surplus value.

Taking in food has become intolerable to Yoon-Hee, whose father the butcher fed her food she didn't want in her childhood and forced sex on her. Like Bess, in Lars von Trier's *Breaking the Waves* (1996), Yoon-Hee suffers, not for Jan, but for the sins of her father.[7] And her refusal of the food Song-Hee makes—her only way of expressing affection and love, it would seem—is intolerable to Song-Hee, who marches Yoon-Hee back into her apartment, empties the food from the trash bag onto the table, and, in an uncanny repetition, tries to force-feed her, as had Yoon-Hee's father. The boundaries of inside and outside are confused, just as they are in the spasm of vomiting by which Yoon-Hee tries to protect herself, evacuating the intolerable, incessantly redrawing the boundary between her and the world that has violated her. She renders the inside outside, vomiting up nothing, because her body refuses to take in anything more from the external world.

In *301/302* a stepfather's incest brings on the abjection of a woman who uses the exclusion of food as a way of tolerating the past, an exclusion that leads to her inevitable death. Yoon-Hee exercises the ultimate control over a life that has escaped from her by orchestrating her own death, a death that is eroticized, ironically, by the cannibalism of Song-Hee, whose passion for cooking and food extends to eating her neighbor. "Food," says Kristeva, "becomes abject only if it is a border between two distinct entities or territories. A boundary between nature and culture, between the human and the non-human." She continues, "The fact remains nevertheless that all food is liable to defile. . . . Food is the oral object (the abject) that sets up archaic relationships between the human being and the other, its mother, who wields a power that is as vital as it is fierce."[8]

The film shows how one woman is so intent on having others eat the food she obsessively prepares that she is willing to kill, and how another woman is so traumatized by the sexual abuse of her past that her body cannot tolerate the incorporation of anything. Song-Hee's threat of "I'll kill you—you have to eat" (I'll kill you if you don't eat) turns into Yoon-Hee's desire to disintegrate, and becomes "I'll kill you, and I'll eat you." Song-Hee's attempt to eat a world including people and dogs to which she otherwise is unable to relate coincides in this instance with the only way in which Yoon-Hee has learned to express her desire, which is to die.

The realism of narrative subsides into a kind of stylized formalism. We are held at arms length from immersion in and identification with the characters because of their sheer idiosyncrasy. Song-Hee's industrial kitchen and complete fascination with food is presented in a way that distances us, rather than drawing us in. As she watches the spinach being pulverized by her food processor with the same mute, fascinated absorption we usually reserve for Hollywood cinema, the displacements are multiple. The camera work lovingly caresses food as art as she puts everything she has into the food she makes and is no longer capable of sustaining any relationship unless it consists of, or is bound up with, appreciation of her food. How far is what entertains or mesmerizes us a product of our gendered normality or abnormality? How far are the food issues that the two central characters display representative of more generalized feminized positions? How far is the production of femininity bound up with rejection or identification with the mother? To take in food in the place of love, or to refuse food as a way of protecting oneself from the trauma of violation, to become overweight or anorexic are both ways of recalibrating one's relation to the maternal, the figure who is supposed to provide both protection and food.

Murder, says Kristeva, "the violence that threatens the living being, and not just society," is one of the elements that previously religious rites and now artists try to purify.[9] "It is no surprise, therefore," Kristeva says, "that in certain unconscious resurgences . . . we can see a relation to violence, death, the corpse, to the fragmented body, to decomposition and sexuality."[10] Food loathing, vomiting, and the butchered body are archetypal expressions of abjection. Here they are engaged in by subjects who find the world intolerable and who attempt to control its dangers by regulating their intake of food in ways that are congruent with their divergent encounters with that world. Song-Hee is trying to compensate her mother's frequent absences in her childhood by filling herself and others up with food. And Yoon-Hee is attempting to exclude the violent trauma of her stepfather's unwanted sexual intrusion, which her mother did nothing to prevent, by erecting a barricade between her body and the incorporation of anything other than water and vitamin supplements.

When Barry Walters accuses the film of being "rather one-dimensional" because "the characterization is restricted to women's neuroses," I am sure he doesn't mean to dismiss all those women who just happen to be neurotic—and there are quite a lot of us. And anyway, as I have tried to show, I disagree. The film is neither about neuroses, nor about obsessionals (as some critics indicate), rather it is about a particular expression of that borderline state, somewhere in between neuroses and psychoses: abjection. The distinctly Shermanesque images of vomit are not the only thing to suggest this.

Subjects can be abjected through the abuse and neglect of other subjects. If the boundaries of the others on whom they are supposed to depend are unstable, unreliable, and permeable, if they mix up the orders of protection with violation, the chances are that these subjects will fail to develop their own boundaries in a coherent way. Subjects can take up their abject positions as a way of protecting themselves from abuse, from traumatic memories, and from the possibility of further incursions and violations. Abjection can occur when a social group unites against a particular subject, or group of subjects, consolidating its boundaries by excluding those it designates as other. Because it is essentially ambiguous, abjection cannot be said to be inherently transgressive. But we can attempt to map the effects of abjection in particular instances and to ask about the political landscape that informs the abject, and how its contours both shape and are shaped by abjection. I have focused on moments of abjection in which the logic of survival or sacrifice for certain subjects not only differs from that of the society in which they are trying to live (or from which they are trying to exit), but radically opposes the norms that these subjects confront. It is this mismatch that I suspect Kristeva cannot account for to the extent that I think we need to account for it. The site of dislocation, this caesura, this stopping point, this abjection of subjects can become abjection of the society that renders them invisible in certain instances, silencing them, whether through murder, suicide, or sexual transgression of the law.[11]

Notes

1. Julia Kristeva, *Powers of Horror: An Essay on Abjection*, trans. Leon S. Roudiez (New York: Columbia University Press, 1982), p. 68.
2. Ibid., p. 57.
3. Ibid., p. 8.
4. *301/302*, directed by Chul-Soo Park (Korea: Arrow Pictures, 1995).
5. Barry Walters, *San Francisco Examiner*, May 3, 1996, http://www.sfgate.com/cgi-bin/article.cgi?f=/e/a/1996/05/03/WEEKEND16113.dtl.
6. Peter Stack, *San Francisco Chronicle*, May 3, 1996, http://www.sfgate.com/cgi-bin/article.cgi?f=/c/a/1996/05/03/DD8368.DTL. Alex Lau, *Movie Magazine International*, 5. 1. 96._http://www.shoestring.org/mmi_revs/301-302.html.
7. Unlike the redemptive bells that ring out in *Breaking the Waves* suggesting that all is well, there is no entirely redemptive moment for Yoon-Hee. If her body is sacrificed in a trope that has become the all too familiar conclusion of female lives, there is no sense of justification, only a sense of the depths of her despair that make it impossible for her to continue to exist in this world. At the same time, there is a radical refusal of the violation that leads to her embrace of death.
8. Kristeva, *Powers of Horror*, pp. 75–76.
9. Julia Kristeva, "Of Word and Flesh," interview by Charles Penwarden in *Rites of Passage: Art for the End of the Century*, ed. Stuart Morgan and Frances Morris (London: Tate Gallery Productions, 1995), p. 23.
10. Ibid., p. 24.
11. I explore the ideas presented briefly in this essay at greater length in *Abjection: Film and the Constitutive Nature of Difference* (Bloomington: Indiana University Press).

CHAPTER NINE

The Taciturn Tongue

On Silence

Brian Schroeder

Meaning is limited silence . . .

—Maurice Blanchot, *The Writing of the Disaster*

Under the vast nocturnal sky, punctuated by countless glinting dots and quivering luminescent bands and streaks, another brighter yet far dimmer and cooler light burns, interspersing the darkness with flickering tongues of flame and shooting embers. Unlike the deep hush shrouding the deafening roar of the stars, however, this glow breaks through the night air, interrupting the still with crackles, whistles, and sputtering pops of various volume. The attending silence of those seated around the fire ring, the primeval seat of human community, is all the more accentuated. In the background, generating their own natural rhythm, the faint sound of animal movements, the whisper of fluttering leaves and grass, the barely audible rustling of garments and clinking of sundry metal objects, even the murmuring, imagined or not, of agitated shades and preternatural forces, fade into a dull white noise for all those except the most attentive.

The restless quiet is suddenly broken by a firm voice discussing the matter at hand. All eyes are focused on the face of this shadowy figure, illuminated by the dancing light and changing hues of the council fire, but it is to the words that the attention is drawn. The others present are taciturn, their speech relegated to the recesses of their own thoughts—until it is their turn to speak.

An ancient carved staff is passed around. No one dares to utter a word until it comes to rest in one's own hands. And should the rod's current holder make no declaration, still none is ventured by anyone else. This silence is more than mere politeness. It is in fact a far graver silence that subtends the moment. To speak out of turn, to upset the rhythm, is to violate the bounds of etiquette and open the portals to internal social strife. Here, silence is respect. But it is also power. Knowing this marks the fixed though fluid boundaries of social difference.

⁂ ⁂ ⁂

The question of community is in large measure the question of the economy of violence. Etiquette is a cornerstone of community. Far more than a matter of mere politeness, etiquette concerns what constitutes proper action, and perhaps even thought. Propriety can be dictated by respect, solemnity, or ceremony; authority, fear, or ignorance at times also condition it. Propriety is a matter of knowing when, where, and how to act; in other words, propriety is tied to a sense of rhythm. In all matters of rhythm, what conditions movement, whether it is that of speech, song, or motility, is precisely nonmovement. With regard to language, especially the dialectic of speech and listening, the rhythm of silence is the play of this nonmovement.

If silence is then linked to etiquette and thereby to community, then it is also connected to an economy of violence, an economy that is both constituted and expressed in part by a certain rhythmic ontology wherein the "proper" oscillation between speech and silence occurs, perpetually differentiating and mediating order and chaos, truth and error, good and evil, law and crime, masculine and feminine, civilized and wild, sanity and madness. According to Deleuze and Guattari, the "refrain" offers a possible solution to the potentially violent and dangerous outbursts of a shattered economy. The refrain is the nonaggressive basis of the territory shared alike by the human and inhuman, the natural art or expression of the world that both preserves autonomy and shields against the moment of a violent backlash within the territorial assemblage. The refrain preserves and defers the "critical distance between two beings of the same species,"[1] a distance that is marked philosophically by Nietzsche and given ethical significance by Levinas. But it is not only a question of keeping a secretly or potentially threatening other at bay, "it is a question of keeping at a distance the forces of chaos knocking at the door."[2] Rhythm marks this critical distance.

Deleuze and Guattari's analysis of the refrain provides a means for remembering the place or space and role of ritual action and thus etiquette. The refrain is fundamentally territorial and thereby a territorial assemblage; it "always carries the earth with it . . . [and] has an essential relation to a Natal, a Native."[3] The movement of cosmological chaotic force to terrestrial force is expressed socially as the relation between *nomos* and ethos that shares the mutual feature of being a distribution of space in space. Deleuze and Guattari appeal to a very Nietzschean notion of chaos out of which are born milieus and rhythms. Chaos is essentially ecstatic and the *Abgrund* from which order, that is, various milieus and rhythms, issue forth. There are various types of milieus (exterior, interior, intermediary, annexed) that are coded, in a flux of periodic repetition, which is to say, in a perpetual state of transcoding or transduction. All living things are composed of milieus that are "open to chaos." Indeed, "rhythm is the milieu's answer to chaos. What chaos and rhythm have in common is the in-between—between two milieus. . . . In this in-between, chaos becomes rhythm, not inexorably, but it has a chance to. Chaos is not the opposite of rhythm, but the milieu of all milieus. There is rhythm whenever there is a transcoded passage from one milieu to another, a communication of milieus, coordination between heterogeneous space-times."[4] Rhythm always occurs and functions in the between of various milieus, not only marking or signing territorial boundaries against intrusion by the stranger, but perhaps more importantly in delineating the territorial boundaries of individuals within the same social grouping.

⁂ ⁂ ⁂

Is not silence most free of the economy of violence that is community, as it seemingly denotes an absolute passivity, a passivity that arguably constitutes the very seat of nonviolence itself? But can this passivity be known? Can it be articulated? If so, what would a speech about silence be? A silent speech? Is that not a nonsensical oxymoron, a paralyzing paradox? "Concerning that about which one cannot speak," writes Derrida, "isn't it best to remain silent?"[5] Derrida writes elsewhere, "A speech produced without the least violence would determine nothing, would say nothing, would offer nothing to the other; it would not be *history*, and it would *show* nothing: in every sense of the word, and first of all the Greek sense, it would be speech without *phrase*. . . . Predication is the first violence."[6] It would seem, on this account at least, that if anything were exonerated from participation in violence it would be silence, and not just any silence, but absolute silence, insofar as such silence would not belong to "being" proper.

Silence only has meaning in relation to that which it is not, that is, language as speech, but it is only through language that the enigmatic signification of the silence of silence is expressed. This is the paradox of silence. We can only understand and interpret the polyvalent paradox of silence by speaking of it and, moreover, out of it. "In brief," states Merleau-Ponty, "we should consider speech before it has been pronounced, against the ground of this silence which precedes it, which never ceases to accompany it, and without which it would say nothing. Moreover, we should be sensitive to the thread of silence from which the tissue of speech is woven."[7] By itself a thread barely constitutes anything, nevertheless it is the stuff that intertwines the inaudible with the audible, much in the manner of his celebrated ontological chiasm of the invisible and the visible.

The line demarcated by this thread conjoins, confuses, both the speaker and the listener. The rhythmic power of speech, indeed of all language, lies not only in its utterance but also in its reception. For this a certain silence is required, a silence that originates not from within but from without. Blanchot writes, "In the silent outside, in the silence of silence which by no means has any relation to language for it does not come from language but has always already departed from it—in this silent exteriority, that which has neither begun nor ever will finish keeps watch."[8] Blanchot here alludes to an often noticed relation between silence and sight, characterizing it as a type of vigilance. But toward what or whom is this watchfulness directed?

The ancient Achaeans, among others, understood the sacrality of ritualistic silence, its rhythm, and thus the reason for and orientation of this sacrality: it was that which preserved the right of the other to speak and, more importantly, to be heard. Silence provided the invisible space for the revelation of one's daemon, god, or gods, and in so providing enabled the subject-vessel to be autonomous, or to maintain at least the appearance of independence. But silence does not stand completely on its own; it is bound to a rhythmic whole. Thus, as Levinas points out, "rhythm represents a unique situation where we cannot speak of consent, assumption, initiative, or freedom, because the subject is caught up and carried away by it. The subject is part of its own representation. It is not so even despite itself, for in rhythm there is no longer a oneself, but rather a sort of passage from oneself to anonymity."[9] In a world where reality was principally construed in terms of fixed positions, temporally and spatially, but also metaphysically and socially, this was no mean matter. Hence the seriousness of the council ritual. Silence denotes more than the invisibility associated with the absence of sound; it also connotes spatiality. Even more than the physical grounds of the temples and groves, silence was the true sacred space, a rhythmically manifested nonspatial space that formed the genuine ground of community.

Community implies relationships, and for a community to flourish it must be sensitive to the needs of the other. But too often those needs are silenced by the violence of force, apathy, or simply ignorance. The sensitivity to which Merleau-Ponty refers above is meaningful only in the context of intersubjective relations. Paraphrasing his words, the other is the thread from which the tissue of community is woven. In assigning an ontological and metaphysical preeminence to vision and light, how often has Western culture lamentably tended to blind itself to the darkened faces of those on the periphery, those on the margins or fringes of society, whose voices, if not completely reduced to silence, are frequently dismissed as the garbled utterances of the barbarian or savage! But the secondary, almost arbitrary status designated to speech and sound by the advance of (a particular) historical consciousness does not completely silence the voices, the cries, of the myriad silent ones. Blanchot poignantly expresses this: "Silence is perhaps a word, a paradoxical word, the silence of the word *silence*, yet surely we feel that it is linked to the cry, the voiceless cry, which breaks with all utterances, which is addressed to no one and which no one receives, that cry that lapses and decries. . . . The cry tends to exceed all language, even if it lends itself to recuperation as language effect."[10] Silence does not only signal a lack of ability to communicate on the part of the oppressed;

it denotes a refusal to listen to the silent voice of the other. The silent voice, however, resounds with a rhythm of its own, vibrating and pulsating through the body, through the very earth itself. De Certeau poignantly notes that Native Americans, for example, have retained in the silence of the "tortured body" and "altered earth" the memory of what European culture has largely "forgotten."[11] But this is not a forgetting in that active sense of which Nietzsche writes; rather, it is a reactive forgetting wherein the sound of silence is repressed precisely by keeping silent, by remaining consciously mute.

To transfigure the reactive into the active, the paralysis of nihilism into the ecstasy of self-overcoming, the no-saying into the great Yes—this is the task and goal of future affirmative willing, adjures Nietzsche; this is awakening. Standing at the bitter end of and staring dumbly down the tracks leading to the Birkenau crematoria, for instance, one finds oneself at the center of the world, seemingly powerless in the full awareness of humanity's capacity for cruelty and horror, suspended between the possibilities of hell and heaven, of inaction and action. Here one is mute in the face of recognition and realization. "Yes, awakening can stop and silence us," writes Lingis, "freezing the continuity and momentum of movements," but it "can also give rise to action"—the action of responsibility. "My action arises when I wake up to *what I have to do*. In the action the I awakens."[12] In doing so, the I gives birth to a new rhythm, a new silence, a new speech, and a new listening—a new I.

❖ ❖ ❖

Silence disturbs, if not frightens, many, and those who command silence are often viewed as the most fearsome because they are generally the least understood. Silence dissipates the veils of meaning, of sense, within which one wraps oneself to stem the blackness of the night, the cries of the other, the pervasive present absence of death. If pure absolute silence *is*, then it is nothing that one can know or experience directly. Even if one denies mediation as the epistemic power proper, to realize the infinite depths of pure silence would be tantamount to becoming absolutely other. It would be nothing short of becoming God—or nothingness.

Indeed, nothing perhaps defines the postmodern condition more than the need to fill the void that is absolute silence itself. Nietzsche characterizes our age as one of nihilism, the legacy of God's complete annulment, but an age virtually ignorant of this death and more so of its causes. Debord declares that ours is the "society of the spectacle,"[13] though surely no time before our own has been as determined and defined by so much relentless sound. Is this not an example of the paradox of silence? The spectacle reduces all to the gaze of the observer, but the silence of this reduction is overwhelming and calls forth the rush of speech to insulate against the terror of silence's indeterminacy.

Nietzsche could name the rhythmic repetition of the silence of silence as the eternal recurrence of the same and know it as his most abysmal and yet most liberating thought, for while in the eternal recurrence life is repeatedly affirmed in its repetition, death is also both continuously staved off and repeated ad infinitum. Could it be that the pure silence left in the wake of God's death can only be known by not knowing the meaning of that silence? Is it not precisely this that most characterizes the present consciousness?

⁂

Silence resounds spatially, despite its apparent temporal dislocation. Is this its secret? And if silence does speak, then it can be said that there is a type of sound to silence. Levinas teaches that "sound is the quality most detached from an object. Its relation with the substance from which it emanates is not inscribed in its quality. It resounds impersonally. Even its timbre, a trace of its belonging to an object, is submerged in its quality, and does not retain the structure of a relation. Hence in listening we do not apprehend a 'something,' but are without concepts."[14] This impersonal quality, however, does not necessarily indicate a nonrelation with the listener, or a relation without affectivity. It could also signify a universal aspect, an issuing forth of sense to all who have the ears to hear, all the while leaving open the nonspatial hermeneutical space.

Silence dictates that we not only recognize it through its opposite, speech, but that we locate it phenomenally, in the earth, the cosmos, in ourselves, and in the other. Nietzsche, Levinas, and Lyotard all refer in their own way to the "listening eye,[15] a term used earlier by Swedenborg,[16] realizing that the meaning of silence cannot be fully reduced to speech but nevertheless cannot be absolutely separated from language if it is to have any signification at all. Knowing when and where to speak is the key to understanding, or at least effectively interpreting, this meaning. Temporality "resounds for the 'eye that listens,' with a resonance unique in its kind, a resonance of silence," writes Levinas.[17] Does this resonance form a sort of language, albeit one without speech—a rhythmic silence? Perhaps it is necessary then, as Merleau-Ponty writes, that "if we want to understand language in its original mode of signifying, we shall have to pretend never to have spoken. We must perform a reduction on language, without which it would still be hidden from our view—leading us back to what it signifies. We should look at language the way deaf people look at those who are speaking. We should compare the art of language with other arts of expression which do not have recourse to language and try to see language as one of these mute arts."[18] Employing here his own listening eye, Merleau-Ponty recognizes what many ancient peoples knew, what the ancient Greeks expressed in the gesture of passing the staff, communicating more than what could be contained in mere words, namely, that the foundation of community is based on the recognition of the etiquette of silence, the opening of a necessary sacred space that allows for free discursive exchange.

Now if existence itself has a meaning, other than the meanings that we assign to it, then it is a secret, at least to most of us. Does the secret meaning of being lie in its silence, a silence beyond language but in which language comes to reside? Following Heidegger's famous claim that "language is the house of being,"[19] Gadamer writes that "being which can be understood is language."[20] If this is so, then it is only because silence is the groundless ground on which this house of understanding is built, and the rhythmic play of silence and speech its building material. The relation between silence and secrecy is intimate, and etiquette demands respect for maintaining intimacy. But etiquette also periodically requires breaking of silence—at the proper time. The secret is as much a matter of knowing when to reveal secrets as it is to keeping them. For this a sense of rhythm is needed. The rhythm of silence attends to the status and well-being of both the self and the other. Therein is community simultaneously constituted and preserved.

⁂

Philosophy is by its very nature opposed to silence and in its own way is an absolute breaking of silence. Indeed, the above said probably brings one no closer to actually understanding the complex saying, with all its multiple levels of meaning, that resides between silence and speech, silence and community, silence and etiquette. In the end, one can only really assert that the silence of silence is a paradox. Perhaps no tradition better expresses that paradox than does Zen, a philosophy that also is not a philosophy, and perhaps it is there that one should finally turn for the ever-elusive meaning of silence.

Of Shakyamuni's followers, tradition holds that only Kashyapa understood the meaning of the Buddha's teaching when the Awakened One held aloft the udumbara flower. Though not in direct reference to Shakyamuni's gesture, the words of Zen Master Unmon are clearly apropos:

> He used no high-flown words;
> Before the mouth is opened, "it" is revealed.
> If you keep on chattering glibly,
> Know you will never get "it."[21]

Etiquette stipulated that Kashyapa not interrupt his teacher, but it also required that a response be given. Kashyapa's silent response mirrored and yet transcended the silence of his teacher's gesture.

Develop the powers of listening, even with the eyes, and silence will flourish. The particular etiquette of silence here opened the sacred space that allowed for the reception of the dharma, or teaching, and the formation of the *sangha*, or community. In the knowing silence of Kashyapa's smile, the meaning of silence was given expression in a resonance louder than any spoken or written words could render. Here, maintaining silence was precisely the rhythmic breaking of silence, the realization of the fullness of the moment—at the *proper* time and in the proper space.

Notes

1. Gilles Deleuze and Felix Guattari, *A Thousand Plateaus: Capitalism and Schizophrenia*, trans. Brian Massumi (Minneapolis: University of Minnesota Press, 1994), p. 319.
2. Ibid., p. 320.
3. Ibid., p. 312.
4. Ibid., p. 313.

5. Jacques Derrida, "How to Avoid Speaking: Denials," trans. Ken Frieden, in *Languages of the Unsayable: The Play of Negativity in Literature and Social Theory*, ed. Sanford Buddick and Wolfgang Iser (New York: Columbia University Press), p. 22.

6. Jacques Derrida, "Violence and Metaphysics," in *Writing and Difference*, trans. Alan Bass (Chicago: University of Chicago Press, 1978), p. 147.

7. Maurice Merleau-Ponty, *The Prose of the World*, ed. Claude Lefort and trans. John O'Neill (Evanston, IL: Northwestern University Press, 1973), p. 45. Elsewhere he writes, "There is no silence that is pure attention and that, having begun nobly, remains equal to itself" (p. 146).

8. Maurice Blanchot, *The Writing of the Disaster*, trans. Ann Smock (Lincoln: University of Nebraska Press, 1995), p. 57.

9. Emmanuel Levinas, "Reality and Its Shadow," in *Collected Philosophical Papers*, trans. and ed. Alphonso Lingis (Dordrecht: Martinus Nijhoff Publishers, 1987), p. 4.

10. Blanchot, *Writing of the Disaster*, p. 51.

11. Michel de Certeau, "The Politics of Silence: The Long March of the Indians," in *Heterologies: Discourse on the Other*, trans. Brian Massumi (Minneapolis: University of Minnesota Press, 1986), pp. 226–227.

12. Alphonso Lingis, *Dangerous Emotions* (Berkeley: University of California Press, 2000), pp. 107, 108.

13. Guy Debord, *The Society of the Spectacle*, trans. Donald Nicholson-Smith (New York: Zone Books, 1995).

14. Levinas, "Reality and Its Shadow," p. 5.

15. Cf. Brian Schroeder, "The Listening Eye: Nietzsche and Levinas," *Research in Phenomenology* 31 (2001): 188–202.

16. Emmanuel Swedenborg writes, " 'To the insides of the ear belong those who have a sight of internal hearing.' That's the nocturnal look, the listening eye." Cited in Jean-François Lyotard, *The Inhuman: Reflections on Time,* trans. Geoff Bennington and Rachel Bowlby (Stanford: Stanford University Press, 1991).

17. Emmanuel Levinas, *Otherwise than Being or Beyond Essence*, trans. Alphonso Lingis (The Hague: Martinus Nijhoff, 1978), p. 30.

18. Merleau-Ponty, *Prose of the World,* pp. 45–46.

19. Martin Heidegger, "Letter on Humanism," trans. Frank A. Capuzzi and J. Glenn Gray, in *Martin Heidegger: Basic Writings*, ed. David Farrell Krell (New York: Harper & Row, 1977), p. 193.

20. Hans-Georg Gadamer, *Truth and Method*, trans. Joel C. Weinsheimer and Donald G. Marshall, 2nd revised edition (New York: Continuum, 1993), p. 474.

21. Quoted in Zenkei Shibayama, *The Gateless Barrier: Zen Comments on the Mumonkan*, trans. Sumiko Kudo (Boston: Shambhala, 2000), p. 175. Master

Mumon cited this poem by Master Unmon in his response to the following koan: "A monk once asked Master Fuketsu, 'Both speaking and silence are concerned with ri-bi relativity. How can we be free and nontransgressing?' Fuketsu said, 'How fondly I remember Konan in March! The partridges are calling, and the flowers are fragrant.' "

CHAPTER TEN

Handy Etiquette

DAVID FARRELL KRELL

The French Lithuanian philosopher Emmanuel Lévinas, with that droll sense of humor and lightheartedness that graces all his works, once tried to prove that murder is impossible. Humanity responded in the predictable manner—by proving that murder is highly likely.

For a period in U. S. academic history that loves to chase loudly after an ethics, hoping thereby to found a lasting and decent politics, discussions of etiquette must seem to be aiming far below the mark—indeed, such discussions must seem apolitical, unethical, downright rude. Yet our time may come to understand that the ethico-political craze in philosophy and theory these days is precisely that, a craze, and an expression of some deep-lying desperation—so that, when all is said and done, what we have to learn how to cherish is the meager hope that human beings may learn civility. If they cannot refrain from murder, let them at least try a touch of *politesse.* Who knows? Etiquette may reduce the killing more effectively than an entire ethico-political police force hiding out in philosophy departments.

Etiquette begins with the simple things, and this chapter is no exception. A minor branch of telephone etiquette is my topic; to be precise, cell phone etiquette. In German, a cell phone is a "Handy," pronounced HEN-dee. Hence the title.

My particular concern is the use of cell phones in high mountains. Yet allow me to set a more familiar stage, a little closer to home. We have all seen and heard the go-getter businessman, the thruster, the aging yuppie, at airport gates. We have all seen and heard him on his cell phone leaving instructions for the incompetents back at the office or preparing the incompetents at his destination for his Coming. He is sometimes good humored, even raucous and jovial, sometimes impatient, but always dependably loud.

Likewise, we have all seen and heard passengers on the bus, subway, or elevated train, letting their loved ones in on the essential happenings of the day:

> —Hi, I'm on the train. . . . Yeah, it's noisy, so I'll have to shout. Can you hear me? Good. I'm on the train. We just stopped at Addison. How's Uncle Theo's hernia? . . . It's those damn dissolvable stitches, I tell you, they never dissolve, and here it is Thanksgiving, and Uncle Theo trussed up like a turkey. . . . Sorry . . . no . . . I know, it's not funny. Oops! Belmont! Gotta go, I'll callya from work.

"I'll callya." In Germany, the most popular cell phones, or "Handies," are fed by *Callya Karten*. These are plastic cards, exorbitantly expensive, on which a secret code number is printed, as though on a lottery ticket. If I rub off the waxy covering and dial that number into the cell phone company they will credit me with a certain number of Euros and I can . . . callya. Some Germans find the use of these American expressions offensive, while others point out that the final stage of imperialism is capitalism.

"I'll callya." It's a new verb, with no object, taking neither the dative nor the accusative; an intransitive verb, well nigh in the middle voice, almost reflexive, but not quite. I'll callya, as in: I'll take a bath, I'll play the lottery, I'll seeya 'round.

There are rules of etiquette governing the use of cell phones in German-speaking lands, however. One of these is never to take your *Callya Karte* cell phone with you on a trek into high mountains. It is quite shocking how many trekkers violate this categorical imperative. The rule does exist. Yet the violators are many, and their number growing.

On a ridge high in the Karwendel Range of Austria, where you would think the bloody things were out of range of even the most rarefied radio waves, you do not have to strain to hear the loudmouth. He is in full trekking gear, toting all the regalia, everything just right, looking sharp, but here is what he is shouting into his cell phone, presumably to loved ones (difficult to imagine!) down in the valley, shouting so loud that the phone seems superfluous:

> —It sure is beautiful up here. Yeah, and the weather's perfect. Blue sky. I said *the sky is blue.* Great weather. This is the third valley we've hiked today, one more beautiful than the next. We sure picked the good ones. We were smart.

You hurry on, trying to get out of earshot now that you know the essential matter, namely, how smart the caller is. Yet the mountain is made of stone, and stone echoes.

> —Yeah, we're really high. I don't know how high, but we're really high. No, I mean *high on the mountain.* Ha, ha! Nothing but rock up here. Yeah, and the sky. Bright blue. Perfect weather.

You hope that his *Callya Karte* is depleting rapidly and that the silence of the mountains will soon be restored. Perhaps the ledge on which he is standing, which he mistakes for a phone booth, will crumble. Hope springs eternal in high mountains. You remember how Nietzsche always dreamed of wandering among icy crags, alone with his thoughts, rapt to the silence, and you wonder how he would respond to the caller—whose voice is still echoing.

> —No trees or nothing. No, we're really high. *On the mountain.* Ha, ha. We're about ready to head back, though. My feet are killing me—it's those bunions, or maybe the gout again. What? I don't care. Sure, schnitzel, if you want. Just go easy on the sauerkraut. You remember what happened last time—phew!

And that, dear reader, is why there are rules of etiquette governing the use of cell phones in German-speaking countries—indeed, rules outlawing their use in high mountains. We have seen why these rules must be respected. Let's start with these rules; later we can eliminate homicide.

CHAPTER ELEVEN

Murder So Bland

The Implosion of Disetiquette

MARK S. ROBERTS

Once a feat of frightful social transgression, of profound disetiquette, the criminal act has, in the postmodern era, become extraordinarily bland and routine. Along with other complex socioeconomic, historical, and psychological factors, it seems that the constant exposure and sheer repetition of criminal acts in modern media and communications has rendered virtually all of these heinous acts commonplace. And, more important, this continuous exposure has provided a sort of mimetic ideal for the act. That is to say, criminal acts today are viewed and treated largely as simple reproductions, copies of other acts, usually ones heard or seen in the media. For example, Charles Stuart, who killed his pregnant wife to collect her insurance and buy a new luxury car, was inspired to perform the murder by a made-for-TV movie.[1] Even stranger, Jesse Anderson later killed his wife by almost exactly duplicating Stuart's crime, rendering a copy of a copy of a copy—one of Plato's greatest consternations. One might also invoke Luigi Ferri, the killer of eight in a San Francisco law firm, who, following his suicide, was found to be carrying a list of TV talk shows in his brief case—talk shows he hoped to appear on to make his case against the law firm. Not to mention a recent grisly L. A. Freeway suicide in which a man first unfurled a banner for the TV helicopters so he could accurately list his grievances.

Given this imagistic treatment of murder, gore, and mayhem—both by participating individuals and the media—one could argue, along with Jean Baudrillard, that the modern criminal act in its constant repetition within the hyperreality of media has imploded, turned in on itself, become merely an image, a bit of information among billions of other bits of information. That is to say, something which can be infinitely reduplicated, since it has lost its uniqueness, its qualities of shock, opprobrium, or transgression.

This has not always been the case, however. In the period between the Renaissance and the height of the industrial revolution, designated by Baudrillard as "the counterfeit," crime took on a distinct significance, serving many unique social, political, literary, and artistic purposes. In the case of Charles Fourier, for example, one finds a marked emphasis on the singular value of the very act of crime. Indeed, with Fourier and the Fourierists, one encounters the early beginnings of an articulated sociology of crime—a theory which seeks to understand criminal acts in terms of social position. In his *Discipline and Punish*, Michel Foucault construes this theory in terms of viewing crime as "a result of civilization . . . and by that very fact, a weapon against it."[2] The Fourierists, it seems, perceived the criminal as a heroic figure fighting against a totally corrupt system that treats his or her "natural robustness" and rebelliousness with violent and repressive means. Effectively, society imprisons and, too often, executes those who reject or disdain its prescriptions. Thus criminality is not rooted in the nature of the individual, as a moral defect, but, rather, it is a means of activism against and resistance to a repressive society. Moreover, an individual will invariably become a criminal or a model citizen based on certain socioeconomic forces at play in the various classes. The high-born criminal would no doubt condemn the low-born magistrate to a lengthy sentence on a prison ship, reversing the existing moral and authoritarian order.

Not only does crime resist the status quo for the Fourierists, but it is also a tonic, a means of awakening the most dolorous, sensuous and dormant passions lying within the individual:

> At bottom, the existence of crime manifests "a fortunate impressibility of nature;" it should be seen not so much as a weakness or a disease, but as an energy that is reviving an outburst of

protest in the name of human individuality, which no doubt accounts for its strange power and fascination.

Without crime, which awakens in us a mass of torpid feelings and half distinguished passions, we would remain still longer in disorder, in weakness.[3]

In short, then, Fourier and the Fourierists viewed crime as a necessary means of rehabilitating a society and civilization which has been perverted by corrupt political institutions. Legislators and various other governmental officials have simply contaminated the natural order of things by imposing false moral codes and by directing the intrinsic passions away from their true objects. Reversing this trend, according to Fourier, requires that individuals render the environment attractive to natural inclinations. Life, labor, leisure, sexuality, and so on. must be organized along the lines of a new environmental plan—a plan that requires a certain regime of association which is consistent with an ancient utopian conception lost in modern times. Vice and crime, viewed in the contemporary world in decidedly negative terms, might, within this regime of association, very well turn out to be virtues, since they would certainly serve to reverse the existing order of things: those false principles of morality that have obstructed the scope of human passions, and thus misdirected them.

For the Marquis de Sade, murder and crime were not only a tonic and a form of social resistance, but also—and above all—a compulsory activity necessary to fulfill the utopic objective of Sade's representation of the most highly developed of all individuals: the libertine. Simply put, the libertine could not live life in its fullest sense until he or she embraced the criminal act and transgressed the codes of customary law. Indeed, for Sade, law (both criminal and civil) was so egregious in its capricious restrictions that it represented one of the most extreme limitations on the human spirit; it placed people in absolute submission to a totally arbitrary legal system and a prohibitive social contract—factors that ultimately weakened individuals' position in society, rather than strengthening it: "The truly intelligent person is he who . . . lashes out against the social contract, he violates it as much and as often as he is able, full certain that he will gain from these ruptures, will always be more important than what he will lose if he happens to be a member of the weaker class; for such he was when he respected the treaty; by breaking it, he may become one of the stronger. . . . There are then two positions available to us: either crime, which renders us happy, or the noose, which prevents us from being unhappy."[4]

Crime rendered us so "happy" that it even led Sade to reduce the entire libertine social organization to a single criminal coterie, which he appropriately named "The Society of the Friends of Crime." Members of this society would resolutely practice virtually every crime imaginable, and, particularly, ones considered most repulsive to those who held fast to conventional notions of law and order. Typically, these crimes would include such monstrosities as rape, incest, sodomy, infanticide, matricide, and torture: "The moral crimes, prostitution, adultery, incest, rape, sodomy, should be perfectly indifferent in a government whose sole duty consists in conserving by whatever means the form essential for its maintenance. If there is a crime in anything it would rather be in resisting the inclinations which nature inspires in us than in combating them."[5] And elsewhere: "The secret is unfortunately only too certain; there is not a libertine the least bit rooted in vice, who does not know how much influence *murder* has on the senses and what extent it determines a voluptuous discharge."[6]

How, one might wonder, could such monstrosities possibly be justified? Although Sade goes into painstaking, sometimes excruciating, detail regarding the reasoning behind his unqualified defense of crime, there are two fairly basic suppositions underlying this belief. The first is rooted in Sade's resolute atheism. He firmly believes that neither the concept of God, organized religion, nor—and especially—the clergy have any legitimate place in the human and natural world. Indeed, as far as Sade is concerned, the immemorial concept of God has perhaps been the most formidable obstacle to civilization's happiness and freedom. The fully invented notion of God presents a distinct set of limits, according to which conventional rules of law are able to fix the boundaries of transgression—to, in effect, authoritatively introduce evil and punishment into the world. We are thus restrained in every worldly endeavor by an arbitrary and entirely corrupt system of belief. Our very possibilities of thought, creativity, passion, imagination, expression, and so on are rigidly controlled and circumscribed by something we, as free individuals, had no part in creating or sanctioning.

In order to reinstate this lost moment of pure freedom and expression, of unrestrained imagination, one must exceed the boundaries of this arbitrarily imposed notion of transgression, demonstrate the pain and suffering that it has caused individuals to endure.[7] In effect, the libertine must fight fire with fire, constantly blaspheming the name and acts of God, twisting the supposed virtuous and moral dictates of religion into hideous monstrosities. The principal means of expressing this distress is, of course, crime. It is through the heinous criminal act, the act that goes beyond every arbitrary boundary of decency, that libertines can eventually gain mastery over both themselves and the imposed social order. Criminal/libertines offer their bodies and their depravity as a sign of both the limits of transgression and the transcendence of those limits. The contemptible impurity of sodomy, rape, incest, coprophilia, pedophilia, murder, and so forth is precisely Sade's foil against what St. Thomas Aquinas called "the government of things in God."[8]

Sade's second defense of crime involves nature and its effective role in human psychology, fate, and action. Nature, for Sade, represents a pure and irreversible force. It operates ineluctably, thus embodying a powerful element of randomness, which often resulted in a perfect symmetry between cruelty and compassion, vice and virtue: "Wolves which eat lambs, lambs devoured by wolves, the strong who sacrifice the weak, the weak the victim of the strong, this is nature; these are her views, these are her plans; a perpetual action and reaction; a host of vices and virtues, a perfect equilibrium, in a word, resulting from the equality of evil and good on earth; an equilibrium essential to maintenance of the heavenly bodies, to vegetation and without which everything would be instantly destroyed."[9]

If there is no difference in nature between good and evil, vice and virtue, then, Sade reflects, there really can be no crimes against nature. The only repugnance we feel regarding crime as being unnatural is not moral, but, rather, results from lack of habit, that is, our being unaccustomed to criminal and vile acts: "Is it not the same with certain foods? . . . Let us accustom ourselves likewise to evil; we will soon find it only charms."[10] The ubiquity of good and evil in nature also tends to absolve the individual from any act of criminal perversion, since it inculcates in one's very fibers the need to act naturally, which of course includes monstrous criminal acts. In this sense, the criminal is no more an immoralist or monster than the saint who bears the martyr's burden. The criminal is only following an ineluctable path fixed in the natural order of things. Sade's parodic counter to St. Jerome the martyr—Jérôme—in *Justine* puts it quite succinctly: "Just think that this depraved nature nourishes itself, sustains itself only through crimes and if crimes are necessary they cannot outrage either nature or the imaginary being whom you suppose to be her mover. . . . All the means which you use to succeed not only could not be criminal, but become even virtuous since the first law which nature inspired in us was to preserve ourselves at whatever price and at whosoever expense it may be."

What, then, could be more natural and useful than crime and criminality? For Sade, practically nothing. They serve an essential dual purpose. On the one hand, the heinous criminal act defies the arbitrary limits of transgression, preordained by an imaginary God and ultimately valorized by organized religion. Each criminal exploit, each act of blasphemy serves to further obliterate the limitations placed on human action and thought. We can only venture beyond by reversing the poles of good and evil, of what is acceptable and what is despised by organized religion, and, subsequently, by society as a whole. On the other hand, crime serves to benefit nature, and is thus not in any way a perversion but a necessity dictated by nature itself. If we are preconditioned to survive, to perpetuate our species, how could any act that accomplishes this program be considered perverse or criminal? Nature simply induces us to follow an agenda, bringing us both good and evil in more or less equal portions. Should we, Sade argues, distinguish between the two so as to judge one natural and the other unnatural? One perverse and the other normal?

The transgressive, upraising, and fashionable aspects of crime were not without their adherents in the nineteenth century as well. The Romantic essayist Thomas De Quincey, for instance, demonstrated a deep fascination with the infinite aesthetic possibilities of crime, particularly mass murder. His chilling, scientifically analytic, and often humorous essay, "On Murder Considered as One of the Fine Arts," begins, satirically, with a kind of disclaimer condemning the various societies formed around evil and vice, particularly those devoted to the promotion of murder. Ironically, he then proceeds to dash off a broad celebration of murder, which runs throughout the body of the essay. His main interests in this most inhuman of crimes are sociopolitical and aesthetic. Regarding the former, he invokes a broad range of sociopolitical phenomena associated with murder, particularly certain statistical data collected from ancient times to the present. His political interest also extends to the social upheaval caused by acts of murder. Murder, De

Quincey argues, totally annihilates the micro-units of social order, destroying those long developed social and political ties that sustain the institutions of family and individual power. His favorite murderer was thus a presumably psychopathic killer named John Williams who in cold blood murdered not one but two entire families in the course of a single hour. De Quincey interpreted these seemingly dreadful acts as expressions of the inevitable breakdown of the family as an institution—something he had continually stressed in his own writings.[11] Williams had not only dispensed with all the family members, literally rendering the traditional nuclear structure and the succession of the family null, but he had also totally destroyed the sanctity of the most private of all spaces, home and hearth. A chilling thought—but one that De Quincey was willing to follow to its conclusion in his compulsive, though ultimately creative, need to reveal the most extreme aspects of this most extreme of all criminal acts.

Another appealing feature of the Williams case was no doubt Williams himself. Apparently he went off to destroy the two families in rather unusual dress: a dreamy evening gown, black silk stockings, and high heels. According to De Quincey's account, he strolled to the crime scene through the streets of London carrying under his overcoat a huge sledge hammer (the grisly murder weapon), further concealed, no doubt, by his billowing gown. Even greater detail of Williams's killing outfit turned up in the trial testimony of the sole survivor of his murder spree: "Mr. Williams wore a long blue frock, of the very finest cloth, and richly lined with silk."[12] Adding humor to injury, De Quincey goes on to point out that Williams was not only a snappy dresser, but also employed the best chiropodist and dentist money could buy. All in all, De Quincey suggests, the man was a supreme connoisseur and artist in his peculiar field: "And, beyond a doubt, in that perilous little branch of business which was practiced by himself he might be regarded as the most aristocratic and fastidious of artists."[13]

A cross-dressing mass murderer is commended for his foppish tastes in personal hygiene and his impeccable choice of murder wear. What could have possessed De Quincey? Driven him so far from the path of what most consider reason, law, and order? In her critical study of De Quincey, Alina Clej suggests several possible answers. First, De Quincey, from his earliest literary endeavors, firmly believed that resistance was a sign of greatness: "His acts of youthful rebellion appear to have been part of the same mystique of sublime power."[14] Any form of resistance to societal norms then became an act of creative defiance—an act by which De Quincey could assert his personal and artistic peculiarity. As a consummate admirer of Milton's Satan, he saw the odd, the eccentric, sheer evil, and criminal activity as expressions of an inner greatness, of a decisive nonconformity: "The greatest obstacles commonly arise in the execution of nefarious designs; whence not unfrequently in deeds of the greatest turpitude a deadly splendor has shone forth from the mind striking terror into nations. . . . A great action, therefore, is not necessarily a fine action."[15]

Another possible explanation for De Quincey's singular penchant for criminal activity lies in his notions of transgression and sublimity. Like Sade before him, he saw transgression as a way of distinguishing oneself from a society enslaved by arbitrary and mediocre rules, by an obligation to rigidly conform to externally conceived societal standards. In this respect, to be a criminal was to be a "hero," at least insofar as one appeared constantly in the police reports and daily newspapers. To celebrate this criminality was to associate oneself with the kind of behavior that contravenes societal norms, and which, ultimately, leads to the discovery of glory and literary and personal transcendence. In De Quincey's mind, criminal transgression opened an entire domain of sublime feelings, because the sublime, as he saw it, always belonged to what is presumably ineffable, unutterable.[16] Hence, to enter the seamy, obsessive, mad world of the mass murderer John Williams was to also recreate the schema of sublimity, to, in effect, express an unqualified empathy with what was commonly viewed as repulsive, unthinkable, inhuman, inexpressible.

The above expressions of crime and the murderous act all presume that they are extreme violations of societal norms. As such, crime is represented as the outermost limits to which social, artistic and literary categories can be extended. Horror, monstrosity, murder, wickedness, repulsion, and gore are unlike any other subject matter; they exceed social norms by the very fact that they are entirely other than what is conventionally acceptable in any society, acts of the most extreme disetiquette.

But, as I mentioned earlier, the structures common to earlier forms of the representation of crime have largely disappeared in the postmodern, information-centric era. Rather, the abovementioned postmodern instances of murder and mayhem are concerned primarily with monitoring faithfully an event as if it was being recorded through some medium, domonstrating a decided concern for how one might appear within another image or screen, inspired, in most instances, by yet another image. In short, the modern murderer/criminal craves to become the medium itself. This presumably being the case, one might seek a possible explanation for this postmodern form of image production in the different ways in which we have come to view human subjectivity vis à vis electronic and informational media, that is, our means of reproducing images of ourselves and our specific relation to these images.

Recently, Mark Poster, in *The Mode of Information*, makes a case for our being cut off from ourselves by our own technologies and inventions. In discussing databases and informational technologies, he argues that the unprecedented spread of database technology has created a "multiplication of the individual"—a new form of subjectivity that has assumed its place alongside the Cartesian vision of the subject. As a result, the Cartesian idea of immanence, mind as superior and distinct from material substance, is no longer conceived as the central model for identity. The self, traditionally viewed as circumscribed within an inner realm, is now, in the postmodern era, grafted onto completely external, impersonal systems. And these systems are composed entirely of electronic information about individuals, databases.

The average database entry, the "additional self," contains hundreds, sometimes thousands of bits of information composing the person's file. A credit information file, for example, might contain pertinent biographical data on a person (age, sex, educational background, and so on), but also a list of every financial transaction he or she has engaged in (including, for example, college loans), as well as, in many cases, extremely personal information like home costs, political affiliations, present salary, criminal records, subscriptions to communist publications, unpaid parking violations, medical conditions, and so forth. In effect, the data bank profile constitutes a subject which is entirely separate from the person, but which, in many instances, touches significant portions of the real subject's life—serves, as it were, as a surrogate for the subject. For example, the database self, due to certain pertinent facts in his file, can be turned down for a mortgage, thus affecting how real subjects live, where their children go to school, who their neighbors are, what kind of employment they are able to accept, and so on. "We see databases . . . as the multiplication of the individual, the constitution of an additional self, one that may be acted upon to the detriment of the 'real' self without that 'real' self ever being aware of what is happening."[17]

Arguing along lines similar to Poster's, Baudrillard suggests that television tends to project us into a space entirely disconnected from our inner lives—a space locatable neither inside nor outside our bodies and minds. This is precisely the point Baudrillard makes when discussing the TV-verité experiment, *An American Family*. The show originally aired on Public Broadcasting stations and was intended as a documentary record of seven months in the life of a typical American family, the Louds. However, some unanticipated, remarkable events occurred as the project advanced. The family began to disintegrate—perhaps due in part to an affair between the director and Mrs. Loud—and the documentary descended into the depths of familial anguish and acrimony, finally ending with the Loud's divorce. What was fascinating about all this, Baudrillard suggests, is that life went on "as if TV wasn't there."[18] What the twenty million viewers who pried into the life of the Louds were treated to, according to Baudrillard, was not the ultimate exercise in voyeurism, but rather the thrill of reality, a glimpse of life at its most hyperreal: "It is . . . a kind of thrill of the real, or of an aesthetics of the hyperreal, a thrill of vertiginous and phony exactitude, a thrill of alienation and of magnification, of distortion in scale, excessive transparency, all at the same time."[19] Thus, TV itself, in the case of the Louds, substitutes, in the eyes of the viewer, for the Loud's truth. TV becomes the very source of the true, becomes the rendering of the truth. The emotions spent by the disintegrating family, by real people in real trouble, are not seen at a distance, effectively absorbed by the viewer, but are rather rendered real through an electronic transference, by the very watching of TV itself. Or, perhaps more accurately, by *being* the watching itself:

> It is entirely different with the Louds: "You no longer watch TV, TV watches you (live)," or again: "You no longer listen to *Pas de Panique*, *Pas de Panique* listens to you"—switching over from the panoptic apparatus of surveillance (of *Discipline and Punish*) to a system of deterrence, where the distinction between active and passive is abolished. No longer is there any imperative to submit

> to the model, or the gaze. "YOU are the model!" . . . You are news, you are the social, the event is you, you are involved, you can use your voice, etc." A turnabout of affairs by which it becomes impossible to locate an instance of the model, of power, of the gaze, of the medium itself, since *you* are always already on the other side. No more subject, focal point, center or periphery: but pure flexion or circular inflection. No more violence, or surveillance; only information.[20]

What Baudrillard proposes here, then, is that media and the information they carry tend to implode reality, drawing us into their rarefied domain. With this implosion, the distance between subject and object is eliminated. We become the event and the event becomes us, leaving us frozen in a hyperreal space consisting of subjects converted into objects and events and vice versa. We no longer participate in the event, but rather, the event participates through us. And this, to be sure, leaves the subject in a unsettled position in its relation to the reality of events. As frozen moments within the vast schema of electronic media and information, we can no longer move up against these events, nor can we absorb them, understand them or react to them. Our capacity to respond to them from a deeper inner level, to respond to them in what might be considered conventional, cathartic ways, is severely restricted, if not entirely effaced. The loss of distinction between the watcher and the watched, the listener and the heard, and so on, eliminates the necessary poles for traditional forms of empathy. There is no longer the possibility of delving into the inner world of the subject, as there is no longer anything secret, dissimulated. Everything you are and will be is already inscribed in the very act of watching, contemplating, listening to, performing, becoming media and information.

All these modes of what Marshall McLuhan once called "extensions"[21] in the end, contribute, I suggest, to the decline of the transgressive force of the criminal act. In the age of electronic information, the very concept of inner/outer, of representational and aesthetic distance has given way to its mechanistic extensions, to media, to the blinding light of pure information. The subject/object-centered language of "the counterfeit"—catharsis, sublimity, shock, transgression, inner, outer, event, spectator, and so on—is no longer fully operative since, in the postmodern era, it has become virtually impossible to locate an instance of the paradigm, the model out of which such language evolves. Baudrillard states it quite succinctly: "No more subject, center or periphery: but pure flexion or circular inflection. No more violence or surveillance: only 'information,' secret virulence, chain reaction, slow implosion and simulacra of spaces where the real-effect again comes into play."[22]

It is thus no great mystery why Charles Stuart, his imitator Anderson, Luigi Ferri, and the L. A. suicide, among numerous others—the modern equivalents of Sade's libertines and the mass-murderer Williams—committed their crimes and acts with such mechanical precision and guiltless detachment. They were simply monitoring the dissolution of TV and media in general into life, seeking to be real participants in a hyperreal drama: an invented or remembered TV story line, the lead story on the five o'clock news. In this respect the postmodern media murderer tends to act in a manner emptied of the traditional modes of causality, of the distinction between active and passive, between human and machine, between media and life, between subject and object, between one's actions and their real consequences. In short, these murderers are unable to transgress the limits of acceptable behavior, to even shock us or themselves, to occasion disetiquette, since these limits require the reestablishment of empathetic boundaries.

Notes

1. The murder was committed in Boston in 1987. For further details see Joe Sharkey, *Deadly Greed* (New York: Simon and Schuster, 1991).

2. Michel Foucault, *Discipline and Punish: The Birth of the Prison* (New York: Vintage Books, 1979), p. 289.

3. Charles Fourier, *Design for Utopia* (New York: Schocken, 1971), p. 18.

4. Marquis de Sade, *Justine*, trans. Richard Seaver and Austryn Wainhouse (New York: Grove Press, 1965) pp. 494–495.

5. Marquis de Sade, *Philosophy in the Bedroom* (New York: Grove Press, 1965), p. 221.

6. Ibid. p. 232.

7. David B. Allison, "Sade's Itinerary of Transgression," in *The Divine Sade*, ed. Deepak Narang Sawhney (Warwick, England: *Pli, The Warwick Journal of Philosophy*, 1994), p. 145.

8. St. Thomas Aquinas, *Summa Theologica*, Question 91, article 1.

9. Marquis de Sade, *Justine or Good Conduct Well Chastised* (New York, Grove Press, 1965), p. 470.

10. Ibid.

11. Josephine McDonagh, *De Quincey's Disciplines,* (Oxford: Clarendon Press, 1994), p. 147.

12. Thomas De Quincey, "On Murder Considered as One of the Fine Arts," in *The Collected Writings of Thomas De Quincey,* vol. 13 (London: A. C. Black, 1897), p. 79.

13. Ibid.

14. Clej, p. 228.

15. Ibid., p. 229.

16. Ibid.

17. Mark Poster, *The Mode of Information: Poststructrualism and Social Context* (Chicago: University of Chicago Press, 1990), p. 56.

18. Jean Baudrillard, *Simulations* (New York: Semiotext(e), 1983), p. 50.

19. Ibid.

20. Ibid., pp. 53–54.

21. See Marshall McLuhan, *Understanding Media: The Extensions of Man* (New York, Signet Books, 1964).

22. Baudrillard, *Simulations*, pp. 53–54.

CHAPTER TWELVE

Branded from the Start

The Paradox of (the) American (Novel of) Manners

HILDEGARD HOELLER

Americans have always had a problem with manners, n'est ce pas? Since I am here mimicking the voice of a European you might think that I mean that Americans famously don't have manners. But, actually, I do not mean any such thing. On the contrary, I mean that the problem with Americans is not that they do or don't have manners—both statements are inevitably true—but that they want to have manners. Wanting to have manners is in itself always a neurotic position since it implies that you both desire them and lack them; thus, in both meanings, wanting manners signifies the belief that one does not have them and should have them. Americans, as a nation, have found themselves always in this neurotic and paradoxical spot. What aggravates the neurosis is yet another dilemma: wanting manners itself (that is, desiring them and recognizing a lack) goes against everything America stands for. It is in itself a breach of manners, if one takes manners to be an action that is silently in tune with a minute emblematic observance of the dominant system and its ideology. Manners, in a European sense (and for everyone else, Westerners seem to have invented the terms "customs" or "rituals") are, after all, a decidedly undemocratic concept, designed to separate classes along unspeakable yet visible lines of taste and behavior, and thus separating the common person from the not so common. A mannered American is then perhaps not an American at all?

This question is too large for a short chapter. However, the neurotic postcolonial struggle with and against manners can be well observed in the development of the American novel of manners, a form that is destined to reenact the dilemma just described. A few observations, necessarily sketchy, about the America novel of manners might then be useful in exploring America's paradoxical relation to manners.

Let's begin, inevitably, with the non-American, British example: Jane Austen, perhaps one of the most perfect and famous novelists of manners. Austen's masterpiece *Emma* (1816) climaxes in an embarrassing breach of manners. That's it. Anyone who expects more for a climax knows nothing about manners: their drama and significance. At the famous picnic on Box Hill, Austen's heroine, freed from the drawing room, makes fun of the loquacious and impecunious Miss Bates, whose never ending rambles have gotten on the nerves of everyone—including the reader who is, thanks to Austen, exposed to pages of her trivial and exceedingly boring chatter. The picnic party, from the beginning, is at odds: there seems a "principle of separation" in the party that no good will could overcome.[1] Frank Churchill, pretending to speak Emma's wishes, suggests a game that should bring the party together: he proposes that everyone say what they are thinking.[2] Emma, horrified by this transgression of manners, refuses such an idea: "Let me hear anything rather than what you are all thinking of."[3] Manners, after all, are there to hide what everyone is thinking. Frank then suggests, again in Emma's name, that "she only demands from each of you either one thing very clever, be it prose or verse, original or repeated; or two things moderately clever; or three things very dull indeed; and she engages to laugh heartily at them all."[4] When Miss Bates responds that she might manage to say three dull things, Emma responds, "Ah! Ma'am, but there might be a difficulty. Pardon me, but you will be limited as to number—only three at once."[5]

At this moment, the novel has reached its climax. While absolutely everyone can understand the impulse to mock Miss Bates, and while few readers won't for a second delight in Emma's witty and still somewhat mannered remark (she does say, "Pardon me," after all), the novel never leaves any doubt that Emma's breach of manners (and our possible readerly delight in it) is a serious mistake: morally, socially, emotionally. The novel's entire structure centers around this flaw—as *Anna Karenina* might be said to center around adultery—assuming this embarrassing act to be a significant, climactic wrongdoing, a betrayal even less forgivable than Anna Karenina's attachment to Vronsky. After all, there is no Karenin, no stifling marriage, no circumstances other than annoyance at Miss Bates's all-too-visible flaw and the temptation of wit at another's expense to excuse Emma's action. And there is an ease, a tastefulness, a well-mannered way in which the novel's dramatic impact and meaning rest on these implicit assumptions, on taking manners extremely seriously. Austen's novel leaves no doubt, without ever saying so explicitly, that manners, tasteful behavior are signs of socially and morally responsible behavior: they are there, to Austen, to express and enact the way in which classes take care of each other, or better, the way in which the upper class takes responsible care of the lower classes and, simultaneously, expresses its own superiority and thus justifies its dominance.

Knightley, the arbiter of good behavior, is the only one who gently, with perfect manners, reproaches Emma. His criticism of Emma goes to the core of Austen's belief about manners: "Were [Miss Bates] a woman of fortune, I would leave every harmless absurdity to take its chance; I would not quarrel with you for any liberties of manners. Were she your equal in situation—but, Emma, consider how far this is from being the case."[6] Knightley reproaches Emma because he needs to see her as his equal—after all he is all along planning to marry her, and manners demand that only equals can speak somewhat openly to each other. Knightley reminds Emma that her behavior toward Miss Bates in the presence of others was so wrong because "many . . . (certainly *some*) would be entirely guided by *your* treatment of her."[7] Emma's witty put-down of Miss Bates fails the standards of manners because it is ungenerous toward someone who is not her equal and because it might guide others into bad behavior as well. Good manners then are the ideal way in which the upper class treats the lower class, and in which it models an ideal way of life to the lower classes.

Yet, there is nothing simple about Austen's view of manners. In Emma's witty put-down of Miss Bates, Austen must be struggling with her own acerbic wit, her daring irony as a novelist. It is, after all, Austen's voice that speaks through Emma, and perhaps this scene implies some vexations, or at least terrible temptations, the author herself feels in her role as novelist. And she, as the writer, speaks the truth even as manners forbid it—never quite openly, more by exposing transgressions of taste. But the novel holds its course as a novel of manners via Knightley, the one flawless character; highest on the social ladder, he exhibits the most unerring sense of judgment and manners, navigating his life among less worthy and well-mannered people with perfect taste and respect, a paternal caring. He in other words exhibits manners in the perfect sense. And he instructs Emma, "[Miss Bates] is poor; she has sunk from the comforts she was born to, and if she lives to old age, must probably sink more. Her situation should secure your compassion."[8] While Austen thus acknowledges the tremendous discipline manners demand, even at times the denial of one's true thoughts, feelings, and wit for the sake of the cohesion of the social body, her take on manners is neither neurotic nor vexed. Knightley reprimands Emma and the novel agrees, even as Emma also speaks for Austen's ironic side. For Austen, manners are the foundations of her writing, her moral and social vision. The novel of manners is as perfect a form for Austen's vision, allowing and containing it, as Knightley is the perfect companion for Emma, loving and instructing her: it is a delightful and reasonable, a tasteful and well-mannered as well as a morally correct marriage of form and content.

Now let's move almost a hundred years ahead in history and across the Atlantic to revisit the issue the novel of manners in the hands of an American writer. Famously tasteful and mannered and moneyed herself, a member of the upper class, Edith Wharton excelled in the Austenesque tradition of ironic realism and the minute depiction of manners. Thus, in her writing we can best observe the full force of the American dilemma about manners. Consider Wharton's masterpiece *The House of Mirth* (1905) in light of Austen's *Emma*. Wharton, too, begins her novel with a tasteful and admirable heroine, who is unmarried for a little bit too long. And Wharton's novel, too, allows few stronger actions than breaches of manners. But Wharton's heroine, unable to find the right match, never gets married, slowly descends in class, and dies by suicide. Tastefully Wharton mitigates this melodramatic ending by never quite allowing her heroine to actually commit suicide, but by showing her not to care enough about life to count her sleeping drops quite correctly. In many other instances in the novel as well, Wharton refrains from less tasteful depictions of inner turmoil, dramatic action, and romantic disclosures.[9] But despite all her efforts, Wharton cannot keep her novel in the same tastefully integrated space of manners as Austen does. The novel constantly struggles with its form, its irony, its realism, because too many, actually almost all, of Wharton's characters are not well mannered but rather "carniverous beasts" and "lower organisms." Furthermore, Wharton's heroine Lily Bart doesn't have the assets Emma has; she has class without money and thus manners without the social position attached to them. This complication of the novel—so unlike Wharton's own life since apparently she did seem to have manners and money and social position[10] but did ultimately choose to live in France—is emblematic of the American dilemma about manners itself. America, Wharton implies, can only house noveaux riches, those tasteless creatures that somehow challenge the ideological and ideal connection between money, social position, manners, and morals on which Austen's novel rests. So the only person with true class in Wharton's novel has no money, and everyone who has money has no manners. The result is devastating: Lily has to die among people who violate manners, and thus herself, throughout the novel.

It is rather unclear, an unsolved mystery, why Lily has class, that is, manners and taste, in the novel. But she does. And she has one thing Wharton did not have (in this sense, Wharton's writing is propelled by a perceived lack in herself): personal beauty. Lily has more of that than any other character in the novel. Indeed, as Austen conflates manners, morals, money, and social position, Wharton conflates manners, taste, and beauty. Perhaps in light of the lack of history, manners have become aestheticized, and the effect is, literally, spectacular. It is all about seeing and exhibiting; but it is not about exhibiting socially responsible, tasteful behavior as in Austen but about displaying, more literally, a beautifully, stunningly tasteful exterior. In Wharton's novel, you wear your manners on your sleeve, so to speak; or even better, your choice of sleeve reveals your manners but so does the shape of the arm it covers. Indeed, manners are expressed most perfectly by the way in which the sleeve is chosen to tastefully reveal and cover the arm. Clothes, appearance, taste, the way one walks and talks, those are the things that determine manners. Thus as in Austen's novel, in Wharton's novel manners are about exhibition: but who exhibits to whom, and who follows whom, becomes a much more vexed issue when class and manners are disentangled. Lily, one might say, is both Emma and Miss Bates: unimaginable to Austen, she is the most mannered woman in the novel but also someone who has sunk from her station.[11]

Wharton's novel thus climaxes in a literal exhibition: the tableaux vivants scene. And the scene reveals that there is a significant difference between exhibiting socially responsible behavior and exhibiting beauty: the former might be instructing, but the latter excites the senses rather than inspires to emulate. Thus, when manners become aestheticized, they always imply their own lethal enemy: desire, one of the very things they are meant to keep at bay. Like the Box Hill picnic, the tableaux vivants scene is designed to bring people together; indeed, it is designed to add people to a social circle from which they have been barred so far. The Wellington Bryses put on this show to become part of the upper crust by seducing these upper-class people to come to their mansion for the spectacular event. In other words, the scene is about a slight reorganization of the social order and its borders. Even though everyone is a noveau riche in Wharton's book, or like Lily a noveau pauper, the New York society Wharton depicts is organized around minute class distinctions and hierarchies that seem to rely on taste. But there is constant flux; like the value of stocks, in which all her characters invest, people's social values rise and fall. Seen from afar, the social order Wharton depicts is random and malleable, but at every moment it appears real and almost fixed for all characters; it is, truly, fixated on Lily by the narrator's standards of manner, which none of the other characters can perceive or adhere to. Thus, most social movements within this order are determined by income and concomitant conspicuous spending. But some characters bring other values to the table: Lily's beauty and class to some degree make up for her lack of money, while Rosedale's Jewishness cannot be overcome by all his money.[12] He rises a bit more slowly than others, just as Lily falls a bit more slowly than others.

Within the novel, this scene is also the climax of Lily's fate and of Wharton's discussion of manners. As the Bryses design this particular kind of (European) entertainment for their entry into the next social echelon, Wharton designs it to exhibit her heroine. From the beginning, we hear that Lily is "in her element": "Under [the painter] Morpeth's guidance her vivid plastic sense, hitherto nurtured on no higher food than dress-making and upholstery, found eager expression in the disposal of draperies, the study of attitudes, the shifting of lights and shadows. . . . But keenest of all was the exhilaration of displaying her own beauty under a new aspect; of showing that her loveliness was no mere fixed quality, but an element shaping all emotions to fresh forms of grace."[13] The term "grace" is important since it hints at the moral element of manners that is still so important in Austen. And, indeed, Lily's superiority to other characters lies partially in her moral grace.

In Lily we—the readers but not the audience in the novel—see a residue of the world Austen depicts. Right before Lily exhibits herself as a tableau vivant, Gerty Farish explains both to us, the readers, and to Selden (the closest Lily comes to having an equal in the novel and the man Lily loves) that Lily had given three hundred dollars to a working girls' club and collected fifteen hundred from the Bryses and Rosedale for that purpose as well. Through Gerty we learn that Lily truly has inner and outer beauty; she is a perfectly mannered, graceful person: "She really can't bear to hurt people's feelings—it makes me so angry when I hear her called cold and conceited! The girls at the club don't call her that. Do you know she has been there with me twice? Yes, Lily! And you should have seen their eyes! One of them said it was as good as a day in the country just to look at her. And she sat there and laughed and talked with them—not a bit as if she were being *charitable*, you know, but as if she liked it as much as they did."[14] Lily exhibits here the kind of compassion and care for the lower classes that Austen associates with perfect manners. Much later in the novel, when Lily herself has sunk into poverty and despair, she meets one of the girls whose life her charity saved. Nettie tells Lily of the importance she has had in her life:

> I'd know you anywhere, I've thought of you such a lot. I guess my folks all know your name by heart. I was one of the girls at Miss Farish's club; you helped me to get to the country that time I had lung trouble. . . . Sometimes when I felt real mean and got to wondering why things were so queerly fixed in the world, I used to remember that *you* were having a lovely time, anyhow, and that seemed to show there was a kind of justice somewhere. . . . I used to watch for your name in the papers, and we'd talk over what you were doing and read descriptions of the dresses you wore. . . . Wouldn't it be too lovely for anything if [my baby]

> could grow up to be just like you? Of course I know she never *could*, but mothers are always dreaming the craziest things for their children.[15]

In this subplot, Wharton clearly alludes to Austen's sense of manners. Lily exhibits the kind of compassion for the lower classes that Knightley teaches Emma in the Box Hill episode. And Wharton shows the response to such responsible manners: Nettie survives, builds a life, and accepts a social order that, in all other regards, must appear unjust and queer. Indeed, seeing Lily contains and stifles a potential revolutionary insight (of thinking why things were so queerly fixed) and makes Nettie accept an undemocratic, un-American world as a form of justice. She furthermore compensates her own discontent by dreaming of an impossible social rise (the American Dream); she acknowledges that dreaming of her baby becoming like Lily is the "craziest thing." In Austen's and Wharton's terms, Lily has exhibited perfect manners and perfect beauty,[16] but Wharton simultaneously shows that such performative visual American manners lead to a celebrity culture posing as justice rather than to a just society.[17]

From Gerty's account of Lily's charitable actions, we move to the actual tableaux vivants scene: an exhibition of the rich for the rich. The entire spectacle speaks of a deep postcolonial neurosis, each American woman trying with every art and artifice possible to fit herself into the picture of a European master: Titian, Veronese, Kauffman, Vandyck, Watteau. "A brilliant Miss Smedden from Brooklyn," writes Wharton with great irony, "showed to perfection the sumptuous curves of Titian's *Daughter*" while "no one . . . could have made a more typical Goya than Carry Fisher." It is not an accident that only Lily selects an eighteenth-century British painter (of manners): Reynolds. Impersonating Reynolds's "Mrs. Lloyd," Lily is seen in her most tasteful and her most vulnerable position: "She had [selected] a type so like her own that she could embody the person presented without ceasing to be herself."[18] Everyone in the party recognizes the superiority of Lily's choice and beauty. The party is stunned by her performance, but no one is up to Lily's standards to respond. Instead the scene elicits unmannered desire that nearly leads to Lily's rape. While Emma fell below her standard in the Box Hill episode, where she should have exemplified flawless manners, Lily exceeds the standards of her exhibition to such a degree that everyone else feels violent want (both desire and lack). A "Miranda amongst Calibans,"[19] Lily exposes herself to both vulgar remarks and appreciation among her friends. But her performance of perfect manners remains unrewarded. Whereas Austen perceives manners as socially responsible behavior that can be fruitfully imitated by the lower classes, the perfect beauty and taste of Lily's performance is unimitable precisely because it is grounded in beauty and taste. Wharton thus brings to light the American dilemma in regard to taste and manners and shows that the sense of lack of taste paired with the power of money and sheer force implies the threat of rape—metaphorical or literal. The vulgar remarks made about Lily's outline are followed by Gus Trenor's attempt to rape her.

In a world where there is no admiration without envy and no reverence without desire to possess, true manners (a combination of taste, grace, and personal beauty) will always be demeaned and destroyed. Hence Lily's slow descent and final suicide. With Lily's death, Wharton apparently abandons the hope for manners in America, bemoans their impossibility, and yet she spends her entire energy of the novel exhibiting them and giving her hopeless American compatriots one more chance to see them, appreciate them, desire them without really believing that they could ever acquire them. Unwilling to marry someone below her standards, Lily dies of a lack of funds and therefore cannot sustain her beauty and grace. In that sense, Wharton directly reflects on Austen's world. Without a Knightley, Lily is lost, vulnerable to the preying eyes of men, the envy of women, and incapable of autonomy. If we read Lily as an embodied ideal of perfect manners (morals, beauty, class), then we can read Wharton's novel as an American statement on manners. The demise of her heroine suggests that manners as Wharton perceives them cannot exist without money, yet money is in the way of such manners. Furthermore true manners are virginal like Lily, unable to link themselves with others, and therefore incapable of building and cohering a social body. They are so unique in America that they are doomed to either stain themselves through association with those who have the money to sustain and afford them, or doomed to die because they are singular and thus ultimately not social and reproducible. In a true paradox, Wharton shows that American manners are a beautiful, tragic impossibility. Her heroine dies, and the author moves to France.

Jumping yet another hundred years ahead, from the beginning of the twentieth to the advent of the twenty-first century, the issue of American manners seems nowhere closer to a resolution; yet, one might wonder, how long can one live with a neurosis of this magnitude and not descend into complete madness? How have Americans dealt with their fate, their being apparently indelibly branded as unmannered, or better, lacking in manners? One might argue that America has embraced the brand, even more has used brand as the key to unlock this neurosis and to fuel an economy that more and more heavily relies on consumption. Tama Janowitz's *A Certain Age* (1999), a remaking of *The House of Mirth,* self-consciously reflects on both earlier novelists of manners[20] and offers us a contemporary "novel of manners [that] would distinguish any decade," according to *Elle.*[21] While Austen put together morals, manners, and class, and Wharton disentangled beauty, grace, and manners from money and desire, Janowitz shows that beauty and money and desire go together through consumption, but that grace has no place in such a mannered world of fashion.

In her story, her Lily/Emma figure Florence is yet another heroine unmarried for just a little bit too long. Like Lily, she is beautiful and fashionable, and, using her assets, she is trying to make it on the New York marriage market, when her own funds are running out. Like Lily she is an orphan whose inheritance is slowly dwindling and who still participates in the life of the upper crust of Manhattan, but only precariously so. Like Lily, Florence becomes a drug addict and descends slowly but surely into poverty and a recognition of her own uselessness. And Janowitz plays out Lily's story in the only logical extension of the upper class and its turn-of-the-century conspicuous consumption: the high end of consumer capitalism, the world of designer brands such as Chanel, Gucci, and Henri Bendel. In those brands and the endless cycle of consumer desire, envy, and more desire, the American neurosis about manners has found its perfect and diseased and somewhat democratized manifestation—the most inexhaustible engine of its capitalist machinery. Janowitz writes, "New York—especially for women but for men as well—was in the convulsive, terminal stages of a lengthy disease, the disease of envy, whose side effects were despair and self-hatred.[22]

Looking back, it is one of those well-mannered, tasteful flaws of Wharton's novel that we never see Lily shopping. Of course, we should have seen her that way since we do hear about Lily's hazardous spending habits as well as her need and desire to be fashionable (more fashionable than others, even though Wharton does not dwell on that either). It is one omission by Wharton that upholds our sense of Lily's uniqueness, her true specialness. In a world of consumption, nothing, by definition, is unique, since it is branded and can be bought; the brand limits the amount of people who can buy, but theoretically anyone can.[23] Florence, like Lily, is beautiful, but she—like a designer gown—is not special; she constantly tries to compete with other women in a seemingly impossible race of similarity and difference, fashion: "She had spent her whole adult life in New York preparing for this. The perfect clothes, the expensive grooming, the sleek pelt of hair, the job in the auction house. There were hundreds, perhaps thousands, of women like herself. . . . They had manners. . . . All at once she was nervous. There were million others more qualified than she."[24] Manners are part of the designer outfit, a brand one exhibits like the *LV* of Louis Vuitton.

And, in a form of postmodern nostalgia, Florence sees the inadequacy of such designer clothing: "Still, no matter what she wore, no matter how expensive or nice, she always had the feeling that the dress or suit was a mere watered-down imitation of what elegance was supposed to be. A hundred years ago money could really buy clothing; things made back then had hand-rolled hems weighted with lead, delicately embroidered buttonholes, better-quality materials. Even the most expensive couture gown nowadays didn't have beadwork of real pearls. And then, too, she always had the feeling that whatever she wore was not quite up to date."[25] Janowitz shows us a world of frantic performance and its never-ending feelings of self-hatred and inadequacy; one is always already an imitation of true elegance as it may have once existed: mass production and its discontents.

Furthermore, Janowitz's world is impoverished by the lack of central locations of exhibition; instead each person's life becomes a stage, many of them without any audience or with a minute audience, smaller even than those at the Box Hill picnic or the spectacle at the Wellington Bryses': a sales clerk, a gallery opening, an encounter on the street—fragments of encounters that do not add up. In Lisa's apartment "there was a quality of emptiness, as if no one really lived here. It was a place constructed for display; without anybody there to view it, apart from her, it was like a theater set without a play."[26] Lacking centrality and a true arbiter of taste, Janowitz's world of manners is an alienated, fragmented world of performances that never translate into reality or beauty. "Inside her were bitter seeds. She was not beautiful on the inside,"[27] writes Janowitz about her heroine, leaving no doubt that we are not dealing with a Lily Bart. Florence's world is apparently a world full of manners—in the guise of designer brands—and no grace. Her protagonist knows that she has no inner values, no morals, no culture, just façade. She lives in a "society without culture or values"[28] and has none herself. "So she had no values. Who here did? . . . So she had no morals. Who did?"[29]

Unlike Wharton, Janowitz does not look to her heroine or her influence on the lower classes for such values. Perhaps here, too, Janowitz corrects Wharton's somewhat skewed vision. Looked at through the eyes of her heroine, the lower classes lack manners without any compensating graces: "The train rattled on uneven tracks, everyone was tossed from side to side, someone wearing one of those hateful backpacks knocked her in the side with it. Someone stank of McDonald's French fries, an immediately identifiable odor of tallow and grease. Someone was slurping a drink. Another was clipping his fingernails; yet another was combing her hair. A whole carful of a species scarcely less evolved, just as ill-mannered, as chimpanzees. The eyes of the commuters were glazed, faces sullen. She shut her eyes in disgust."[30] If Wharton uses naturalism to express her contempt for the brutish nouveaux riches, Janowitz uses her naturalist venom for Florence's view of the everyday person—Americans, in the most common sense. But while we might reject Florence's vision as lacking grace—it is a far cry from Lily's kindness to the working girls—the novel nowhere contests this image of meaningless, unappealing commonness of American life. Janowitz's novel seems to suggest that while there is no grace inside Florence's world, there is no grace outside of the upper crust either. At least the upper crust has style, something to protect it from the true Americanness of everyday working life, public transportation, and fast food.

Showing that an American novel of manners cannot exist without British people, Janowitz explicitly tackles the postcolonial neurosis of American manners, the need to look back to the original (as Lily impersonates Mrs. Lloyd): "These were examples of the simpering idiots who were taking over New York. More than two hundred years ago there had been a Revolution; the Americans threw the Brits out. Now they were welcomed back, ushered back, swooned over—the descendents of the same fops who sneered and looked down on the colonists."[31] Americans, according to Janowitz, have never overcome the "foppery" of British society, have never truly revolutionized themselves. Over and over, Florence, the American heroine, feels provincial in knowledge and experience: "It was awful to have worked so hard to acquire a veneer of New York sophistication but, due to circumstance, be basically provincial underneath. Her friends—her acquaintances—were widely traveled; Paris, London, Prague, all these places were nothing to them."[32] New York sophistication, in other words, does not exist without the old-world metropoles from which it merely borrows.

In what appears to be a savage critique of New York society and American manners, Janowitz seems to disentangle the ideological constructions of both Austen's and Wharton's novels. Manners seem to have become nothing more than designer labels. In some ways, one might surmise then that the novel finally solves the American neurosis about manners by trivializing manners to such a degree that they are void of all ethical dimension, meaningless affectations—a postmodern performance, a form of shallow, parodic insanity. Yet, they do seem to be more desirable than sitting in the subway and wearing a mediocre backpack, a sign of unmannered death Janowitz seems to look at with the same disgust as her shallow heroine.

But in one central aspect, the author's and the heroine's views diverge, and Janowitz surprisingly introduces grace into her novel. Even as the novel seemingly deconstructs manners à la Austen and Wharton, it ultimately reinstates the very connection between socially responsible behavior and class that we saw in both earlier novels. Florence is empty, but another character in the novel isn't. Grace is not beautiful in the heroine's eye, but it is the prerogative of the upper class in Janowitz's novel nonetheless. Flirting with, but ultimately rejecting a postmodern parodic view of manners, Janowitz offers us one ideal character, a Knightley of kinds, who loves the heroine but cannot make her good. Darryl Lever, a "brilliant" and "Harvard-educated" Russian immigrant lawyer, is, on second reading, truly the central character of the novel—a Knightley of kinds who is polite, tasteful, and gracious to the point of self-sacrifice. While he is in love with Florence, she cannot see him as others do: as gorgeous, brilliant, witty, and kind. Darryl is messy and unfashionable, quite unlike the glamourous, designer-attired Raphaelo, whom Florence desires. Florence, fooled by the designer idiom of her world, cannot see Darryl for who he is. When Darryl stops at his parents' house, an old mansion on Long Island, Florence is unable to guess the connection: "The house was so splendid Florence thought for a minute it was some old hotel or country club—what was Darryl doing here?"[33] While Florence cannot recognize "a good thing," the novel ultimately upholds Darryl as a standard of true manners: of taste and grace. He is the escaped character of a nineteenth-century novel: loving classical music, being polite and cultured, and sacrificing his Wall Street career for working with the homeless in New York. The nineteenth-century reference is even more obvious since Darryl, like so many nineteenth-century fictional characters, contracts consumption through his work with the homeless. Like Lily, he needs to die. In the end, frustrated by Florence's lack of love and ethics, he marries the only other rich eligible girl in the novel, who nurses him in his terrible and fatal illness.

Ultimately then Janowitz reconnects social grace and upper-class status and disentangles them from style and fashion to come full circle—back to Austen, back to the metaphorical Brits, back to the Old World, back to the neurosis. Despite her name, Florence is nothing more than an aspiring and always lacking American girl. Florence's beauty and style are not the same as true class and manners; indeed, her middle-class background makes her unable to recognize class when she sees it. Her obsession with fashion as a form of manners blocks her from seeing the real thing—the self-sacrificing high-class Russian—and leaves her in an unreal, empty world of signs.

Surprisingly, thus, none of the novels can separate manners from social grace, and neither Janowitz nor Wharton believes that Americans can have true manners. While Austen can connect them wholeheartedly, both Wharton and Janowitz struggle. The American aestheticization and final commodification of manners is apparent in both of their novels. But manners, the two novels insist, cannot maintain themselves as such. Both novels flee back—in light of all contrary evidence—to a view of manners none of their realistic characters upholds: Lever is as unconvincing and unviable in that regard as Lily. Both exceptional characters are depicted against a world in which manners seemingly exist only as fashions and signs. Yet, both novelists reconnect true manners to social grace and to a world that is not, ultimately, American: an undemocratic world of an upper class taking care of the lower class, a static nineteenth-century worldview in which, ideologically, class privilege is fortified and justified by conflating taste and grace. Manners then, amazingly, have remained conceptually unchanged. These novels suggest that no brand can change the fact that manners continue to be an utter, central paradox for Americans—an impossibility, a perpetual want that defines America's neurosis and its frenzied consumer economy.

Notes

1. Jane Austen, *Emma* (New York: Signet, 1980), p. 291.
2. Ibid., p. 293.
3. Ibid.
4. Ibid., p. 294.
5. Ibid.
6. Ibid., p. 298.
7. Ibid.
8. Ibid.
9. For a detailed discussion of Wharton's dialogue with sentimental fiction and the language of emotion and passion see my discussion of *The House of Mirth* in *Edith Wharton's Dialogue with Realism and Sentimental Fiction* (Gainesville: University Press of Florida, 2000), pp. 96–125.
10. The saying "keeping up with the Joneses" relates to Edith Wharton's family: she was born Edith Newbold Jones.
11. Austen does partially deal with this issue in the character of Jane Fairfax—arguably the Lily Bart of the novel and, significantly, Miss Bates's niece. Ultimately the novel cannot resolve this contradiction and makes narrative choices to avoid it as a central theme. It loves Emma in the same indulgent way Knightley does, who will not consider Jane Fairfax as a possible marriage partner.
12. For a detailed reading of the anti-Semitism of Wharton's novel see my article " 'The Impossible Rosedale': 'Race' and the Reading of Edith Wharton's *The House of Mirth*," *Studies in American Jewish Literature* 13 (1994): 14–20.
13. Edith Wharton, *The House of Mirth* (New York: Signet, 1980), p. 138.
14. Ibid., p. 140.
15. Ibid., pp. 324–326, 328.
16. It is interesting to note that the issue of perfection comes up in the Box Hill scene as well. Mr. Weston offers the conundrum of two letters expressing perfection: *M* and *A*, Emma. This highly ironic moment hints at the ideal of manners Austen embraces and Emma, at this moment, falls short of.

17. This result is due to Wharton's sharp perception rather than an inherent or conscious democratic impulse.

18. Wharton, *The House of Mirth*, p. 141.

19. Ibid., p. 142.

20. Tama Janowitz, *A Certain Age* (London: Bloomsbury, 1999). For example, on page 129 Janowitz's heroine thinks about both Wharton's and Austen's heroines.

21. Ibid., back cover.

22. Ibid., p. 113.

23. Janowitz does not deal with designer outlets yet, a further deconstruction and democratization of designer names; she does, however, mention repeatedly that her heroine buys the designer items on sale.

24. Janowitz, *A Certain Age*, pp. 104–105.

25. Ibid., p. 240.

26. Ibid., p. 309.

27. Ibid., p. 161.

28. Ibid., p. 298.

29. Ibid., p. 286.

30. Ibid., p. 302.

31. Ibid., p. 285.

32. Ibid., p. 151.

33. Ibid., p. 62.

CHAPTER THIRTEEN

"Make Yourself Useful!"

SHANNON WINNUBST

"Make yourself useful!"

A stinging command. One that rings and reverberates all across whitened, westernized, colonized lands. Lodged deeply in our cultural psyches, it rings and rings and rings, leaving us nothing but guilt in its wake.

The grasp of utility is deep, deeper than the late-nineteenth-century European systems of ethics could begin to convey. John Stuart Mill merely systematized what had already been stirring in cultural practices of northern and western Europe across the prior three centuries. And Max Weber then cast its net yet further, easily and appropriately, sealing the twin triumphs of capitalism and Protestantism, and further hiding the true victor, utility. By giving vague cultural sensibilities proper names—"Utilitarianism" and the "Protestant Work Ethic"—the power of categories settled utility yet deeper into our cultural fabrics. And, in the ultimate act of a totalizing grasp, it even delimited itself, setting the (alleged) boundary of its own reach: aesthetics lay beyond it.

Or so utility said. And so we, dutifully at the beginning of the twentieth century, championed the radically solitary domain of aesthetics as the last frontier safe from the vagaries of the market. Whether we are still lured by the "art for art's sake" mantra or we have seen through the political nihilism that results all too easily from it, the vague sense that aesthetics is the singular realm beyond the grasp of utility persists. Grappling with the seeming impossibility of thinking or living without utility, we most easily turn to aesthetics. "What is not useful?" After much searching, we comfort ourselves with the discovery of "style, aesthetics, art." This is, after all, surely what Nietzsche had in mind when he beckoned us to turn away from the grave seriousness of morality towards art, "where the lie is sanctified."[1] Is not the sanctifying of the lie, the undermining of the grand epistemologies of truth, not also an evading of utility, modernity's most forceful form of truth?

It is a tempting solution, with radical possibilities. But perhaps also too obvious and simple. As Michel Foucault's method, if not his explicit response, demonstrates, this valorizing of the aesthetic as the realm exempted from the powerful barometer of utility may itself be an enactment of utility's power. Indeed, as Georges Bataille argues over and over, utility may not be so easily eluded.

Foucault repeatedly demonstrates the subtle mechanisms of boundary construction and controlled transgression performed in the emergence of categories. In volume one of *The History of Sexuality*, for example, he shows over and over how a normalizing category emerges through the careful construction of what lies beyond it. As an exemplar perhaps, heterosexuality emerges as a category of identity only against the emergence of homosexuality, the category of (apparent) transgression that finally serves to reinscribe the heterosexual as the norm. Bataille outlines similar functions in volume 2 of *The Accursed Share*, where he shows how behaviors are eroticized via prohibitions, demonstrating again how the transgression of set boundaries reenforces the category transgressed. For Bataille (following Levi-Strauss), the exemplar is incest, where the prohibition against intergenerational sexual contact within biological families actually serves to eroticize familial ties, ensuring the continued flow of erotic energy in this otherwise closed container. And finally, in more recent texts, Judith Butler helps to open the field of queer theory by using these strategies to show how the grasp of the sex/gender distinction in feminist theory effectively controls the kinds of transgressions against the normative heterosexual matrix, limiting it to homosexuality rather than trans- or bi- or multisexualities. In all of these texts, we learn to read categories as performative entities that, in delimiting their own boundaries, ensure that the transgression of the category will only further solidify the category.

It is an old lesson by now. And, here, it presents us with the possibility that our very conception of the aesthetic as something beyond or outside of the useful is itself an effect that further blinds us to the deep grasps of utility.

I want to explore how this deep grasp of utility—the valuing of that which is useful as the ultimate criterion for all actions, thoughts and even desires—reaches inside all of us in these whitened, westernized lands in ways that exceed our usual demarcations of utility's realms. I want to explore how utility operates within us not as a rational response to moral questions, nor as an ethical response to religious duty, nor even as a civilized response to economic imperatives—but as a much deeper sensibility about aesthetic style. A much deeper sensibility about the world and its rhythms and our places in it. A sensibility that is written on and in and through our bodies, shaping us to fulfill its needs without even the question of our consent. An imperative aesthetic style. An unwritten code. An etiquette.

⁂

"Make yourself useful, *boy.*"

Listen to the southern twang, the mean trace of slavery's history lingering in that last word, that damning last word which is always implied if not spoken in the command itself: "boyyy." It pulls the command right out of the sky of abstractions and slams it squarely on the ground. This ain't about no lofty ideals—this is about bodies. Bodies of control and bodies to be controlled. Bodies of discipline and bodies in need of discipline. Bodies of power and bodies that obey. Bodies and histories. That simple, far from innocent "boyyy" cuts the demand straight into its fundamental register—the old but hauntingly familiar voice of the patronizing white overseer that never seems to die. Whether spoken sternly by a parent to a child, frankly by a boss to an employee, reprimandingly by a teacher to a student, or jokingly by a friend to a companion, it is the same voice speaking and the "boyyy" is at the end of every sentence. This command of utility, whenever and however spoken, is about bodies—black, brown, white, yellow; queer, female, trans, disabled, poor; Jewish, Catholic, Muslim, Hindu. It is about bodies and the ways that utility cuts the social mapping of power directly into them.

If etiquette is the proper comportment of the body, these social mappings of power should be readily legible in the codes of its practices.

Whether one knows which fork to use, for example, has always been one of the most simple locators of social class. But if we place utility in this realm of etiquette, we may begin to see how utility and etiquette work together to draw the maps of some of our most salient categories of identity and difference. Reading utility as a primary force in shaping proper comportment, we begin to see how this imperative shapes all bodies—racializing, sexualizing, gendering, classing, even spiritualizing and nationalizing according to how bodies fall on either one or the other side of the command, "Make yourself useful, boyyy."

The stories with bodies of color are all too easy to tell, belying the ways that racism lurks literally just beneath the skin in the United States. Brown bodies are lazy, black bodies even lazier. White folks marvel at the hard work of Mexican day laborers as they toil away in their yards and bathrooms and garbage cans: "That Mexican sure does work hard, don't he?" The surprise belies the expectation. Black bodies are seen only in crime reports, drug zones, and welfare lines. Their usefulness all dried up post-Emancipation, they are no longer even expected to work. And then the yellow bodies, who have mistakenly taken the command of utility to the other extreme—working much too hard, far too useful, displaying their zeal for success in extraordinary bad taste. One must know how to appear with just the right amount of usefulness to gain entrance to those cherished boardrooms. To work too hard is not in good taste and, accordingly, not highly valued, leaving the physical laborer with one of utility's most perverse twists: it takes three jobs of hard, physical labor just to pay the bills. It is not by accident that the bodies in those boardrooms all look alike, behave properly, and display just the right amount of usefulness to ensure their lives of luxury.

Sexualized bodies fare only slightly more subtly than racialized ones: the queering of that "boyyy" as the effeminate one who cannot protect himself has always echoed through its racialized tenor. (We hear this most clearly in the contemporary voice of that white overseer, the white police officer poised on the brink of violently sodomizing his catch.) The perversion of queer bodies lies in their categorical refusal of the act that renders sexuality meaningful—the act that renders it useful. An affront to all "natural" sensibilities, a sexuality that categorically precludes reproduction can be nothing but a breach of etiquette. The reverberations surface with humorously literal aberrations of taste:

queens with cartoonish femininity on parade; gay men with "too much" taste and a perfectionism that paralyzes; lesbians with bad haircuts and no taste at all. Again, the simple balance between too much and not enough is missed, but here it is biologically impossible: these sexual bodies cannot be useful. Granted, the categories are shifting as the lesbian baby boom takes cultural root. But the lesbians in flannel shirts and combat boots have only been eclipsed by lipstick chic as the much promised polymorphous perversity has finally arrived: transsexual bodies will truly never be of any use at all.

Utility's gendering of bodies may seem old hat and obvious by now. Surely, we know that masculine bodies are the ones that work hard and produce useful commodities for the marketplaces—whether economic, intellectual, political, spiritual or moral. Masculine bodies produce things. Conversely, feminine bodies are put on their pedestals because they were never even made for working. As Bataille voices that which should perhaps remain unspoken (if the phallus is to remain veiled): "The prostitute [as] the perfection of femininity, is the only being who logically should be idle."[2] Feminine bodies perform their femininity perfectly when they behave as beautiful bodies untainted by even a trace of material servitude. In fact, it is through this purity from utility that female bodies become the natural arbiters of good taste and the quintessential consumers, locking the role of shopper as the subject position that bridges the 1950s ideal housewife to the sixteen-year-old female target of all contemporary marketing. How do women fit into the closed economy of utility? We shop 'til we drop. And yet are women not simultaneously the exemplary commodities exchanged? And is not the exchange value determined precisely by their disavowal of such roles? Following Irigaray here, we see that feminine bodies perform the merging of aesthetics and utility perfectly: it is in their beauty that feminine bodies are deemed valuable. It is in their complete disavowal of all crass utility that feminine bodies are judged useful to the (specular) economy.

Finally, we may see this reign of utility at work most brutally in the realm of spiritual lives—or what we should properly call religion. Only those religious practices that issue into some moral statement about the world, some clear evaluation of behaviors, ideas, choices, or lifestyles, are worthy of the very name "religion." All others, whether meditative practices or pagan aesthetics, whether ritualized prayer or goddess festivals, only defame the concept of religion when they claim it for themselves. As the fount of all values, proper religion must exercise the power of a transcendent to master the world—to master the world and nature and all unruly desires. It is the place in which we learn the fundamental practices of discipline, spelled out before us in clear and distinct moral principles.

These are, of course, cartoons. Cartoons intended to laugh at the arrogant voice that might actually speak them. But in that sad laughter we hear ugly truths. We hear the ways that racism, heterosexism, sexism, and nationalism write themselves upon our bodies through the register of utility. We hear the many forms that utility assumes: economic, reproductive, biological, moral—even aesthetic. Fundamentally, these forms write themselves on our bodies through demanding that we become just exactly the right sorts of tools—the sort of (white) tool that labors without showing it, exploits the work of (black, brown, female) others while disavowing their abilities to work, supplies just the right amount of products (children), and declares itself pure and dedicated to clear, distinct principles of mastery and control (over nature, over others, over the world). It is the Enlightenment utopia. And it writes itself on our bodies in the very ways we conduct ourselves from moment to moment, day to day, week to week. It writes itself upon our bodies in the kinds of tools that we become.

⁂

In suggesting that the command of utility is written on our bodies, I am suggesting that it infects our senses of style, taste, and etiquette. Perhaps the fundamental corporeal register in which we can witness this ruling of etiquette is temporality: timing is everything.

A basic lesson of childhood is about timing. We learn rather quickly not only which parent to ask for what, but more importantly when to ask for it. Whether we get two, five, ten, or twenty dollars for the night's activities, whether we get to spend the night at Joni's or Joey's house, whether we get to go to the movies or the skating rink all hinge entirely on the fragile balance of timing. We learn to read the rhythms of the adult world with an unspoken precision. And this precision writes itself on our bodies with greater and greater force as we slowly enter that world of adult bodies.

Temporality frames the space of etiquette. Whether it is gauging the window of fashionable tardiness or delivering the joke at its singular moment of possibility, one's style is constituted fundamentally through one's relation to proper timing. The range of proper timing varies from place to place and community to community: urban time is certainly not what suburban time is, not to mention rural or small-town time; single time varies from coupled time; middle-class time differs from working-class and again from upper-class time; children's time seems infinitely longer than adult time; and, of course, the infamous "CPT" ("Colored Person's Time") or even "QST" ("Queer Standard Time") differ considerably from the punctuality of good old-fashioned white Protestant time. Nothing conscious, nothing intentional, and yet speaking more loudly than any of our professed values or aesthetics—temporality gives us away. It tells where we came from and where we are placed in this world. It tells what kinds of tools we are.

One way to connect the (seemingly) totalizing realm of utility with the systems of domination that we all embody is thus to investigate its temporality. As an activity that is determined by the ends that it obtains, utility is driven by a temporality of anticipation. It directs consciousness always toward the future, assuming an intentionality that can both be mastered and master conditions necessary to achieve the desired end, usefulness. The endpoint of one's activities is expected, anticipated, and awaited as the final judgment of all moments leading toward it. This is teleology at its strictest definition, where the telos must manifest itself in clear and distinct ways—in useful ways. Implying that these ends can be obtained, this temporality of anticipation also assumes that it will recognize its final achievement. It is satisfaction that is deeply anticipated, and this satisfaction is expected to be recognized with certainty. The temporality of utility embeds us in a deep anticipation of satisfying certainty.

But the effects of this temporality of anticipation on the present often seem to run at odds with this promised endpoint. Utility's temporality, in its demanding march toward its singular goals, performs some of the hallmarks of colonialism's divide and conquer strategies. Each and every moment in a consciousness driven by utility is sequestered off into its individual role in the grand movement toward achievement. Utility divides our experience into separable moments that fall neatly into sequential lines, all leading toward the final point of use. The shirt is ironed so that the body will appear orderly, so that the voice will be heard authoritatively, so that the argument will persuade, so that the position will be obtained, so that the money will be earned, so that the economy will flourish, so that the citizens will buy more shirts to be ironed. Unbothered by any circularity that appears through a general perspective, utility operates comfortably in this closed economy, dividing each moment discretely from the next, reducing the meaning of the present qua present to a nonsensical question.

The present is judged, clearly and distinctly, by the role that it plays in the achievement of useful ends. The present is judged by the future, framed by the future anterior—the perspective of the "will have been"—that already reads each moment as if the future moment of utility has already been achieved. Beautifully performing Western metaphysics and its repeated reduction of the present to a fleeting juncture between past and future that ontologically resists conception, utility thereby totalizes its grasp, seeping into each discrete, sequential moment through the implicit judgment of that moment's usefulness—a judgment that the singular moment itself can never adequately answer. Utility claims to ground itself and provide its own certainty, rendering each singular moment vulnerable to a judgment whose final criterion operates on general principles that necessarily supersede the singular moment: the value of each singular moment requires a judgment that the singular moment can never provide.

Judgment and mastery thus structure utility's temporality of anticipation. And the experience of consciousness embedded in this temporal structure is appropriately demarcated. Having itself always already assumed the form of a tool, consciousness structured by utility demands that experience should answer it in the form of a tool. The world should present itself to us in useful ways and when it fails to do so, it is the human mandate to shape it accordingly. An exemplary performance of a phallocentric specular economy, it issues into the forms of racism, sexism, classism, heterosexism, and nationalism that were parodied above but sadly saturate our cultural practices: the temporality of anticipation provides one of the more subtle tools of judgment and mastery at work in each of these systems of domination.

But what if we refuse to reduce ourselves to tools?

Wouldn't this be, simply, in bad taste?

⁂

> If the world insists on blowing up, we may be the only ones to grant it the right to do so, while giving ourselves the right to have spoken in vain.
>
> —Georges Bataille, *The Accursed Share*

Living now, at the dawn of the twenty-first century as it is called in whitened, westernized lands, a dawn that is promising a century still more bloody than the last and bloodiest yet, such a line as Bataille's sounds absurd at best, perverse at minimum. To resign ourselves to the world blowing itself up seems the very worse kind of aestheticizing of violence that modernism could have bred. But it is not exactly resignation that Bataille is voicing. To be resigned requires that one was involved, invested. And to give oneself the right to speak in vain certainly does not imply involvement—but rather the right, the space, not to be involved. Never to have been invested. Not to be running on the same rails of time and efficiency and meaning that the world proclaims. Not to be, as an enactment of the most concise rejection that late capitalism (suspiciously) offers us, useful.

To do these things is, as our glimpses and cartoons show us here, far from simple. It cannot be, for example, merely the act of celebrating laziness or deliberately choosing activities that result in sheer absurdity, such as debauchery or acts of self-destruction. To do these things is to be shunned by this society in the simplest and most straightforward of manners: it is to reenforce the normalizing power of the very society one hopes to escape. It is not to create a space beyond that society—or beyond utility.

The call of Bataille, and of Foucault and Nietzsche and Butler and Irigaray and so many others of their ilk, is more subtle. As I hinted above, Foucault turned in his later texts to a celebration of style, to the art of caring for the self, as a turn away from the normalizing ethics of rationalist modernity. Nietzsche also turned in his later works toward a sense of the aesthetic and style that would not collapse into the conceptualized realm of good taste I have sketched here. While I hope to have intimated that a turn to aesthetics cannot be a naïve claim to step beyond the grasp of utility, the attempt to live one's life with the sort of style suggested by texts such as Nietzsche's and Foucault's may nonetheless disclose the frayed limits of utility's totalizing grasp.

Taste, as I hope to have already implied, is one of the longest reaching tentacles of whitened, westernized ethical and moral precepts. It is all that I have cartooned above about the ways that utility, the hallmark of these precepts, writes itself into our racist, sexist, heterosexist, classist, and nationalist ethics—and, more frighteningly, into our bodies. To have good taste is to mirror the dominant and dominating world back to itself. It is to behave properly, which means ultimately to make oneself useful in exactly the sort of veiled manner that allows power to emerge in this phallocentric, white supremacist world. It is to make oneself just the right sort of tool that can, in turn, manipulate all other tools to its own ends. It is to have just the right timing—not to mention the right race, sex, sexuality, class, nationality, and religion. To have good taste is a primary way to mark one's location in this culture. It is a mark of how well we have learned to be properly useful and, thereby, to perpetuate systems of domination.

In its Nietzschean vein, style becomes the attempt to create one's life—to create one's values, relations, spaces, and temporalities—in ways that are not reducible to these ethical or rational precepts. This is not, again, merely to negate rationality or morality in a silly pantomiming of the irrational and immoral as more worthwhile. It is not to engage in this sort of reverse valorization of opposites, nor in the anticipated transgression of categories that only reinstates the original category's power. Rather, it is to move beyond this logic of negation. It is to step away from it, not against it—to step aside, with light feet. It is to untangle and surpass utility's apparent totality, along with its shaping of our bodies, our taste, our very temporality.

As we have already encountered, the temporality of utility operates within the demonstrable. The imperative of recognizable and certain satisfaction structures utility as its defining moment. Out of this temporality, social power emerges as utility's strongest tool to shape human experience to its own needs and demands. Because it can be recognized, because utility lodges us in a closed economy with set parameters that enable us to know when it has been achieved, utility presents the social map of power with a clear and distinct barometer. Is this body useful? We can answer that question, definitively and with damning—racist, sexist, classist, heterosexist, and nationalist—consequences. Utility thus grounds our social configurations of power.

But it can only do so in its own closed economy. Utility cannot see outside of itself. As we have witnessed here in its insidious control of aesthetics—indeed, of our very corporeal habits and rhythms of etiquette—utility totalizes social relations precisely through foreclosing the possibility of any space or thing beyond it. Socially enmeshed in it, we cannot even conceive of thinking outside of it: the simple question of the utility (professionally, politically, culturally, even aesthetically) of this very chapter surfaces with unremarkable ease. But, at the very same time, utility is not as totalizing as it might wish to appear. It is not the exemplary performance of Hegelian dialectics that it fools us into thinking it is in our cultural practices and habits. Utility falls short. The closure of its boundaries presents itself too explicitly. The very neatness of its system suggests that it has suspended any account of its own condition of possibility—namely, its own demarcation.

Utility functions as a totalizing logic only within the closed boundaries of its own criteria. That is, only insofar as we fail to question why we might want to buy more shirts—or enter the cherished boardroom or produce our 2.5 children or cite an ethical imperative or even look like the Aryan fantasy—does utility entangle us entirely in its web. But, while it may be exceedingly difficult, particularly given the seductive social power that it would cost us, it is not impossible to ask such questions. It is not impossible to locate this blindspot in utility's logic.

Reading utility as a restricted kind of teleology, we begin to see that utility actually cannot account for its own telos. As in the shirt-ironing example, circularity eventually emerges. The immediate teloi of utility (appearing well coiffed, attaining the position) eventually close in on themselves, offering no telos beyond the ones that utility already assumes. That is, utility cannot account for why it is itself finally useful. Rather, it can seduce us into its material effect, which is considerable, and blind us to these ontological questions. But this blinding, as I hope to have invoked here, comes only with the perpetuation of numerous systems of domination and the foreclosure of this more general questioning about purpose and ends.

This is, of course, its crucial blindspot. It is only in foreclosing any account of its own overarching telos that utility sets its own boundaries and begins totalizing the economy it has closed for itself. It is only from this basis that utility can be idealized as the sort of unquestionable value that it has become in whitened, westernized lands. And, of course, it is in this idealizing that it further exercises its social—and aesthetic—power. It is in this idealized state that "good taste" emerges as one of utility's most insidious tentacles, shaping our desires to place ourselves squarely in this culture where utility parades so effectively as beauty. But, true to the dynamics of blindness and insight, this insight into utility's blindspot weakens its otherwise blinding material effects. If utility only totalizes its grasp through its seductive material effects of power and its foreclosure of its own condition of possibility, cracks emerge in its own closed economy. It is no longer totalizing.

To create a style, rather than a taste, of resistance to domination is then possible. While it is undoubtedly difficult, involving practices that jar us from patterns as unconscious as our embodied, subtle temporalities of anticipation, it is nonetheless possible. As Bataille warns us, "It is not easy to realize one's own ends if one must, in trying to do so, carry out a movement that surpasses them."[3] But if the alleged ends are shaped by utility, it is possible. And this may be our best attempt to foil and undercut our placements in this culture of domination, opening fresh ways to becoming antiracist, antisexist, antihomophobic, anticapitalist. It may be our best attempt to cultivate styles of quintessentially bad taste and develop an etiquette—not an ethics—of resistance.

Notes

I am grateful to Jennifer Suchland and Amy Wendling for astute readings of this chapter and a few of the more interesting observations therein.

1. Friedrich Nietzsche, *On the Genealogy of Morals,* trans. Walter Kaufman (New York: Vintage, 1989), p. 153.
2. Georges Bataille, *The Accursed Share,* vol. 2, trans. Robert Hurley (New York: Zone Books, 1993), p. 146.
3. Georges Bataille, *The Accursed Share,* vol. 1, trans. Robert Hurley (New York: Zone Books, 1991), p. 21.

CHAPTER FOURTEEN

The American Guest

KEVIN MACDONALD

Die Freie Gebrauch des Eignen das Schwerste ist.

—Hölderlin

Giving Thanks

Every November, countless numbers of Americans travel within the space of forty-eight hour days to celebrate Thanksgiving. There is a veritable crush of humanity on the roads, on trains, and in airports as people make their way to the inevitable endpoint of Thanksgiving dinner, like so many millions of frenzied birds rushing home to roost before the end of what must have been a monumental day. Indeed, millions of real birds are then sacrificed in this annual ritual of harvest reunion and repast, as millions of people experience the mixed emotional landscape of family togetherness and alienation. Mothers, fathers, sons, daughters, uncles, aunts, nieces, nephews, cousins, and friends find themselves in a situation that is, we are told, a commemoration—through repetition—of the Pilgrim Fathers' gratitude in having lived through the first year of colonial settlement. What American school child has not been fed this myth, this story that serves as a kind of cultural *arche*? Is it not a tale to be remembered with a lesson to be learned? And what is that lesson, precisely?

It is highly likely—no, almost certain—that there is no precise lesson here. We know that stories like this, whether it be the story of Thanksgiving, the story of Christmas, or say, the story of Columbus, are all exercised upon us like so many spells and incantations with the effect of putting us into a trance which can serve many purposes. Whose purposes? Again no exact answer can be given. Sometimes it is the purposes of another; sometimes it is our own purposes that are served. The institution of Thanksgiving, however, does bring into focus how Americans are disposed toward the phenomena of gratitude. That may be one of the lessons posed by the story of Thanksgiving, a lesson on saying thank you, an exercise in grace.

It is a story of helplessness and succor, of please and thank you. We know the story well enough. The Pilgrims, having some inexperience in matters of New World survival, were near starvation in their first year. The Native Americans, for all intents and purposes, came to the assistance of the Pilgrims, teaching them as well as feeding them. Thanksgiving undoubtedly has its historical roots in the tradition of the harvest feast. But the facts of the case are rather interesting, and have no little bearing on the subject that falls under our consideration in this chapter. In the traditional, more finely detailed account of the first Thanksgiving, a Native American named Squanto plays a rather significant role. Squanto is often pictured as the helpful Indian who was willing to save the colonists from a potential disaster. Most us are not aware of the fact that this same Squanto had been captured and enslaved by English slave traders some years previous to the pilgrim landing, and was basically shuttled back and forth between Spain, England, and the New World until he ended up on the Massachusetts coast, once again a free person. Whatever his real motivation, if ever such a thing could be discovered, it is noteworthy that our friend Squanto practiced a form of graciousness toward these settlers, people who were intent on establishing their own domain regardless of the existence of the native peoples. The graciousness of Squanto is all the more remarkable considering that he must have had some experience of European hostility and rapacity. As we know, it is not Squanto who is remembered on Thanksgiving, it is our good fortune in being so blessed with plenty for which we give thanks. But do Americans really know how to say please and thank you; do they really know how to say grace?

Freeway

Let's pause here for a moment. Do we really need to be grateful? Why should anyone be thankful for anything? Haven't we outgrown this superstitious transaction of request and appreciation? It is quite conceivable that as our society moves toward its apotheosis in the age of the DSL connection, gratitude will become passé. Perhaps many might think this is a state to be wished for, a society free of gratitude. Consider the American motorist, who stands, or rather drives, at the very vanguard of the movement to liberate us from gratitude. What does the behavior of this being demonstrate to us? If anything it shows us that gratitude is superfluous, that it is perfectly possible to live without it. Our highways, with their innumerable signs, lights, and symbols, allow us to follow our individual paths according to the logic of traffic engineering. There is no need to be polite. Why say "please" when one's vehicle can act as a gesture of a demand, naked and without the need of a mediating gesture of supplication? System, machine, and engineered movement strip away the veneer of politesse and replace it with a refined and ferocious will to arrive, a pure intention to move. The articulation of gratitude takes up time after all. The turn signal is not so much read as a request as it is seen as an alert, perhaps even a threat of danger. What takes place on the highway is replicated more and more everywhere else. The need for speed and information continually erodes and erases any context wherein supplication and gratitude could take place. In place of a request met by the grace of a god, host, or stranger, there is an increasing analysis of request, subjecting the need of the supplicant to mathematical and economic criteria. A prayer is answered with the assistance of a scoring system. We are grateful when our credit is good, and thank God if the HMO covers the hospital bills.

"Please" and "thank you" have become mere rhetorical devices, the words themselves nothing but simple ornamentations that serve any number of singular pragmatic purposes. They have been relegated, like so many other everyday practices of their kind, to the domain of the polite and the considerate, knowledge of which has become a kind of techne, a technique of managing the friend, the enemy, or the client. This domain is separated off from what we designate as the "ethical," which is somehow of greater importance by virtue of the fact that it is the domain somehow pertinent to the preservation and living of life itself. The theme to be traced out here is that gratitude may perhaps be closer to the bone of life and the living of it than we would like to admit. We might have to see gratitude as a practice, and not as a mere emotion or institution. It could be phrased in this manner, with much hesitation and some caution—where Heidegger in Being and Time mentions and delineates the "Inauthentic" read "Ungrateful." So is the authentic therefore the grateful? Such a correlation would be easy to make, and the temptation is strong to reach just such a conclusion. However, it would be more appropriate to the nature of grace itself to state that the grateful is what it is precisely because it is radically uncertain of its status as either authentic or inauthentic. "One merely accepts the gift, one does not ask who the giver is," as Nietzsche says in the Gay Science. One suspects that the ungrateful thinks of itself as authentic, and furthermore is disposed to even make such a distinction in the first place. If I may borrow the language of Bataille, the ungrateful is a participant in a restricted economy, where please and thank you must be met with the appropriate responses or acknowledgement of debt and credit that go without saying in this form of transaction.

If we briefly examine the phenomenon of road rage we can see this ingratitude at work firsthand. The boundless anger which many drivers experience would seem at first glance to be a mere psychological problem. The automobile has, as is obvious to everyone, become a multivalent symbol functioning on many levels. This includes of course any representative power that accrues to the vehicle as an icon. What is it, however, about the automobile and its use that opens up this bottomless reservoir of anger? When we sit in our automobile not only are we shielded from others, the automobile also installs us into a sense of entitlement, we are in a position in a most definite sense of the word. The car opens up on a new level of possession where there is a fiction of independence, where one is no longer tied to the interactions that interrupt and commit us to the social.

The car is the concept of the individual right made visible. The anger that erupts at the slow driver in front of us, or when someone is too close behind us, or someone is careless signaling, is not simply a reaction to a lack of consideration, but a response to our impotence revealed in the violation of our right to the road. Ingratitude is revealed the moment this impotence is broached, the moment the vulnerability of the thankless is revealed. For those without grace, nothing is guaranteed, not even a place in the sun—precisely because it is the ungrateful and thankless who demand a guarantee of the absolute right. Furthermore is not the idea of the guarantee itself derived from the thankless? This is not a moral judgment of those without gratitude. It is to state that gratitude, or rather a return to it, is necessary if we do not want to submit to a culture of rights without life.

So what is there to be grateful for? Why say please and thank you at all? If gratitude has something to recommend it to us, what could it be?

Psycho Killers: At the Table, at the Door

Let me reiterate in different terms: living well is a matter of having good manners—knowing the appropriate nature of please and thank you, knowing how to say grace, knowing what gratitude is, having grace, being grateful, developing a sense of grace. Let us propose an example of what it might mean to live with gratitude, an example which is not perfect, but which nevertheless might indicate some marks of the gracious. Epictetus, who had known slavery as well as intellectual respect in his life, had this sense of grace in mind when he wrote in his manual, "Behave in Life as you would at a banquet." This famous metaphor from Epictetus illustrates a pattern that is found throughout his manual in other images supplied by him. It of course was a way of describing what the Stoics called "Apatheia," or, as it is sometimes translated, "detachment." Is not this apatheia descriptive of a release from the pathos of ingratitude, the disease of self-absorption in any guise? In other words the Stoic approach was to recognize the gift in its emphatically transitive state. This recognition hinges upon a realization that gratitude must never presume upon the nature of the giver, that there will always be a radical impossibility of pronouncing what is given and what is not. The freedom of the Stoic is found in the acceptance of this very impossibility, a gratitude for the gift of pure life—and here the purity of it must remain essentially unknown and yet radically gratifying. The Stoics, or at least Epictetus, were masters of gratitude by surrendering to the unknown and unknowable gift of life.

We Americans, on the other hand, think other cultures insane for practicing what we so clumsily call the "guest ethic." It is a well-known fact that in many cultures, past and present, the guest is viewed as a sacred presence, possibly even a god who comes to test our graciousness. The guest does not have to say the magic word; the guest is already "magic," if by that we could understand the guest as being a living test of the graciousness, of our gratitude to life. The guest is a gift who reveals our vulnerability to and immersion in the absence of gratitude. In some places, such as in certain areas of Siberia, all the guest has to do is to simply walk in unannounced, stranger or not, to receive the requisite treatment of full hospitality. Curiously, the human response to life in many places has been to accept it and celebrate it in a ritual where the "stinginess" of nature (to recall Hume) is left unaddressed or denied. In its place there have been erected various temples of codes, strictures, and requirements that can be rudely shoved under the name of "hospitality."

If a stranger arrives at our door, we might even be tempted to shoot the person, if we're armed, or at least not answer the door, if we're not. It is not just the city folk who exhibit such rudeness, to make an answer to someone I can hear saying, "But there is danger on the other side of the door!" Witness the case of Yoshinori Hattori, a Japanese exchange student who was shot to death in 1992 by a suburban homeowner in Baton Rouge, Louisiana, because he wouldn't leave the man's property with the proper speed and decorum. The student, who thought he was at the right address for a Halloween party, apparently did not understand the nature of what was being communicated to him, which was a warning to go away or else. Mr. Hattori was not vindicated in the courtroom. After a trial that lasted several months and received national attention in the press, the homeowner was acquitted.

A final plea for the necessity of gratitude—a last exhortation to say thank you. There is a scene in the movie *Apocalypse Now* that is in some respects the most barbarous one of all in this disturbing, provocative, and at times pretentious film. In it, the main character, Captain Williard, must sit down to a polite dinner with two army officers and a civilian who looks like someone who either sells insurance or overthrows governments. During the course of the meal, which is carefully choreographed in the film, all of the traditional etiquette of the American mealtime is set out on display, like a shelf of figurines, delicate and absurd. It is a meal over which the death of Colonel Kurtz is plotted on the pretext that Kurtz himself has become a murderer, that his methods have become unsound. The crime that Kurtz has committed is, of course, the crime of having become a living exemplar of the logic of the American guest unwound to its ultimate, inescapable conclusion—that there is a violent ingratitude in the American quest for liberation. This lunch table scene suggests the essence of hypocrisy that tints the American guest the ineradicable color of ingratitude or the color of murder. That is the outcome, the last conclusion, of the ungrateful—that which does not please us must die, even though we may be very polite as we kill. This tableau gives us the essence of the American guest as the guest who is ultimately insane with gracious ingratitude. So we live with style and recognize the importance of treating others right, but woe befall the thief of the parking space, or to the bandit of the place in line. Like Captain Willard we accept our mission to wipe out the purveyors of unacceptable conduct while politely passing assorted fruits of the slaughter. However, contrary to Nietzsche's prescription, we see ourselves, the Americans, as those who would know exactly how to place please and thank you. The American guest brings the gift of freedom, for which we should all be thankful. But be careful. For even if this gift is itself an opportunity to experience the gratitude for life, there are conditions for its acceptance that we may find a burden. Would we want our Thanksgiving dinners to recur eternally? I think not.

So kill us if you must, if we have offended you, if we stand in your way, if our manners are bad enough to warrant our execution. Perhaps we take our freedoms for granted in saying such unlovely things about our honored guest, and so we deserve your cries of execration. At least we are resolved to die graciously.

CHAPTER FIFTEEN

A Place Where the Soul Can Rest

bell hooks

Street corners have always been space that has belonged to men—patriarchal territory. The feminist movement did not change that. Just as it was not powerful enough to take back the night and make the dark a safe place for women to lurk, roam, and meander at will, it was not able to change the ethos of the street corner—gender equality in the workplace, yes, but the street corner turns every woman who dares lurk into a body selling herself, a body looking for drugs, a body going down. A female lurking, lingering, lounging on a street corner is seen by everyone, looked at, observed. Whether she wants to be or not she is prey for the predator, for the Man, be he pimp, police, or just passerby. In cities women have no outdoor territory to occupy. They must be endlessly moving or enclosed. They must have a destination. They cannot loiter or linger.

Verandas and porches were made for females to have outdoor space to occupy. They are a common feature of southern living. Before air-conditioning cooled every hot space the porch was the summertime place, the place everyone flocked to in the early mornings and in the late nights. In our Kentucky world of poor southern black neighborhoods of shotgun houses and clapboard houses, a porch was a sign of living a life without shame. To come out on the porch was to see and be seen, to have nothing to hide. It signaled a willingness to be known. Oftentimes the shacks of the destitute were places where inhabitants walked outside straight into dust and dirt—there was neither time nor money to make a porch.

The porches of my upbringing were places of fellowship—outside space women occupied while men were away, working or on street corners. To sit on one's porch meant chores were done—the house was cleaned, food prepared. Or if you were rich enough and the proud possessor of a veranda, it was the place of your repose while the housekeeper or maid finished your cleaning. As children we needed permission to sit on the porch, to reside if only for a time, in that place of leisure and rest. The first house we lived in had no porch. A cinderblock dwelling made for working men to live in while they searched the earth for oil outside city limits, it was designed to be a waiting place, a place for folks determined to move up and on—a place in the wilderness. In the wilderness there were no neighbors to wave at or chat with or simply to holler at and know their presence by the slamming of doors as one journeyed in and out. A home without neighbors surely did not require a porch, just narrow steps to carry inhabitants in and out.

When we moved away from the wilderness, when we moved up, our journey of improved circumstance took us to a wood-frame house with upstairs and downstairs. Our new beginning was grand: we moved to a place with not one but three porches—a front porch, a side porch, and a back porch. The side porch was a place where folks could sleep when the heat of the day had cooled off. Taking one's dreams outside made the dark feel safe. And in that safeness, a woman, a child—girl or boy—could linger. Side porches were places for secret meetings, places where intimate callers could come and go without being seen, spend time without anyone knowing how long they stayed. After a year of living with a side porch and six teenaged girls, Daddy sheetrocked, made walls, blocked up the door so that it became our brother's room, an enclosed space with no window to the outside.

We sat on the back porch and did chores like picking walnuts, shucking corn, and cleaning fish, when Baba, Mama's mama, and the rest had a good fishing day, when black farmers brought the fruit of their labor into the city. Our back porch was tiny. It could not hold all of us. And so it was a limited place of fellowship. As a child I felt more comfortable there, unobserved, able to have my child's musings, my daydreams, without the interruptions of folks passing by and saying a word or two, without folks coming up to sit a spell. At Mr. Porter's house (he was the old man who lived and died there before we moved) there was a feeling of eternity, of timelessness. He had imprinted on the soul of this house his flavor, the taste and scent of a long lived life. We honored that by calling his name when talking about the house on First Street.

To our patriarchal dad, Mr. V, the porch was a danger zone—as in his sexist mindset all feminine space was designated dangerous, a threat. A strange man walking on Mr. V's porch was setting himself up to be a possible target: walking onto the porch, into an inner feminine sanctum, was in the eyes of any patriarch just the same as raping another man's woman. And we were all of us—mother, daughters—owned by our father. Like any patriarch would, he reminded us from time to time whose house we lived in—a house where women had no rights but could indeed claim the porch—colonize it and turn it into a place where men could look but not touch—a place that did not interest our father, a place where he did not sit. Indeed, our daddy always acted as though he hated the porch. Often when he came home from work he entered through the back door, marking his territory, taking us unaware.

We learned that it was best not to be seen on the porch often when he walked up the sidewalk after a long day's work. We knew our place: it was inside, making the world comfortable for the patriarch, preparing ourselves to bow and serve—not literally to bow, but to subordinate our beings. And we did. No wonder then that we loved the porch, longed to move outside the protected patriarchal space of that house that was in its own way a prison.

Like so much else ruined by patriarchal rage, so much other female space damaged, our father the patriarch took the porch from us one intensely hot summer night. Returning home from work in a jealous rage, he started ranting the moment he hit the sidewalk leading up to the steps, using threatening, ugly words. We were all females there on that porch, parting our bodies like waves in the sea so that Mama could be pushed by hurting hands, pushed through the front door, pushed into the house, where his threats to kill and kill again would not be heard by the neighbors. This trauma of male violence took my teenage years and smothered them in the arms of a deep and abiding grief—took away the female fellowship, the freedom of days and nights sitting on the porch.

Trapped in the interstices of patriarchal gender warfare, we stayed off the porch, for fear that just any innocent male approaching would be seen by our father and set off crazy rage. Coming in from the outside I would see at a distance the forlorn look of a decimated space, its life energy gone and its heart left lonely. Mama and Daddy mended the wounded places severed by rage, maintaining their intimate bond. They moved away from Mr. Porter's house into a small new wood-frame structure, a house without a porch, and even when a small one was added it was not a porch for sitting, just a place for standing. Maybe this space relieved Dad's anxiety about the dangerous feminine, about female power.

Surely our father, like all good patriarchs, sensed that the porch as a female gathering place represented in some vital way a threat to the male dominator's hold on the household. The porch as liminal space, standing between the house and the world of sidewalks and streets, was symbolically a threshold. Crossing it opened up the possibility of change. Women and children on the porch could begin to interpret the outside world on terms different from the received knowledge gleaned in the patriarchal household. The porch had no master; even our father could not conquer it. Porches could be abandoned but they could not be taken over, occupied by any one group to the exclusion of others.

A democratic meeting place, capable of containing folks from various walks of life, with diverse perspectives, the porch was free-floating space, anchored only by the porch swing, and even that was a symbol of potential pleasure. The swing hinted at the underlying desire to move freely, to be transported. A symbol of play, it captured the continued longing for childhood, holding us back in time, entrancing us, hypnotizing us with its back-and-forth motion. The porch swing was a place where intimacies could be forged, desire arising in the moment of closeness swings made possible.

In the days of my girlhood, when everyone sat on their porches, usually on their swings, it was the way we all became acquainted with one another, the way we created community. In M. Scott Peck's work on community-making and peace, *The Different Drum*,[1] he explains that true community is always integrated and that "genuine community is always characterized by integrity." The integrity that emerged in our segregated communities as I was growing up was based on the cultivation of civility, of respect for others and acknowledgement of their presence. Walking by someone's house, seeing them on their porch, and failing to speak was to go against the tenets of the community. Now and then, I or my siblings would be bold enough to assume we could ignore the practice of civility, which included learning respect for one's elders, and strut by folks' houses and not speak. By the time we reached home, Mama would have received a call about our failure to show courtesy and respect. She would make us take our walk again and perform the necessary ritual of speaking to our neighbors who were sitting on their porches.

In *A World Waiting to Be Born: The Search for Civility*,[2] M. Scott Peck extends his conversation on making community to include the practice of civility. Growing up in the segregated South, I was raised to believe in the importance of being civil. This was more than just a recognition of the need to be polite, of having good manners; it was a demand that I and my siblings remain constantly aware of our interconnectedness and interdependency on all the folk around us. The lessons learned by seeing one's neighbors on their porches and stopping to chat with them, or just to speak courteously, was a valuable way to honor our connectedness. Peck shares the insight that civility is consciously motivated and essentially an ethical practice. By practicing civility we remind ourselves, he writes, that "each and every human being—you, every friend, every stranger, every foreigner is precious."[3] The etiquette of civility then is far more than the performance of manners: it includes an understanding of the deeper psychoanalytic relationship to recognition as that which makes us subjects to one another rather than objects.

African Americans have a long history of struggling to stand as subjects in a place where the dehumanizing impact of racism works continually to make us objects. In our small-town segregated world, we lived in communities of resistance, where even the small everyday gesture of porch sitting was linked to humanization. Racist white folks often felt extreme ire when observing a group of black folks gathered on a porch. They used the derogatory phrase "porch monkey" both to express contempt and to once again conjure up the racist iconography linking blackness to nature, to animals in the wild. As a revolutionary threshold between home and street, the porch as liminal space could also then be a place of antiracist resistance. While white folk could interpret at will the actions of a black person on the street, the black person or persons gathered on a porch defied such interpretation. The racist eye could only watch, yet never truly know, what was taking place on porches among black folk.

I was a little girl in a segregated world when I first learned that there were white people who saw black people as less than animals. Sitting on the porch, my siblings and I would watch white folks bring home their servants, the maids and cooks who toiled to make their lives comfortable. These black servants were always relegated to the back seat. Next to the white drivers in the front would be the dog and in the back seat the black worker. Just seeing this taught me much about the interconnectedness of race and class. I often wondered how the black worker felt when it came time to come home and the dog would be placed in front, where racism and white supremacy had decreed no black person could ride. Although just a child, witnessing this act of domination, I understood that the workers must have felt shamed, because they never looked out the window; they never acknowledged a world beyond that moving car.

It was as though they were riding home in a trance—closing everything out was a way to block out the shaming feelings. Silent shadows slouched in the back seats of fancy cars, lone grown-up workers never turned their gaze toward the porch where "liberated" black folks could be seen hanging together. I was the girl they did not see, sitting in the swing, who felt their pain and wanted to make it better. And I would sit there and swing, going back and forth to the dreaming rhythm of a life where black folks would live free from fear.

Leaving racialized fear behind, I left the rhythm of porch swings, of hot nights filled with caring bodies and laughter lighting the dark like june bugs. To the West Coast I went to educate myself, away from the lazy apartheid of a jim crow that had been legislated away but was still nowhere near gone, to the North where I could become the intellectual the South back then had told me I could not be. But like the black folks anthropologist Carol Stack writes about,[4] who flee the North and go south again, yearning for a life they fear is passing them by, I too returned home. To any southerner who has ever loved the South, it is always and eternally home. From birth onward we breathed in its seductive heady scent, and it is the air that truly comforts. From birth onward as southerners we were seduced and imprinted by glimpses of a civic life expressed in communion not found elsewhere. That life was embodied for me in the world of the porch.

Looking for a home in the new South, that is, the place where jim crow finds its accepted expression in crude acting out, I entered a real-estate culture where material profit was stronger than the urge to keep neighborhoods and races pure. Seeking to live near water, where I could walk places, surrounded by an abundant natural tropical landscape, where I can visit Kentucky friends and sit on their porches, I found myself choosing a neighborhood populated mainly by old-school white folks. Searching for my southern home, I looked for a place with a porch. Refurbishing a 1920s bungalow, similar to ones the old Sears and Roebuck catalogue carried for less than seven hundred dollars with or without bathroom, I relished working on the porch. Speaking to neighbors who did not speak back, or one who let me know that they came to this side of town to be rid of lazy blacks, I was reminded how the black families who first bought homes in "white" neighborhoods during the civil rights era suffered—that their suffering along with the pain of their allies in struggle who worked for justice makes it possible for me to choose where I live. By comparison, what I and other black folk experience as we bring diversity into what has previously been a whites-only space is mere discomfort.

In their honor and in their memory, I speak a word of homage and praise for the valiant ones, who struggled and suffered so that I could and do live where I please, and I have made my porch a small everyday place of antiracist resistance, a place where I practice the etiquette of civility. I and my two sisters, who live nearby, sit on the porch. We wave at all the passersby, mostly white, mostly folks who do not acknowledge our presence. Southern white women are the least willing to be civil, whether old or young. Here in the new South three are many white women who long for the old days when they could count on being waited on by a black female at some point in their life, using the strength of their color to weigh her down. A black woman homeowner disrupts this racialized sexist fantasy. No matter how many white women turn their gaze away, we look, and by looking we claim our subjectivity. We speak, offering the southern hospitality, the civility, taught by our parents so that we would be responsible citizens. We speak to everyone.

Humorously, we call these small interventions yet another "Martin Luther King moment." Simply by being civil, by greeting, by "conversating," we are doing the antiracist work of nonviolent integration. That includes speaking to and dialoguing with the few black folk we see from the porch who enter our neighborhood mainly as poorly paid, poorly treated workers. We offer them our solidarity in struggle. In King's famous essay "Loving Your Enemies," he reminded us that this reaching out in love is the only gesture of civility that can begin to lay the groundwork for true community. He offers the insight, "Love is the only force that can turn an enemy into a friend. We never get rid of an enemy by meeting hate with hate; we get rid of an enemy by getting rid of enmity. By its very nature, hate destroys and tears down; by its very nature, love creates and builds up. Love transforms with redemptive power." Inside my southern home, I can forge about the world of racist enmity. When I come out on my porch I become aware of race, of the hostile racist white gaze, and I can contrast it with the warm gaze of welcome and recognition from those individual white folks who also understand the etiquette of civility, of community building and peace making.

The "starlight bungalow"—my southern home for now, given the name assigned it in the blueprint of the Sears and Roebuck 1920s catalogue (as a modern nomad I do not stay in place)—has an expansive porch. Stucco over wood, the house has been reshaped to give it a Mediterranean flavor. Architecturally it is not a porch that invites a swing, a rocking chair, or even a bench. Covered with warm sand-colored Mexican tiles, it is a porch that is not made for true repose. Expansive, with rounded arches and columns, it does invite the soul to open wide, to enter the heart of the home, crossing a peaceful threshold.

Returning to the South, I longed for a porch for fellowship and late-night gatherings. However, just as I am true to my inner callings, I accept what I feel to be the architectural will of the porch and let it stand as it is, without added seats, with only one tin star as ornament. It is a porch for short sittings, a wide standing porch, for looking out and gazing down, a place for making contact—a place where one can be seen. In the old Sears and Roebuck catalogue, houses were given names and the reader was told what type of life might be imagined in this dwelling. My "starlight bungalow" was described as "a place for distinct and unique living." When I first sat on the porch welcoming folk, before entering a dwelling full of light, I proclaimed, in old-South vernacular, "My soul is rested." A perfect porch is a place where the soul can rest.

Notes

1. Peck, M. Scott, *The Different Drum: Community Making and Peace* (New York: Touchstone, 1998), p. 34.

2. Peck, M. Scott, *A World Waiting to Be Born: Civility Rediscovered* (New York: Bantam, 1994).

3. Ibid., p. 106.

4. Stack, Carol, *Call to Home: African Americans Reclaim the South* (New York: Basic Books, 1997).

CHAPTER SIXTEEN

Slurping Soda, Twirling Spaghetti

Etiquette, Fascism, and Pleasure

DON HANLON JOHNSON

At this point in our battered histories, what might justify troubling ourselves about such a dainty subject as etiquette, a topic seemingly more appropriate for Miss Manners and the latest advice book on how to be a success in the upper realms of global capitalism? There are both dramatic and intimate answers to this question. The dramatic response has to do with how etiquette figures in the structuring of power; the more intimate, with how the practices of etiquette make communal life—meals, conversations, dancing, sports, erotics—more pleasurable. Let us begin with the more intimate.

Not too long ago, I was on my first snowshoe hike with a friend on a cross-country ski trail in the Sierras. Not used to the situation, I was slogging along over tracks made by skiers touring the area. My friend informed me that it was bad manners to walk on the grooves because it impeded the glide of the skiers. A year later, I took up cross-country skiing myself. Trails in resorts are groomed by large tractors with a device in the front that cuts two sets of parallel tracks on opposite borders of a large smoothed trail in between. The tracks, I was told, were followed as one would drive in traffic, staying to the right. As I struggled to learn how to control my movements down the steeper slopes, I would glide around a blind corner, see people coming up the wrong direction, and, not having sufficient control, would have to fall down to prevent myself from hitting them. Or as I would round a bend, there would be a large group standing chatting, blocking the trail, and again my only resort was to hurl myself ingloriously into the snowbank, sometimes hurting myself. Over the weeks as I got a sense of the situation, I came to appreciate the choreography of the tracks, how being observant of the appropriate directions and keeping off the tracks when not in them left room for the graceful and sensual strides that make cross-country skiing so attractive. The manners of the course were designed to promote the inherent pleasures of the activity.

During the same period of time, I was also engaging in an exercise program called White Cloud Yoga or Gyrotonic, a brilliant system designed by Juliu Horvath, a former Olympic athlete from Rumania. At one point in his career, he had gone to a hatha yoga retreat which affected him so deeply that he was inspired to develop a synthesis of the strengthening regimes he knew from Olympic physical training with the depth of consciousness and bodily release that he found in hatha yoga. He began to craft baroquely complex Nautilus-like machines that are designed to evoke the infinite ranges of muscular movement within the body. Unlike practices using standard Western machines, however, his devices evoke endless complexity. The regimen he teaches encourages people to use the machines in the manner of hatha yoga, slowly and precisely enough that one is constantly in touch with one's inner experience, allowing the maximum stretches, rotations, and expansions to take place. After a lifetime of avoiding such systems because I found them either painful or boring, I found this system sensually pleasurable and almost miraculously effective in toning my aging muscles.

After six months of working with a highly skilled and sensitive trainer learning a sequence to follow, I arrived for my hour-long session in the midst of a tightly scheduled day. My trainer was sitting in a corner of the studio with three other exercitants in a circle where they were doing some sort of self-massage which I had not seen before. He softly ordered me to join them. The instructions had a heavy overlay of exotic interpretations: "massaging the webs between your fingers evokes the movements behind your ankles," "pressing the backs of your calves relieves the pressure in your brain," and so on. Since I often do such movements myself, I did not want to waste my very constricted time and the considerable fee I was paying doing such things. After about fifteen minutes, becoming increasingly restless, I said, "May I ask a question?" My trainer, a gentle yogic person with whom I had been working fruitfully for these many months, turned toward me like an angry dog and growled, "No, this is not the place to ask questions." I continued, "But how long are we going to do this?" He looked at me angrily and said I was disrupting the concentration of other people. "You should know after all these months that you may ask questions only of me privately after we are finished." I replied, "But I've never done this before, I didn't know how long it would last." He rapidly finished the session and stalked away, visibly furious. I called after him asking if he was mad at me. He snapped back, "I'm not allowed to be angry!"

I tell these two stories because each is a recent version of two very different kinds of etiquette familiar to me over my lifetime. In the snow, the rules are clearly meant to enhance the pleasure of the skiers; to deliberately violate them implies unkindness and disrespect for others, even physical harm. In the workout studio, rules, many of which I didn't even know, were mysterious in function. When I was charged with violating one under the argument that it interfered with others, the justification seemed spurious. The studio is like any exercise studio: people coming and going, phones ringing and being answered, people chatting about their latest lover or good meal. It was not a zendo with an atmosphere of silent concentration. In that situation, it was difficult for me to see how my question would disturb the others. Moreover, the rule was being used to cajole me into putting up with an activity which I did not want to do and for which I was paying; it was a maneuver of power, having no discernible relation to the pleasure I typically experience in doing the work. I was in the all too familiar situation of not knowing, assuming I was lacking a kind of mastery of the system that was mysterious and accessible only through deference to authorized protectors of the secrets.

> 150. The grammar of the word "knows" is evidently closely related to that of "can," "is able to." But also closely related to that of "understands" ("Mastery" of a technique).
>
> 151. But there is also *this* use of the word "to know": we say "Now I know!"—and similarly "Now I can do it!" and "Now I understand!"
>
> —Ludwig Wittgenstein, *The Philosophical Investigations*

Over the past three decades, I developed a close friendship with three people from the old upper class. In my relations with them, both in larger social settings and in more intimate ones, I got a very different sense of manners. Because they have been raised from infancy within a circle of expert formality, they are masters of the art, making the rules seem natural and effortless. Like being in the presence of the masters of any art, I learned simply from being with them how to maneuver in various social gatherings more easily than from books or direct advice. Their mastery of etiquette, learned in childhood, has the purpose of removing any of the worries and discomforts that might distract from enjoying the pleasures of conversation and food. They embody a difference between graciousness and sheer formalism. One can follow all the rules and be a dour dinner companion; in the back wilderness, the grim follower of rules can mar the feelings of awe evoked by mountain ridges and bright winds. Mastery of good manners ensouls the rules with good humor and concern for others. Masters of the art give precedence to function over form, a sense that the pleasures of being together are of more value than selecting the correct fork for the escargots.

It was very different in my family. Etiquette was for my parents what English was for their forebears, a fully formed, complex, unknown system that had to be learned with great difficulty, and then always with a trace of awkwardness. My parents, children of immigrants, seemed always to be struggling to figure out what the rules were and how to implement them if they were to continue to move up the socioeconomic slopes. In that struggle, they always seemed to feel themselves as outsiders lacking mastery of the rules, not knowing what to do. When my family made a shift in my early childhood from lower working class into the middle class, etiquette came to represent the complex set of mysterious rules that were required of anyone who was longing to be accepted. They seemed to govern every aspect of social behaviors: the setting of the table and the appropriate moves to be made when sitting there, the proper kinds of clothing for different occasions, the correct forms of address, formats of letters, postures and gestures, and who knows what else. Pierre Bourdieu accurately described my childhood situation:

> In opposition to the free-and-easy working-class meal, the bourgeoisie is concerned to eat with all due form. Form is first of all a matter of rhythm, which implies expectations, pauses, restraints; waiting until the last person served has started to eat, taking modest helpings, not appearing over-eager. A strict sequence is observed. . . . Through all the forms and formalisms imposed on the immediate appetite, what is demanded—and inculcated—is not only a disposition to discipline food consumption by a conventional structuring which is also a gentle, indirect, invisible censorship (quite different from enforced privations) and which is an element in an art of living (correct eating, for example, is a way of paying homage to one's hosts and to the mistress of the house, a tribute to her care and effort).[1]

I was born toward the end of the Great Depression into a family that was just struggling to survive: my father was working in the Del Monte cannery, his father was a carpenter, my mother's father was a clerk in a downtown men's clothing store. We lived in a lower working-class neighborhood in a house my father built around the corner from a house my grandfather had built. My grandparents had immigrated from Scandinavia when they were young adults. Their house had an Old-World feel, permeated with smells of coffee sitting all day on the heater, meatballs and soups always simmering on the stove, casual eating of ample amounts of food, prepared for the hard-working men. I don't remember "places being set" or any talk of propriety. There was an informality with meals usually being taken at a cozy nook in the kitchen. Nor do I remember vulgarity or rudeness.

Our house was very small—two bedrooms, one bathroom, small dining room, and a very small den which was soon converted into a bedroom when my mother's father moved in with us when he lost his job. After World War II ended and my father began to make more money in the booming California heavy-construction industry, the first thing that changed in our house was tableware. My parents bought a full set of sterling flatware engraved with *J*, gold-edged Lenox china, fine damask, and Swedish crystal. They purchased an expensive membership in the Del Paso Country Club. When old friends came for dinner, we now crowded around the table in our tiny dining room set elaborately according to the rules prescribed by Emily Post, a new reference book in our house shelved next to the Bible. Despite my parents' slow upward move into the comfortable middle class, they remained in this small house in an increasingly depressed and crime-ridden neighborhood for forty years, traveling the world, buying fine clothes, eating excellent food served on an increasing array of fine dinnerware, financing my college education.

The writer Richard Rodriguez, four years younger than I, grew up a few blocks away in a slightly better middle-class neighborhood; we both graduated from the same Christian Brothers High School. Though from a different ethnic heritage, he describes in his memoirs of Sacramento a similar feeling of the struggles of his parents to create a new identity as Americans. "My mother and father," he writes, "(with immigrant pragmatism) assumed the American tongue would reinvent their children."[2] Proper English had to be accompanied by proper manners for the reinvention to be successful.

The first time I remember clearly becoming aware of etiquette as an agreed-upon, highly defined, and very complicated body of rules was in seventh grade just at the end of World War II. I had gone to public schools until the end of sixth grade, when my parents transferred me to a Catholic elementary school. Like most kids finding themselves at that erotically charged age in a totally strange community, I felt very uncomfortable with boys and girls who had known each other for at least six years. They were all Catholics, mostly from working-class families, whose grandparents, like mine, had been born in the Old World. A few weeks into the school year, I received an invitation in the mail to a Halloween party at one of the girls' houses. It was the ordinary kind of kid's invitation you buy in drugstores, a playful design of pumpkins and goblins with blanks filled in with the date and time of the party. I could feel my mother nervously rising to a very important social occasion as she tried to figure out the appropriate way for me to respond. The stakes seemed higher than one might expect. She got out her Emily Post to consult the section on responses to invitations. Because there were no directions for pubescent Halloween parties, she followed its instructions for replies to invitations for weddings, formal parties and teas, having me painstakingly copy in black India ink this prescribed reply on the required blank ivory card:

Donald Hanlon Johnson accepts with pleasure your invitation to a
Halloween party on October Thirty-First,
Nineteen Hundred and Forty-Six,
at Twelve Hundred and One "K" Street
from Seven to Nine O'clock Post Meridian.

Then she took me to Weinstock and Lubin's Department Store, where I was fitted out in a tan double-breasted linen suit, a white shirt with French cuffs, a tie, and leather wing-tip shoes. I arrived at the party. A small modest house like ours. The boys and girls, all easily familiar with each other, were wearing the casual clothes you might expect. I have a photograph of me standing there looking like a newly arrived immigrant on Ellis Island in my ill-fitting suit and bewildered facial expression. I sensed that the formal reply and my dress had provoked some gossip about my weirdness. I did not understand; did not know how to do it; was in no sense a master of the techniques I thought were required just to have fun with my classmates.

After I graduated from college, by then thoroughly schooled in Emily Post, I entered the Jesuit novitiate to begin my studies for the priesthood and the long years of initiation into the religious order. Each Saturday morning, Fr. Joe Meehan, husky, a dry-humored, Irish San Francisco priest who would have done well as a fire chief or democratic ward boss, would enter our lecture hall, draw out a large white linen napkin, a set of silverware, plates, delicate cups, and crystal, ordering them properly on the desk in front of him, purse his lips as he seated himself daintily, and give us lessons on how to use the utensils, the proper glasses for red and white wine, how to wipe excess food from one's lips and dispose of olive pits, how to stifle possible burps—all in good Irish wit. I was puzzled about why we, who were devoting our lives to becoming mystics and missionaries charged by the Pope with bringing the message of Jesus to the furthest reaches of the world, were having these classes in secular niceties. It was only much later that I came to realize that we were being educated to sit among the upper classes who funded our vast networks of high schools and universities. Most Jesuits, like myself, came from working-class families. Their parents, however, had not been as concerned as mine about the manners of the upper classes. Learning the language of elegant tables was a missionary strategy every bit as important as learning the language of the country in which one was living—Japan, China, India, Russia. A burping bumpkin with food hanging from his chin would hardly be effective in his mission to insinuate Christian doctrine into the best homes where power lay.

❖ ❖ ❖

During the writing of this chapter, my eight-year-old son seems coincidentally to be going through an etiquette stage of development. He hears from our neighbors on green cards from England, who have three children, how much looser manners are here in California. From other Japanese friends with two boys who live nearby, and from my own stories of Japan, he knows that manners there are different from here and England. He knows, for example, that Japanese pride themselves on developing muscular lips to slurp soda with a potent sound. He has heard me talk about the sucking concerts at Tokyo noodle counters and he has watched our friends slurp. He has been to France and Italy and knows that Europeans twirl their pasta around a fork with the help of a large spoon before they bring it quietly into the mouth. As we were eating dinner together at home recently he said to me, "I never want to live in England." "Why is that?" I asked. "They have too strict manners," he replied. "I want to live in Japan where they slurp." He continues, impishly putting his finger in his nose then into his mouth, "Would they like this in England, Dad?" "How about this?" letting out a huge burp, then a fart. "Would Grandma like it if I did this?" he says, getting up and running boisterously around the table.

Bourdieu argues that manners define

> a whole relationship to animal nature, to primary needs and the populace who indulge them without restraint; it is a way of denying the meaning and primary function of consumption, which are essentially common, by making the meal a social ceremony, an affirmation of ethical tone and aesthetic refinement. . . . This whole commitment to stylization tends to shift the emphasis from substance and function to form and manner, and so to deny the

> crudely material reality of the act of eating and of the things consumed, or, which amounts to the same thing, the basely material vulgarity of those who indulge in the immediate satisfactions of food and drink.[3]

His otherwise brilliant analysis misses a point here, probably because he lived in a much more rigidly constructed society. My son's behavior is not accurately described as animal in nature, or as crudely material. It is in fact uniquely human, saturated with trickster humor, cross-cultural insight, and devices cleverly designed to upset his grandmothers, and adult guests who appear in his eyes to be a little too serious. This is not the behavior of our pet dog. My concern as a father is not to abstract him from his body, but to help him gain respect for others, a sense of their needs as well as his own. My work is to create a more pleasurable social situation where he is not disrupting our meals by commandeering all the attention so that others are unable to interact without focusing solely on him, or by emitting offensive odors and sounds. In that sense, learning manners is like learning the rules of cross-country skiing, playing a musical instrument, or dancing, practices that make human interaction more pleasurable. These strategies do not need to have the primary aim of making one less animal or bodily, but less aggressive and narcissistic.

Norbert Elias argues that the rules of etiquette are like the rules of dance; what he calls "figurations," the creative forms that shape particular communities out of many individuals:

> One should think of a mazurka, a minuet, a polonaise, a tango, or rock 'n' roll. The image of the mobile figurations of interdependent people on a dance floor perhaps makes it easier to imagine states, cities, families, and also capitalist, communist, and feudal systems as figurations. By using this concept we can eliminate the antithesis, resting finally on different values and ideals, immanent today in the use of the words "individual" and "society." One can certainly speak of a dance in general, but no one will imagine dance as a structure outside the individual or as a mere abstraction. The same dance figurations can certainly be danced by different people; but without a plurality of reciprocally oriented and dependent individuals, there is no dance.[4]

I had trouble with both social dances and manners, always feeling like I had five thumbs and sprained ankles. Like social dances, manners can make people feel clumsy and ill at ease, envious of their betters, enhance their fun, lead to wonderfully erotic encounters . . .

For me and many of my contemporaries, the 1960s were among other things a rebellion against the figurations of the previous generation, both their etiquette and social dances. I found myself revelling in free-form rock-and-roll and table manners. The first time I took LSD, I indulged in the ecstatic pleasure in devouring a wonderful meal like a dog, shoveling the food in my mouth with my bare hands, slurping, smearing the juices over my face. I let my hair grow unkempt, wore shaggy clothes, belched and farted at will. When I paid my first visit to the Esalen Institute in Big Sur at that time, I encountered the Fritz Perls Gestalt community, who believed that manners were inauthentic. If you said "good morning" to people, they looked at you with a cold stare letting you know what a phoney they thought you were. I felt as awkward and uncomfortable at Esalen in those years as I did at the seventh grade Halloween party. It was the beginning of a new figuration in America that might be called the "do-your-own-thing" figuration, which has polluted our social life, leaving us with insensitive drivers, loud babblers in small restaurants, and hikers in the back country peeing directly in the clear streams, leaving toilet paper beside the lupine, polluting the majestic sounds of the winds with their cell phones.

In 2002, the research group Public Agenda, funded by the Pew Charitable Trusts, released a study entitled "Aggravating Circumstances: A Status Report on Rudeness in America." It found that 80 percent of the adults surveyed believed that lack of respect and courtesy is a serious problem in American society. The president of the group reports, "Lack of manners for Americans is not whether you confuse the salad fork for the dinner fork. It is about the daily assault of selfish, inconsiderate behavior that gets under their skin on the highways, in the office, on TV, in stores and the myriad other settings where they encounter fellow Americans."[5]

⁂ ⁂ ⁂

Eros and etiquette?

A far-fetched link for Westerners where eroticism, like violence, is mistaken as primitive and animalistic. Best when done spontaneously, wildly, following one's passions, whose only formalities should be based on medical safety. Pornography more than aesthetics. And yet, think of the frustration at insensitive comings and goings.

Michel Foucault brought to light the radical contrast between Western and Asian discourses on erotics. If one wishes to find the major texts on sexuality in the West, one turns to the overstuffed libraries of Christian moral theology and popular medicine, in which the exclusive concerns are sins and bodily pathologies, with sexuality confined to the urogenital tract. In cultures from Japan to Turkey, by radical contrast, one finds the treasures of erotic poetry and fiction, painting and sculpture, and sophisticated texts giving directions for erotically based meditations. Instead of the crass pornography that litters our bookstores and browsers, there are the gardens of earthly delights cultivated by skilled artists and spiritual teachers. In those traditions, emphasis is on deliberate and systematic intensification of the infinite variety of pleasures available in refined erotic activity. Sexuality encompasses the whole body in harmonious concert with other bodies, and involves breathing practices, conscious direction of bodily excitations, stretching muscles, directing attention of various bodily regions, visualizations, and chanting. At the same time, the practices are done within an atmosphere of cultivating fundamental spiritual qualities like nuanced thoughtfulness, kindness, authenticity, love, and respect—the soul of etiquette. Mastery of erotic manners enhances the intensity of sexual pleasure just as mastery of social graces enhances the delights of conversation over dinner.

A confusion of etiquette and morals in Christian Europe is partly to blame for our debased notions of eros. Etiquette and moral virtue are so close they are often mistaken for each other. The Greek term for ethics, εθος, meant customs, the way a community organized itself, Elias's "figurations." Aristotle's *Ethics* argued that the study of customs was important to determine which particular practices led to what he defined as the shared goal of all human activity, happiness, and how those practices might be refined. In that original sense, etiquette was linked with gentlemanly satisfactions rooted in a harmonious (patriarchal, of course) community. As in China and India, the study of the figurations of human behavior had to do with the fullest development of the human community, allowing the ultimate flowering of its capacities of pleasure and wisdom.

In the thirteenth century, Thomas Aquinas and a host of medieval theologians transformed Aristotle's goal of well-oiled humane intercourse into the pursuit of the salvation of one's eternal soul created by a God who laid down laws defining goodness and its pursuit. They created a synthesis of classical Greek ethical philosophy with the great body of rules found in the ancient Christian Penitentials, documents that detail every possible sin and the conditions for its forgiveness. My guess is that few laymen have any sense that this weird strain of reasoning about human foibles exists in the dark halls of the monasteries and the Vatican. The early Penitentials were the first attempts to spell out the complexities of sin, degrees of seriousness, and the specific penances that would lead to their forgiveness. As literary texts, they bear more similarity to the writings of Baudelaire and de Sade than to cleaner philosophical tracts. In Bosch-like fantasy, they fantasize in bizarre detail any sin that any cleric might commit in his wildest flights of desire. In a not atypical passage, for example, the first Irish monks wrote, "Anyone who eats the flesh of a horse, or drinks the blood or urine of an animal, does penance for three years and a half. Anyone who drinks liquid in which there is a dead mouse does seven days' penance therefor. Anyone who drinks or eats the leavings of a mouse does penance for a day and a night. Theodore says that although food be touched by the hand of one polluted or by dog, cat, mouse, or unclean animal that drinks blood, this does no harm."[6] One might think that this prescription had more to do with manners than with morality: disgusting behavior, not to be done in public. But these prescriptions typically enter a realm where the disgusting is elided with the morally reprehensible: "He who sins with a beast shall do penance for a year; if by himself, for three 40-day periods; if he has clerical rank, a year; a boy of fifteen years, forty days. He who defiles his mother shall do penance for three years with perpetual exile."

Here you can see the dubious conflations of radically different kinds of behavior (sex with sheep and with one's mother) that have something to do with the sad state of morality of priests and bishops exposed in recent years. It is as if the cataloguing of thousands of fantasy trees obscured the forest of love and respect.

The transformation from the humane view of Aristotle to the theological view of medieval scholasticism left intrinsic contradictions. On the one hand, Jesus's discourses emphasized love and care for other people. In that sense, etiquette clearly bears on morality inasmuch as its rules are concerned with embodying intentions of kindness and respect.

Despite that foundational message, the overwhelming emphasis in Catholic moral theology was not on nurturing the human community, but on obeying the imagined dictates of God, often in behaviors that have no discernible relationship to the well-being of other human beings. Nowhere is that confusion of morality and etiquette more apparent than in the realm of erotics.

When I was in the final stages of my Jesuit initiation, about to be ordained and put into the confessional, our most important preparatory course was in moral theology. It was an infamous course, talked about for years during our preparatory training, with covert references to its kinky sexual content. Like the ancient Penitentials, the course indeed had a tone of surreal and twisted sexual fantasy. Although we dealt with all the sins proscribed by the Ten Commandments and the six special commandments of the Roman Church—stealing pears off local trees, lying, blaspheming, disobeying parents, tax evasion—the emphasis was on "sins of the flesh." We discussed every possible kind of sexual activity and imaginable orifice, with large and small animals as well as different kinds of humans. Our textbook, used in Catholic seminaries throughout the world, was the up-to-date version of the Penitentials. Its author was German Capuchin Friar Heribert Jone. It was translated and "adapted to the laws and customs of the United States of America" by Friar Urban Adelman in 1963. We examined intricacies of masturbation skirted in high school religion classes: it is alright for a man, wrote Friar Jone, "to wash, go swimming, riding, etc. even though one foresees that due to one's particular excitability in this regard, pollution will follow. Similarly, it is lawful to seek relief from itching in the sex organs, provided the irritation is not the result of superfluous semen or ardent passion. In case one doubts about the cause of the itching he may relieve it. It is likewise lawful in case of slight itching if only slight sexual stimulation is experienced therefrom."[7]

Friar Jone prided himself on a modernist sensibility in finally having arrived at a nonsexist definition of "pollution" as "complete sexual satisfaction obtained by some form of self-stimulation." He boasts of his formulation: "By evading reference to 'semination' our definition evades the various controversies concerning the specific difference of this sin in men, women, eunuchs, and those who have not reached the age of puberty, since only men are capable of secreting semen in the proper sense of the word."

The argument justifying these weird imaginings was that since we were about to enter the dark confessional to hear the full catalogue of human waywardness, we had to be prepared to diagnose every imaginable sin, and judge its degrees of seriousness to determine the appropriate penance. And the sins that most concerned the "Fathers of the Church" were masturbation and various forms of intercourse. Only very late in the history of moral theology did sins like social injustice and inflicting state-sanctioned torture begin to gain attention, and still now remain on the margins of Christian moral concerns.

By striking contrast, Buddhist, Taoist, and Hindu discourses about erotic behavior are more in the realm of etiquette and configurations: how to increase the intensity of pleasure and mystical insight, how to approach one's own body and one's partner's, touch, breathe, engage bodily surfaces and orifices, use flowers, perfumes, oils, music, and dress. The rules here, like good table manners, are about enhancing the pleasures of congress.

While it is true that Asian monastic communities observe celibacy, the practice is far more informal than in Catholicism. From my observations of rimpoches and gurus, it is more a matter of etiquette than of morals, practiced as a matter of refinement, but like rules of etiquette, often transgressed in the dark of the night or a private bedroom. The obsessive imaginings characteristic of European moral texts find their parallels in Hinduism and Buddhism only in the complex metaphysical texts outlining the myriad levels of consciousness one traverses in intricate practices of meditation. There are certainly moral prescriptions in these traditions, but by comparison to the Catholic tradition, they are minimal in content, dealing, for example, with obligations of husband to wife and children, and the duties of various stages of growing older.

⁂ ⁂ ⁂

We move now from the dinner table and the bedroom to the cells of political torture and fields of slaughter.

The dedication page of Norbert Elias's analysis of the so-called civilizing process is haunting:

> Dedicated to the Memory of My Parents
> Hermann Elias, d. Breslau 1940
> Sophie Elias, d. Auschwitz, 1941 (?)

I cannot believe this was written without deliberate and grief-stricken irony that the behaviors which he is about to describe so dispassionately in the following volumes, identified as the marks of high civilization, characterized the very men who supervised the murder of his parents.

Natural tendencies toward humane behaviors can indeed find in manners a help toward their flowering, but such behaviors are by no means guaranteed by mastering the manners themselves. In our own generations, we have seen masters of etiquette engineer extreme horrors. The chilling film *Closetland* gives an accurate fictional portrayal of what typically happens in educated and skilled political torture. With Philip Glass's music hauntingly in the background, Alan Rickman plays the torturer of a young woman author of children's fantasy books who is charged with using the metaphors of her books to criticize an anonymous regime. He is elegantly dressed in a grey suit, white shirt, and tie; he has impeccable manners, punctuated by the briefest blow here, a sudden piercing there, an electrode quickly shoved into the woman's orifices, but without giving up for more than a moment his exterior graciousness. His exquisite refinement is what makes the physical pain of the torture even more horrible. Countless real instances like this throughout the world are not the acts of individuals out of control in bloodlust, but highly educated manifestations of civilized, even scientific reason. Like the Holocaust, this kind of behavior requires sophisticated chemists and biologists, architectural and transportation engineers, psychiatrists, physicians, the kinds of professionals who staff our tax-supported School of the Americas in Georgia, the Harvard of schools for political torturers from favored allies around the world.

In tandem with Elias's work on manners, one might read the older Austrian Wilhelm Reich's *Mass Psychology of Fascism*, which offers a link between obsession with etiquette and political madness. Why, Reich asks, did the masses support Hitler? He argues that certain kinds of figurations produce a character that habitually and automatically looks outside the self for direction. If these figurations are effectively broadcast to the point where they seize hold of the imagination of the masses, they succeed in producing a habitual self-defeating identification of the masses with oppressive hierarchical power. Longing to belong to a world whose rules elude them, conditioned to strive to be something they do not understand, they lose contact with their own humane feelings for others: "At first it is only the idea of being like one's superior that stirs the mind of the employee or the official, but gradually, owing to his pressing material dependence, his whole person is refashioned in line with the ruling class. . . . He lives in materially reduced circumstances, but assumes gentlemanly postures on the surface, often to a ridiculous degree. He eats poorly and insufficiently, but attaches great importance to a 'decent' suit of clothes. A silk hat and dress coat become the material symbol of this character structure."[8] Reich argues that vast numbers of clear-thinking, good-hearted Germans who could see the horrors coming were unable to rally enough strength to stop them because they assumed that people are moved primarily by reason, when in fact it is the costumes, music, symbols, the hypnotic cadences of Hitler's speeches playing on primal fears:

> The revolutionary movement also failed to appreciate the importance of the seemingly irrelevant everyday habits, indeed, very often turned them to bad account. The lower middle-class bedroom suite, which the "rabble" buys as soon as he has the means, even if he is otherwise revolutionary minded; the consequent suppression of the wife, even if he is a Communist; the "decent" suit of clothes for Sunday; "proper" dance steps and a thousand other "banalities," have an incomparably greater reactionary influence when repeated day after day than thousands of revolutionary rallies and leaflets can ever hope to counterbalance. Narrow conservative life exercises a continuous influence, penetrates every facet of everyday life.[9]

The more dramatic and less intimate answer to my original question of why study the delicate subject of etiquette at this dark period in history rather than leaving it for Miss Manners[10] is that it is one factor in developing a contemporary mass psychology of fascism, stripping bare any illusions that people dressed in well-pressed suits and ties, behaving with easy courtesy and urbane humor cannot be vicious terrorists or devout thieves. Focus on minute rules of behavior can distract the gentleman or woman, and the communities under their sway, from the reasons for the rules, the nurturance of the human community. Like the pedophilic priest and his protector bishop schooled in the subtleties of Heribert Jone, well-mannered government, military, and global corporate executives have learned to shut off their feelings for the humans they are abusing, let alone the earth that supports us, no matter how much they apologize or shed tears of seeming grief.

Notes

1. Pierre Bourdieu, *Distinction: A Social Critique of the Judgment of Taste*, trans. Richard Nice (Cambridge, MA: Harvard University Press, 1984), p. 196.

2. Richard Rodriguez, *Brown: The Last Discovery of America* (New York: Viking Penguin, 2002), p. 113.

3. Bourdieu, *Distinction*, p. 103.

4. Norbert Elias, *The History of Manners: The Civilizing Process*, vol. 1, trans. Edmund Jephcott (New York: Pantheon, 1978), p. 262.

5. "Land of the Mean, Home of the Rage," *San Francisco Chronicle*, April 3, 2002, p. 2.

6. "The Penitential of Cummean," II, 6, *The Irish Penitentials*, ed. Ludwig Bieler (Oxford: Oxford University Press, 1963).

7. Rev. Heribert Jone, *Moral Theology*, "Englished and Adapted to the Laws and Customs of the United States of America" by Rev. Urban Adelman (Westminster, MD: Newman Press, 1963), p. 228.

8. Wilhelm Reich, *The Mass Psychology of Fascism*, trans. Vincent Carafagno (New York: Farrar, Straus & Giroux, 1970), p. 47.

9. Ibid., p. 69.

10. I followed Miss Manners's daily columns while working on this piece, and came to respect her. She is constantly reminding her questioners that it is not the rules that count, but respect and care for others.

CHAPTER SEVENTEEN

Make It Look Easy

Thoughts on Social Grace

KARMEN MACKENDRICK

I am inclined to think of etiquette as ethics in the diminutive—a set of smaller, perhaps less binding, terms of conduct. But this is not to suggest that etiquette is any less important than ethics; it functions, rather, much as mercy does in relation to justice—as a strange set of not-quite-rules, at once outside of laws and yet built into them, which makes the law not only more functional but somehow better. This is a somewhat roundabout way of suggesting that etiquette functions interpersonally (that is, in the realm of most versions of ethics) as a form of grace. The *Oxford English Dictionary* lists fifty-nine senses of "grace"; the term is certainly, if not ambiguous, at least highly polyvalent. But I suspect a common thread among senses of grace that may illuminate them for us, suggesting something of the place of grace in etiquette, the value of those small kindnesses and social flourishes that never reach the level of being required. The first thing I should like to undertake in this essay is to suggest that there is this common sense of grace stretching across the widely varying places in which we find it—a sense characterized by lightness, generosity, and responsiveness; understandable in terms of mobility, an odd proportionality, and (as I've suggested) a curious relation to laws or organizing principles. In so doing, I'll look at several senses of the term. My second objective is to observe that grace, which seems to lie outside and even to contradict those orderly laws, is in fact what makes them humanly possible—and that this is key to the relation of etiquette to ethics.

Perhaps oddly, we may begin considering grace with an observation on epistemology. It can be useful to conceive of knowledge in spatial terms; that is, to think of realms or spaces of knowing.[1] More precisely: imagine a *system* of knowing, a tabular knowledge, with all of the kinds of things there are to know neatly laid out in their proper places, in proper relation to one another. One fairly obvious point, at least once we begin to think about it, is that the kinds of things there are to know and the ways they are arranged are mutually implicated. When we know all the things there are to know, we know too how they fit together. Well, perhaps we don't know all of them, but we know where the spaces are and are confident we can fill them in (this, of course, is before the poststructuralism undermines that confidence altogether).

Of course, space implies not merely order but also direction. Like the tabular sense of space, the vectored sense implies at least the potential of completion. Spaces are there to be crossed, rather like roads before chickens. Space is a realm in which to order things, statically according to law; or it is distance to be crossed and thereby finished with. But neither mappable topography nor orderly container works as spatial image for grace—wherein space is elastic, reversible, and responsive. Here the relevant spatiality—even one as abstract as the epistemological—is surprisingly, delightfully open. This, ever so elegantly, messes up everything.

And in fact, among the things we know or suspect, depending upon our disciplinary backgrounds and intellectual dispositions, is that perfect systematicity is not only currently unavailable but in fact unattainable. One might react to this with frustration, maybe even abandoning whatever epistemological project might be at stake. But I recall an article I read some months ago in the *New York Times*—I fear I did not anticipate writing the current chapter and so did not save the article—in which a scientist, I believe an astronomer, responded to the possibility of knowledge's being not only unsystematizable but incompletable with great satisfaction. She (or he) said, in effect, what a depressing possibility it would be to think that we could know it all, ever be done with the pleasures of searching. If we can't know it all—not by virtue of sheer quantity of information but by the very nature of knowing—there is always more to draw us forth. Thus in incompletion is the seductive possibility of motion, a possibility here understood as at least indefinite, and possibly infinite.

This is not to deny the pleasures of order or of knowing things. And the possibility of grace, which I think is precisely what's inherent in that openness, doesn't contradict those pleasures. Instead, this first, intellectual variant of grace is that which, belonging to some particular order of knowing (the openness of one discipline is not precisely that of another), nonetheless goes beyond what is given to knowledge. If knowing it all is impossible, then at the same time the possibilities for coming to know may be infinite—even though necessarily laid out by disciplinary rules. The rules tell us where the spaces are, and the spaces don't await filling so much as open the possibility for further movement.

Moving into a more common sense of the term, suppose we take space literally, as a realm in which we can dance, move about, respond to chance, so that movement across space is not straight but back and forth, distance both overcome and sustained. Such grace may be understood as a mutuality of response between spaces and bodies. When one dances, space presents itself as elastic, malleable. It opens, inviting the stretch of limb; it enwraps, making even the still body the center of anywhere. Between dancers, grace is found in the added possibilities of bodies moving together, making new formations, new entries and wraptures, possible. Without this possibility, we cannot move: even the most efficient crossing of space demands some interaction with it. Thus tabular containment gives way to rearrangement, and the distance is neither crossed and finished nor left indifferently uncrossed. Dance draws space around the body and extends the body into space.

Social grace, in parallel, is drawn to the happiness of another without denying the discontinuity of the other from the self. Social grace is a dance with other persons; one sees and one takes the chance to add small pleasures, small beauties to the interpersonal space between. In making the other at ease, perhaps even happy, one draws her toward oneself; one is drawn to her as in invitation to these small graces, these ornaments on what is necessary in interaction. Certainly there are rules; as in many disciplines and dance forms, there are more rules than nature would give us by far, and more rules even than ethics demands. Yet the intent of these rules is the ease and pleasure of knowing, rather than the malicious marking of the unknowing; they must always be adaptable, fluid. Etiquette demands both the rules and the spaces.

The elasticity of space means that one can play with space itself, drawing and being drawn; its reversibility means that either of these movements implies the other. The space of chance and the response to chance form one another. Grace moves between chance and response, a movement both of acceptance and of possibility, creating the possibilities it accepts precisely by making space for them. This opening of and movement in space makes the space itself possible; the motility that might threaten systems is necessary to their very possibility.

Again, grace—entailing a sense of the possibilities of spaces and of what to do with them, how to evoke as well as how to respond—demands rules. It would be difficult, for example, to be truly delighted by the inexhaustible possibilities of scientific knowledge unless one already had some of that knowledge—and, more importantly, some grasp of the methods by which it might be attained and understood, ways of knowing that might tell one why a body of knowledge is not solely a series of facts to be ordered and completed. One form of the grace of knowledge is just this openness, this inviting quality that ways of knowing present to those who have made those ways part of themselves. Rules serve similarly to train us in other graces. Someone trained in dance is not necessarily graceful (as I ruefully attest from personal experience). But the training does multiply our awareness of space as open to possibilities. The rules of etiquette, perhaps counterintuitively, likewise make ease and pleasure in interaction possible.

Context, however, is key in every one of these cases. Drawing and infolding space can be graceful, but it can be important and graceful to leave space open, as well. I am not the least graceful if I move into a space that has no room for movement, imposing myself on the overcrowded.[2] Grace only works if it works with what there is, even in remaking it. A graceful body responds differently to the space open to it and to the touch of what coinhabits that space. The socially gracious respond to others; they interest themselves in the comfort of others. All those elaborate concerns with rightly ordered introductions and properly utilized forks fit here too: they are matters of style[3] and of ease. One's knowledge of what to do—in fact, the very existence of a proper something to do—and a good sense of context make for social graces, and for the possibility of opening easy spaces for others to move. We are drawn to what is graceful; we want to share in its motion. Grace in its very responsivity is compelling; it draws and part of its attraction is precisely that it is attracted, not to us perhaps but to some facet of the world, in a confident acceptance of possibility that already constitutes an invitation.

There is a curious and important unproductivity at work here. Despite the upsurge of interest in international business etiquette, grace remains inefficient and unproductive, gratuitous in more than the etymological sense. Efficiency means working with laws, by which results follow expectedly and we are enabled to get on with things. The responsiveness of grace is one reason it can't come under law (even though law needs it)—and a reminder that rules (as in etiquette) aren't laws (as in ethics). What is graceful will always depend upon which one—which one moves, which space is opened, which responds, which is responded to. To move gracefully across a bare stage entails an altogether different set of bodily motions than to move gracefully through a crowded dining room. To respond to the possibilities of biochemical research demands something other than detailed knowledge of archaeology. Social grace too must respond, to the person, to the situation, even to oneself (it is gracious, when one has strep throat, to avoid human contact altogether). It always carries with it the possibility of redirection; graceful movement is always light. And without this lightness, without what lies necessarily outside law and disorders the tables thereof, law itself becomes impossible.

What is graceful is always disproportionate[4] in being unnecessary, inefficient, unproductive, and unmerited. Yet it is also perfectly proportioned, moving to perfect its space and form possibilities of beauty. Here too we see its double character: not fitting into any order, yet making that order possible—humanly, liveably possible rather than merely conceptually possible.

These two senses, that of openness and that of unmeritedness, are not so far apart. Law keeps order; grace exceeds it.[5] Grace retains the character of the gift, given gratuitously. Emmanuel Levinas writes of "a generosity nourished by the desired [which] is a relationship that is not the disappearance of distance, not a bringing together"[6] but also a movement toward, not apart.[7] To insist upon giving is not generous; redirection is lightness in action. There is a lot of etiquette in Levinasian ethics.

And so, oddly, grace is wholly unjustified; to justify one must point to reasons, grounds, causes, laws. Pure formalism (ethical or legal) is not only inhuman, it is unliving, neither human nor divine: Friedrich

Nietzsche notes, "If God wished to become an object of love, he should have given up judging and justice first of all; a judge, even a merciful judge, is no object of love."[8] In religious terms, grace is concerned not to justify but to redeem,[9] and perhaps it redeems our social spaces as well, beyond the rigid ordering of ethical behavior.

So I would argue that etiquette is precisely the element of ethics that involves grace. Our eagerness to have its rules right is reflected in that remarkable proliferation of intercultural etiquette books (especially but not exclusively for business use) earlier mentioned. The idea is that people have rules to follow in interaction, rules that tell us what to do, and the better we know these the easier it will be to get along (and presumably turn a profit, which point I leave aside as not being of quite such direct concern to the present project). This gives the impression that etiquette is a kind of knowing that fits best into the tabular model, where the rules are set forth in a neat and orderly system and anxiety is reduced by the confidence that knowing brings.

But the point of etiquette's rules is to smooth ethical spaces, not to foreclose them; to both ease and to ornament, to impress but not negatively; rather, as with physical grace, to please.[10] Social graces can never be ethically required, yet are more than irrelevant frills.

The key is this: in the possibility of grace, which disrupts or lies outside of (which disruptively opens the very possibility of an outside to) any system, that nonetheless makes a system possible. The law alone is unlivable[11]—this is a commonplace criticism of Kantian ethics in particular, as Kant virtuously attempts to provide an ethical option for every possible action. Without the grace of mercy, no system of justice could remain in act; in fact, without grace, no system of law is ever just. I do not mean simply that we would be unhappy under it; I mean that it would be impossible, incomplete to the point of insufficiency (no system can contain every possible circumstance and variant, yet no set of circumstances is identical to any other, nor any judgement just which leaves them wholly out of account). This openness is likewise fundamental to the possibility of ethics. Without the possibility of new conceptual spaces, rethinkings, no advance in the systematic sciences is possible: rigidified knowledge destroys learning; in fact, knowledge itself, through which our learning must move if we are to come to know it, is impossible. Without the possibility of dance's topographic seduction, no space permits bodily movement; even the most efficiently disciplined movement must contain some small sinuous possibility if it is to move at all—otherwise, the transition is impossible, as perfect efficiency would have us arrive at point B from point A without any need to slide between them.

Ethics by itself is no way to live. Without etiquette, which is not ethics, no system of ethical rules can hold: ethics is about human behavior, and we cannot continue to interact without grace notes. It would be absurd to impose with the stringency of an ethical requirement the small, useless gestures that make up the social graces. We have all known, surely, people whose ethical character was unarguable and unshakeable, who were yet very difficult to cope with as human beings, because their systems left them no room for interactions which were unnecessary and situationally responsive—those who are so busy being good they have nothing left with which to be gracious.

We might say that grace is the avoidance of systematic rigidity, of stiffness, perhaps. It is the ability to keep manners from becoming mannered. One must always, my overworked ballet teacher used to insist, make it look easy. So too says Count Baldassare Castiglione in his sixteenth-century guidelines for courtiers. Listed in "A Breef Rehersall of the Chiefe Conditions and Qualitites in a Courtier" is the requirement "To do his feates with a slight, as though they were rather naturally in him, then learned with studye: and use a Reckelesness to cover art, without minding greatly what he hath in hand, to a mans seeminge."[12] So too says Miss Manners, who indeed regards etiquette in certain senses a matter of ease: "It is a great deal easier to settle conflicts on the superficial ground of manners than to fight them out as matters of morals."[13] "Make it look easy," probably a command to lie, can never be an ethical imperative. It belongs rightly in the diminutive, to etiquette. But without it, our ethics is no ethics, no way to behave, no ethos by which a human being can—or by which, at any rate, any civilized human being ought—to live.

Notes

1. In *The Order of Things,* Michel Foucault writes of spaces of knowledge, spaces both opened by and opening the way for certain forms of discourse. It is largely to his discussion there that the present remarks are indebted.

See Michel Foucault, *The Order of Things: An Archaeology of the Human Sciences* (New York: Vintage Books, reissue), 1994.

2. Miss Manners points out this contextuality in her discussion of good manners in an urban setting, where in regard to others on the street one ought to "Observe the condition that they are invisible, because it is impossible to live in a city where you are constantly being required to participate in social encounters not of your own choosing." In small towns, of course, this politeness comes across as rude or hostile. Judith Martin (Miss Manners), *Basic Training* (New York: Crown Books, 2000), p. 49.

3. See Judith Martin (Miss Manners), *Miss Manners' Guide for the Turn of the Millennium* (New York: Fireside Books, 1990), p. 140.

4. As St. Thomas Aquinas says, grace is always "exceeding what is commensurate with nature." *Summa Theologiae,* in *Aquinas on Nature and Grace,* in *The Library of Christian Classics*, vol. 11, ed. and trans. A. M. Fairweather (Philadelphia: Westminster Press, 1954), Q114.A.5.

5. See, for example, John 1:17, Romans 5:20–21.

6. Emmanuel Levinas, *Totality and Infinity,* trans. Alphonso Lingis (Pittsburgh: Duquesne University Press, 1969), p. 34.

7. Ibid, p. 62.

8. Friedrich Nietzsche, *The Gay Science,* trans. Walter Kaufmann (New York: Vintage Books, 1974), sec. 140.

9. See, for example, Galatians 5:4. All biblical citations are from *The Oxford Catholic Study Bible,* multiple authors and translators (New York: Oxford University Press, 1990.)

10. This is an old tradition; the *Book of the Courtier* demands not only those graces we already consider social, but skills in music, dance, athleticism, languages and games. Count Baldassare Castiglinone, *The Book of the Courtier* (Rutland, VT: Everyman's Library, 1994), 367f.

11. On which compare Maurice Blanchot, *The Step Not Beyond*: "The law kills. Death is always the horizon of the law: if you do this, you will die. . . . Grace does not save from death, but it effaces the mortal condemnation in making of the *saltus mortalis* . . . the careless motion that concerns itself neither with condemnation nor with salvation, being the gift that has no weight." *The Step Not Beyond,* trans. Lycette Nelson (Albany: State University of New York Press, 1992), p. 25.

12. Castiglinone, *The Book of the Courtier,* p. 367.

13. Judith Martin, *Guide to the Turn of the Millennium*, p. 152.

CHAPTER EIGHTEEN

Etiquette and Missile Defense

ROBIN TRUTH GOODMAN

From a widespread appeal to family values as an answer to perceived social dissolution,[1] to a repeated call to end the bipartisan bickering in Washington, to the press's disapprobation of negative add campaigns without defining what counts as negative, to the current mainstreaming of the belief that social and political criticism of policy is both uncivil and unpatriotic, to suggesting that character-training programs be implemented in schools as the solution to youth violence, even to the culture wars on canon, the mainstream media have made etiquette newsworthy. The current popular obsession with wayward behaviors marks a growing sense of insecurity that finds its parallels in an economy where futures are uneasy,[2] where the social net, labor and environmental rights, and protections against the business cycle have disappeared,[3] where jobs are flexible and short-lived.

Like behavior, the market is disorderly. The unruly 1960s has led, right-wing moralizers would argue, to behavioral disarray, with presidents who smoke pot and get blow jobs, and the civility of a former era of integrity, respect, and sexual propriety needs to be restored. Some have argued that terrorism has resulted from this mismanagement of values, either because the terrorists themselves have not learned the proper behavior of tolerance, or because changing academic practices—feminism, gay and lesbian studies, postmodernism, cultural studies, multiculturalism—have incited divine wrath and punishment. The democratization of culture and the multiculturalization of curricula testify to an incipient moral anarchy, such pundits claim, furthered by a dissipation of religious values, a loss of community, an adherence to relativism, and an unraveling of standards. Lost are the social institutions that, such nostalgic dreamers claim, fixed meaning. Disrupted is a time when everyone and everything had its place.

The irony is that the same people who are calling for a lessening of state interventions in the economy are also advocating an increase in state interventions on the body. As state sovereignty is being dismantled by increased capital influx and influence, the neo-con right calls for a return to traditional values, more state regulations on marriage, the development of abstinence-only programs in schools, and the like. Part of this comes out of an ideological assault on the poor as the causes of their own problems, making poor people's behavior seem not a product of cuts in supports or growing unemployment but rather a dangerous social cancer that needs discipline and threatens to unravel the "good values" of yesteryear.

Etiquette has been made to stand for a particular conglomerate of seemingly contradictory meanings within a neoliberal culture. It responds to a threat of chaos, a panic over the idea that values and codes of understanding have become terrifyingly uprooted as controls and codes of understanding have been happily unmoored, a running-for-cover in an age which seems to be reveling in the end to governmentality:

> Behind the expanding insecurity of the millions dependent on selling their labour, lurks the absence of a potent and effective agency which could, with will and resolve, make their plight less insecure. Fifty years ago, in the Bretton Woods era (now ancient history), when they thought of the way global affairs were going, people in the know spoke of *universal rules* and their *universal enforcement*—of something we ought to do and will do eventually; today they speak of *globalization*—something that *happens to us* for reasons about which we may surmise, even get to know, but can hardly control.[4]

Growing stronger is a widespread fear that the weakening of the nation-state has undermined universal morality, creating uncertainties and an unpredictable future, alongside a firm conviction that if people were only left to themselves, without the state's strong-armed imposition of immoral texts and cultural differences, they would behave appropriately in the universal interest and according to protocol. Yet contradictorily, particularly under the Bush administration, the freedom of choice promised in market freedoms and deregulation can only be enforced on people through threats of military punishment or longer prison sentences exhibiting that the state sovereignty, severely damaged through market reforms, can still appear strong and functional (even when, as mostly happens, these measures do not accomplish what they set out to accomplish, do not diminish crime, stop people from having sex, or stop the proliferation of weapons of mass destruction when projects for their development exist in the first place).

This chapter reads through an editorial page of *The Wall Street Journal* in order to explore how the talk about etiquette is producing a sense of radical chaos which, in turn, creates an uncertainty about the state's role in routing out the immorality and violence of the free market. Etiquette represents the ever-growing demand for regrounding, to the point of inflicting punishment and pain. At the same time that it depends on a faith in radical freedom where people act solely on the principles of preleviathan free will and self-determination—where, in short, they have choice—it demands, too, that free will and self-determination adhere completely to the moral guidelines, rules, and protections of what is assumed naturally right and good, the law.

For example, just yesterday I was walking back from the gym when I saw a middle-aged white man walking toward me. He was screaming at the top of his lungs, noticeable because he was breaking all the rules of etiquette, whatever those might be on a New York City street, in the Village, on a beautiful spring day. I stopped to stare at him. He looked straight at me, and screamed, "The light says WALK!" as though it were an imperative. Just as he was dismissing convention, he was seeking an authoritative power to replace it, calling in the state to do so, phrasing the desire for restored meaning as both a subjunctive conditional and a command.

Much academic writing has considered the role of etiquette, specifically as it puts in place a consensual, inarticulable, class-based code of behaviors embedded in the social relations of production under capitalism. Most notably, Pierre Bourdieu has theorized how "cultural capital," or habits of the body, is instrumental in maintaining socialized class differences and power domination.[5] According to Nikolas Rose, during World War II the field of professional psychology discovered that disciplining attitudes through group behaviorism would lift morale, and this finding was translated into factory management, where the "subjective commitments of the worker were to be incorporated within the objectives of the firm."[6] "At work," explains Rose, "unconscious conflicts, unsuccessful repression of thwarted instincts, and unexpressed emotions could be found at the root of many industrial problems. . . . The question of industrial efficiency was, at root, one of mental hygiene—the diagnosis and treatment of the minor mental troubles of the manager of the worker before they produced major and disabling problems; the promotion of correct habits in light of a knowledge of the nature of mental life; the organization of the factory itself so as to minimize the production of symptoms of emotional and mental instability and enhance adjustment."[7] Etiquette was one of the ways which management used to get labor to identify with the needs of management during industrialization. Richard Sennett has explored the public performance of class replacing sumptuary laws of dress and comportment as critical masses congregated with strangers in the growing urban centers of the eighteenth- and nineteenth-century western Europe. As a man was no longer recognized familiarly and his reputation no longer built out of his family name, vestments, and ancestry, gestures served to codify strength of character and trustworthiness.

Nancy Armstrong has discussed how, with the rise of the popular press and leading toward the advent of the novel, eighteenth-century conduct books for women "enabled a coherent idea of the middle class to take shape,"[8] producing a sense of female domestic propriety, taste, virtue, leisure, and privacy as separated from the economic and the public. Ann Laura Stoler has shown how eighteenth-century manuals of conduct and child rearing were seen to preserve a proper white culture as the culture of governance and superiority in colonial Malaysia.

> I use the Indies to illustrate . . . how a cultivation of the European self (and specifically a Dutch bourgeois identity) was affirmed in the proliferating discourses around pedagogy, parenting, children's sexuality, servants, and tropical hygiene: micro-sites where designations of racial membership were subject to gendered

> appraisals and where "character," "good breeding," and proper rearing were implicitly raced. These discourses do more than prescribe suitable behavior; they locate how fundamentally bourgeois identity has been tied to notions of being "European" and being "white" and how sexual prescriptions served to secure and delineate the authentic, first-class citizens of the nation-state.[9]

Stoler argues that such instructional regulation was the precursor to Foucault's history of the disciplined body in *The History of Sexuality*.[10] Clearly, etiquette is about class, and particularly with maintaining recognizable and differentiable bodily practices and stable structures of knowing and belonging. Etiquette serves to manage working populations—both on the international and national levels—by producing cultural aspirations to middle-class status: "To differentiate oneself is always, by the same token, to bring into play the total order of differences, which is, from the first, the product of the total society and inevitably exceeds the scope of the individual. In the very act of scoring his points in the order of differences, each individual maintains that order, and therefore condemns himself only ever to occupy a relative position within it. Each individual experiences his differential social gains as absolute gains; he does not experience the structural constraint which means that positions change, but the order of differences remains."[11] Historically and culturally, etiquette substitutes for ritual in scripting a certainty of meaning onto a newly secularized world filled with ambiguities. Contrasted with, on the one hand, elaborate displays of adornment of the old aristocracy and, on the other, the public bodies of newly industrial laborers, bourgeois etiquette reads the inner moral rectitude defining middle-class sensibilities transparently through staged public uprightness and bodily management. This chapter shows how these values which have historically defined the social place of etiquette are presently working ideologically within the free market imaginary to redefine the role of the state within the politics of contemporary culture. Additionally, I suggest that etiquette reveals these traditional class, race, and gender exclusions within right-wing ideological rhetoric about the future of free market democratization.

Nowadays, it is popular to talk about the loss of etiquette, and to link such loss to what is seen as the dismantling of the foundations of culture, the restructuring of what counts as knowledge, and the redefining of citizens' values through extension of what gets included as canonical text. "We are witnessing the proletarianization of the dominant minority,"[12] announces Charles Murray, a fellow at the American Enterprise Institute and cowriter of the contentious study *The Bell Curve*, in a *Wall Street Journal* editorial on February 6, 2001.[13] In a signed editorial entitled "Prole Models," Murray is writing in the *Journal* to protest the popular white singer Eminem's consideration for a Grammy Award, evoking the responses of such defenders of elite culture as Lynne Cheney,[14] the vice president's wife, with her long career of voicing opposition to all creative expression not lined up with her moralizing on the preservation of ethical values through the preservation of canon.[15] Murray worries here that the Eminem event portends a culture of decadence signifying civilization's demise.

The parallels of Murray's claims with Nazi doctrine on decadent art do not need elaboration. Murray is, in fact, arguing that civilization is upheld through the manners of a white elite. Eminem, for him, represents the emptying out of elite codes of conduct, as intellectual trendsetters imitate the conduct of "trash." In other words, white values are endangered as they absorb the "violence, cheating and vulgarity"[16] of the underclass, in this case clearly, though not explicitly, of black rappers and hip-hop.

According to Murray, the result will be, following a long line of colonialist warnings, the loss of propriety in women.[17] Women, Murray contends, have started behaving "sluttish,"[18] causing divorces and illegitimacy, because they have adopted the social anarchism of those Murray is referring to as the proletariate: "As late as 1960, sleeping with one's boyfriend was still a lower-class thing to do. Except in a few sophisticated circles, a woman of the elites did it furtively, and usually with the person she expected to marry."[19] Murray does not fret over the sexual behaviors of men, though he never explains why men's sexual acts do not threaten civilization. Instead, men's public social postures are scrutinized. Murray assesses men's business practices, nostalgically lamenting the loss of the cult of the American gentleman, where "one was brave, loyal and true," not asking for legal contracts but instead trusting an agreement on a handshake.

In his descriptions of the current crisis of culture, Murray does not mention that both Eminem and the advent of the prole itself are not products of the contagious virus of inner city styles, but rather of elite corporations that promote and profit from vulgarity and violence. The culture that Eminem's manners have absorbed does not arise like a plague from the dregs of industrial workers' cultural depravity but rather from a broad-based selling of violence as a politics of enforcement for free-market policies and a socialization process that categorizes social place through habits of the body and of speech. Unlike Murray, however, other contributors to the *Journal*'s editorial page recognize this. For them, Europeans are complaining about American violent and vulgar behavior just as right-wing warriors like Murray are criticizing the cultures of rap and hip-hop. "In 1960," Murray complains, "four-letter words were still unknown in public discourse. Among the elites, they were used sparingly even in private. The use of vulgar language among adults was *declassé*. . . . Technical mastery of craft is not at issue here, just as it is not at issue for 'South Park' or the average MTV video. At issue is the cultural significance of choosing to approve the vulgar and the illiterate, both of which used to be classic indicators of the underclass."[20] Meanwhile, further down on the page, in an article entitled "Why Are Europeans Still Fighting Missile Defense?" Kenneth Adelman[21] chides the Europeans for reproaching the American debasement of language: "Europeans faulted President Reagan for his 'harsh rhetoric' toward Moscow, such as calling the evil empire 'the evil empire.' "[22] Celebrated on the same page as it is condemned for its manifest cultural depravity, language vulgarity here stands in for adherence to the free market and to unilateralism.

Adelman's commentary goes on to appropriate, in the figure of "American," the uncivilized cultural codes which Murray, in the editorial just above it, attributes to the impolite underclass, to black culture, to degeneracy and criminality, and to the primitive. Murray treats the impolitic of violence and the loss of outrage at poverty as signs of degeneracy, a vacuum in elite codes of behavior, and, contingently, a sign of civilization's demise: "Within the underclass, the vacuum has been filled by a distinctive, separate code. Call it a thug code: Take what you want, respond violently to anyone who antagonizes you, gloat when you win, despise courtesy as weakness, . . . take pride in cheating, deceiving, or exploiting successfully. The world of hip-hop is where the code is openly embraced."[23] At the same time, Kenneth Adelman gloatingly rebukes the Europeans for openly opposing U.S. allowances for violence, exploitation, discourtesy, and disrespect for the poor: "European leaders didn't relish American badgering to boost their defense budgets—which stayed shamefully low compared to U.S. outlays. And, of course, European leaders couldn't stand Reaganomics, with its bold plans to trim taxes and cut wasteful government programs, or its votes against the United Nations regulatory schemes."[24] While condemning the popularization of violence, such anxieties over etiquette justify building cultures of violence to protect and spread American lifestyles while chastising the Europeans for not allowing us our military fun.

In the current administration, missile defense has been central to the building of Secretary of Defense Donald Rumsfeld's career in both the private and the public sectors since the Ford administration: the Rumsfeld Commission had announced in 1998 that both North Korea and Iran, and probably Iraq, would be able to develop long-range missiles by 2010. As reported in a post-September 11 *U.S. News & World Report* article,

> It was a routine evening in the control room deep inside Cheyenne Mountain, near Colorado Springs, Colo., where U.S. Space Command keeps its eye on the heavens. Then, just after 9 p.m., alarm lights began flashing. Analysts scrambled. A computerized wall-size map showed the cause—U.S. spy satellites had detected the heat pattern of a rocket launch from North Korea. . . . The rocket carried a "third-stage" booster that could have lifted it into deep space and, once there, to U.S. territory. . . . It hardly mattered that the text was a failure. . . . That launch, on Aug. 31, 1998, revolutionized the missile defense debate. It effectively changed the question from *whether* to build a missile defense system to *how* to build it.[25]

Though the subject seemed to fall out of public scrutiny when Clinton declared a moratorium on testing due to the failures of previous tests, it was revived again after the terrorist attacks of September 11, 2001, when President Bush himself—against both intelligence and Pentagon assessments—declared that the attacks proved the need for Star Wars-type nuclear protections (when, in fact, they proved quite the opposite: the need for better intelligence on the part of the executive branch and protections against conventional aggressions. Even the *U.S. News & World Report* team suggests, "What enemy needs intercontinental ballistic missiles . . . when he can use commercial airliners as weapons of mass destruction?"). Though talk of missile defense seemed to dissipate during the Afghanistan invasion, it reemerged when plans and preparations for an invasion of Iraq were escalating (even though the situation in Iraq again "proves" that missile defense need not be on the top of anyone's Christmas list). This return to the talk of Missile Defense has been accompanied by an explosive growth in deficit spending during the current Bush administration alongside large cuts, throughout the United States, in social spending. In other words, the talk of missile defense underlies the bolstering of the military and corporate defense subsidies at the expense of the public. Yet, according to Adelman, the Europeans need to quit stalling and copy the American system. Adelman's picturing of the market builds on Murray's sense of hip-hop thuggery, and Adelman's thirst for deregulation is expressed as a desire for the loss of etiquette which Murray deems as the depravity of African-American culture. Ironically, both writers promote antiblack agendas: Adelman calls for an appropriation of inner-city culture to be used against both people of the inner city (cuts in public supports) and Third World nations while Murray deplores and rejects black culture outright and advocates its further ghettoization (if not extermination) in the name of safety.

Unlike Murray, Adelman believes that the snooty Europeans are better off when they imitate the much less uptight military posturing of the Americans (exactly the kind of imitating that Murray fears) and stop their preachy moral superiority by supporting missile defense and free markets. Having realized the mistakes of their initial hesitation, he observes, "European governments of all stripes have succumbed to some degree of Reaganomics, though none (of course) accept the label."[26] Though it is clear now that Reaganomics serviced the rich and impoverished the poor,[27] and that the Europeans were slow to adopt its policies because of their long and popular traditions of social democracy and welfare states (under which, most would argue, most people were better off),[28] Adelman claims that European resistance to free markets and missile defense stems from a cultural stagnation due to their reluctance to change and their loss of outrage against poverty. Change would mean imitating American behaviors: "Deploying a serious missile defense system is something new. Novelty constitutes something of a cultural divide: Americans embrace most anything new, while

Europeans eschew almost anything new."[29] In other words, like the Eminem that Murray lambastes, the Americans are introducing, through free markets and missile defense, new styles of governance and new claims to power, and the stodgy Europeans need to relinquish their old habits of propriety, declass, and embrace the novel violence.

In making an argument in favor of a missile defense system and the free markets it would protect, Adelman is calling in the state to defend, in the name of American values and the preservation of civilization, the very types of behaviors which Murray, on the very same page, calls in the state and the law to oust in the name of American values and the preservation of civilization.[30] Murray reprimands the defunct state itself for inducing the destructive values, suggesting that only with a reformed and revitalized state would the healthy morals and habits of the elite return. "I urge," he writes, "that the following statement is not, at bottom, a partisan one: Bill Clinton's presidency, in both its conduct and in the reactions to that conduct, was a paradigmatic example of elites that have been infected by 'the sickness of proletarianization.' The survival of our culture requires that we somehow contrive to get well."[31] The unclean state here causes the demise in morals and the declassing of the elite. Though unspecified, it is safe to assume that Murray is not reproaching Clinton for his reprehensible behavior in testing a missile defense system, imitating the prole vulgarity of playing with guns and dangerous explosives which Adelman praises.[32] Murray restricts Clintonian signs of decadence to the undisciplined body rather than to geopolitical injustice and economic redistribution schemes that funnel money to the most wealthy, reproducing the underclasses.

On the very same page, Adelman intimates that the free market ("Reaganomics") is what builds a vulgar culture in which American technological superiority and mastery reside. Whereas Murray yearns for regulations on the vulgar identities that the free market produces in celebrities like Eminem, Adelman revels in these identities, lauding them as the foundation of a specifically American ingenuity. Whereas Murray calls for some kind of authority to protect the elite body against the vulgar freedom of the market, Adelman wishes for such elite checks on the vulgarities of market freedom to disappear.

An ambiguity arises here about whether, according to the *Wall Street Journal*, etiquette is the treasured possession of a deserving few, as

Murray believes, or it is easily acquired by anyone with a will, as Adelman professes, or whether etiquette should be jettisoned as an antiquated reminder of a disciplinary state (only acceptable when it disciplines others), as Adelman seems to imply, or it will redeem the future which is falling into decay. Etiquette is culturally wielded as a promise of social mobility: higher class positions are as easy to come by as learning word inflections and correcting eyebrow movements, for example. In 1926, Upton Sinclair presented etiquette as a problematic sign of an open economy which anyone could access. In his novel *Oil!*, the Groartys find oil on their small plot of land, and Mrs. Groarty immediately goes out to buy "The Ladies' Guide: A Practical Handbook of Gentility" at a discount, spending some of her future oil earnings, and she leaves it displayed on the coffee table of her tiny home for all to see. However, right away, something in the instructions does not fit: "Mrs. Groarty had had no clothing suitable for the occasion, so she had been driven down-town in her husband's Ford, and had spent some of her oil expectations for an evening gown of yellow satin. Now she felt embarrassed because there was not enough of it, either at the top where her arms and bosom came out, or below, where her fat calves were encased in embroidered silk stockings, so thin as to seem almost nothing. It was what they were wearing, the saleswomen had assured her; and Mrs. Groarty was grimly set upon being one of them."[33] The novel returns to the Groartys in its final pages, and still "The Ladies' Guide, a Practical Handbook of Gentility" is on the coffee table, though now faded. Alongside is a pile of legal documents testifying to the Groartys' efforts to acquire any kind of profit from the oil found on their own land, but to no avail: "The Groartys had entered a community agreement, and then withdrawn from it and entered a smaller one: then they had leased to Sliper and Wilkins, and been sold by those 'lease hounds' to a syndicate; and this syndicate had been plundered by a man whom Mrs. Groarty described as the worst skunk of them all, and he had gone and got a lot of claims and liens against the property, and actually, people were trying to take some money away from the Groartys now, though they had never got one cent out of the well."[34] Passing into ever more private and exclusive holdings, etiquette gives a false sense of possibility to everyone that all people can integrate within a social contract of middle-class prosperity which ultimately excludes many, releases violence, diminishes opportunities, disenfranchises, and discriminates. As Sinclair's novel suggests in contrast to the *Wall Street Journal*, it could be different.

Notes

1. For a more in-depth discussion of how this works to blame social problems on private individuals, see Robin Truth Goodman and Kenneth J. Saltman, *Strange Love: Or, How We Learn to Stop Worrying and Love the Market* (Lanham, MD: Rowman & Littlefield, 2002).

2. "National governments find themselves in environments not merely of risk but of radical uncertainty. In economic theory, risk means a situation in which the costs of various actions can be known with reasonable probability, while uncertainty is a situation in which such probabilities cannot be known." John Grey, *False Dawn: The Delusions of Global Capitalism* (New York: New Press, 1998), p. 74.

3. "The incomes of most Americans have stagnated. Even for those whose incomes have risen economic risk has increased perceptibly. Most Americans dread a mid-life economic dislocation from which—they suspect—they may never recover. Few think now in terms of a lifelong vocation. Many expect, not without reason, that their incomes may fall in future." John Grey, *False Dawn*, p. 111.

4. Zygmunt Bauman, *In Search of Politics* (Stanford, CA: Stanford University Press, 1999), p. 20.

5. For example, "Symbolic power cannot be exercised without the contribution of those who undergo it and who only undergo it because they *construct* it as such. But instead of stopping at this statement (as constructivism in its idealist, ethnomethodological or other forms does) one has also to take note of and explain the social construction of the cognitive structures which organize acts of construction of the world and its powers. It then becomes clear that, far from being the conscious, free, deliberate act of an isolated 'subject,' this practical construction is itself the effect of power, durably embedded in the bodies of the dominated in the form of schemes of perception and dispositions (to admire, respect, love, etc.) which *sensitize* them to certain symbolic manifestations of power." Pierre Bourdieu, *Masculine Domination*, trans. Richard Nice (Stanford, CA: Stanford University Press, 2001), p. 40.

6. Nikolas Rose, *Governing the Soul: The Shaping of the Private Self* (London: Free Association Books, 1989, 1999), p. 73.

7. Ibid., p. 69.

8. Nancy Armstrong, "The Rise of the Domestic Woman," in *Feminisms: An Anthology of Literary Theory and Criticism*, ed. Robyn R. Warhol and

Diane Price Herndl (New Brunswick, NJ: Rutgers University Press, 1993), p. 897.

9. Ann Laura Stoler, *Race and the Education of Desire: Foucault's* History of Sexuality *and the Colonial Order of Things* (Durham and London: Duke University Press, 1995), p. 11.

10. "Eventually the entire social body was provided with a 'sexual body,' although this was accomplished in different ways and using different tools. . . . It is at this point that one notes the introduction of a new differentiating element. Somewhat similar to the way in which, at the end of the eighteenth century, the bourgeoisie set its own body and its precious sexuality against the valorous blood of the nobles, at the end of the nineteenth century it sought to redefine the specific character of its sexuality relative to that of others, subjecting it to a thorough differential review, and tracing a dividing line that would set apart and protect its body. . . . The theory of repression would compensate for this general spread of the deployment of sexuality by its analysis of the differential interplay of taboos according to the social classes." Michel Foucault, *The History of Sexuality: An Introduction,* vol. 1, trans. Robert Hurley (New York: Vintage Books, 1978), pp. 127–128.

11. Jean Baudrillard, *The Consumer Society* (London: Sage, 1998), p. 61.

12. Charles Murray, "Prole Models," *Wall Street Journal,* February 6, 2001, p. A18.

13. I would like to thank my student, Devorah Stern, from Queens College of the City University of New York, for bringing this article to my attention.

14. "Lynne Cheney, not usually known as a feminist, singled out Eminem as a 'violent misogynist' at a Senate committee hearing on violence and entertainment. Eminem's lyrics, she argued, pose a danger to children, 'the intelligent fish swimming in a deep ocean,' where the media are 'waves that penetrate through the water and through our children . . . again and again from this direction and that.' Pretty sick stuff. Maybe it comes from listening to *Marshall Mathers,* but maybe it's the real Lynne Cheney, of lesbian pulp-fiction fame, finally standing up." Richard Kim, "Eminiem—Bad Rap?" March 5, 2001, retrieved from http://www.thenation.com/doc.mhtml?i=20010305&s=kim).

15. *The Nation* describes her thus: "The right-wing warrior who used her post at the NEH to fight the Republican culture wars of the eighties; the ideologue who, after continuing to serve as head of the NEH through the Bush years, resigned following Clinton's election and moved to the American Enterprise Institute to write Op-Ed hit pieces, and later co-hosted the now-defunct CNN show *Crossfire Sunday*—she was the one 'on the right.' . . . At the NEH, Cheney . . . perfected a method of attack that depends more on hyperbole than accuracy. One of her first campaigns was aimed at a PBS series, *The Africans,* that she called 'propaganda' because it described Africa's historic

problems as a consequence of European exploitation. She insisted on removing the NEH's name from the credits and refused to approve endowment publicity funding for the series—actions she termed 'a defense of free speech.' The controversy enabled her to seize the limelight for her own brand of political correctness. . . . Cheney's initiatives at the NEH aroused cries of dismay from much of academia, but she stumbled only once, in her effort to pack the advisory panel of the NEH with right-wingers, who lacked the requisite qualifications—especially Carol Iannone. Iannone had gained fame for a *Commentary* article in which she said that giving National Book Awards and Pulitzer Prizes to African-American women writers like Toni Morrison and Alice Walker sacrificed 'the demands of excellence to the democratic dictatorship of mediocrity.' " John Wiener, " 'Hard to Muzzle': The Return of Lynn Cheney," *The Nation,* October 2, 2000, retrieved from http://past.thenation.com/issue/001002/1002wiener.shtml. It seems contradictory, and yet immensely believable, that such language would serve as credentials for defending etiquette in the arts.

16. Murray, "Prole Models," p. A18.

17. I would not want anyone to understand here that I am defending Eminem in this regard. Not only his lyrics, but also his movie (*8 Mile,* directed by Curtis Hanson, 2002) make reprehensible statements about women. In *8 Mile,* white women are seen as trophies for the successful rappers, and black men who fuck white women are severely punished for being out of line and transgressing property boundaries. Objectifying women maintains the propriety of race, class, and heterosexuality. Therefore, though I do believe that Eminem's misogyny needs to be criticized, I also think that censorship is most often simply a more legitimate form of misogyny, not the answer to it. What needs to be asked, then, is why the corporations that distribute such products want to promote such misogyny, what they stand to benefit from it, and why popular audiences are pleased by it—in other words, why it works and what it accomplishes.

18. Murray, "Prole Model," p. A18.

19. Ibid.

20. Ibid.

21. Assistant to George W. Bush administration's Secretary of Defense Donald Rumsfeld in the Ford administration and arms control director and ambassador to the U.N. in the Reagan administration.

22. Kenneth Adelman, "Why Are Europeans Still Fighting Missile Defense?" *Wall Street Journal,* February 6, 2001, p. A18.

23. Murray, "Prole Model," p. A18.

24. Adelman, "Europeans Still Fighting," p. A18.

25. Kevin Whitelaw, Mark Mazzetti, and Richard J. Newman, "Wishing Upon a Star," *U.S. News & World Report,* Nov. 19, 2001.

26. Adelman, "Europeans Still Fighting," p. A18.

27. "The average weekly earnings of the 80 per cent of rank-and-file working Americans, adjusted for inflation, fell by 18 per cent between 1973 and 1995, from $315 a week to $258 per week. At the same time, between 1978 and 1989 the real annual pay of American corporate chief executives (CEOs) increased by 19 per cent, or two-thirds in post-tax terms." Gray, *False Dawn*, p. 114.

28. "According to the Thatcherite understanding of the role of the state, its task was to supply a framework of rules and regulations within which the free market—including, crucially, the labour market—would be self-regulating. In this vision, the role of trade unions as intermediary institutions standing between workers and the market had to be altered and weakened. . . . Partly as a result of these policies, there was an explosive increase in part-time and contract work. Many low-skill workers earned less than the minimum needed to support a family. . . . At the same time, entitlements to welfare benefits were restricted across the board. . . . The fragility and decline of the traditional family increased throughout the Thatcherite period. . . . Still more striking was the growth of an underclass. The percentage of British (non-pensioner) households that are wholly workless—that is, none of whose members is active in the productive economy—increased from 6.5 per cent in 1975 to 16.4 per cent in 1985 and 19.1 per cent in 1994. . . . Between 1992 and 1997 there was a 15 per cent increase in unemployed lone parents. . . . Between 1992 and 1995 Britain's prison population increased by nearly a third (to over 50,000). . . . Thatcherite policies also promoted a striking growth in economic inequality. . . . Since 1977 the proportion of the population with less than half the average income more than trebled. By 1984-5 the richest fifth's share of after-tax income—43 per cent—was higher than at any time after the war." Gray, *False Dawn*, pp. 28–32.

29. Adleman, "Europeans Still Fighting," p. A18.

30. The other topic included on this page is an unsigned editorial called "Progressive Plunder" about how the tax code unfairly targets the rich and how Clinton was unfair in raising taxes for the most wealthy Americans. It never states that the richest 1 percent made significantly more under Clinton than in the Reagan/Bush years, even after the steeper tax schedule. Nor is it stated here who the *Journal* thinks should pay for this missile defense system once taxes on the very wealthy have been lowered.

31. Murray, "Prole Model," p. A18.

32. The Pentagon's budget "a decade after the fall of the Berlin Wall and with no credible enemy in sight—sat at $268 billion during the Clinton years. . . . That's four times more than Russia spends and about eight times more than China." Ken Silverstein, *Private Warriors* (New York: Verso, 2000), p. ix. Then there is the special $112 billion Clinton authorized in 1999 for the

Pentagon over the next six years and the political consensus of the necessity for a missile defense system (even as feasibility tests have failed) and the $400 billion appropriation for three new tactical aircraft programs and the continued expenditure of $2.5 billion per plane on the B-2 bomber—a plane designed to penetrate the air defenses of the Soviet Union, a nation that no longer existed.

33. Upton Sinclair, *Oil!* (Berkeley: University of California Press, 1996), p. 27.

34. Ibid., p. 507.

CHAPTER NINETEEN

Odysseus Lies

THOMAS THORP

Withdrawal

In "The Work of Art in the Age of Mechanical Reproduction," Benjamin wonders whether art is not rendered mute when withdrawn from the culture that gave it voice. The case of oral traditions might seem to be the extreme instance of such a dislocation. Because it is a written text, the very artifact created in an effort to preserve an oral culture's stories and songs can represent the song only by erasing it as an oral performance. And yet what is mute is not illegible. Even in the written representation, the logical outline of a community created by the oral/aural performance marks the text. In the written form that claims to be a repetition, or preservation, the oral logic withdraws, but the traces of that withdrawal are still legible if we can learn to read the acts of human and political representation that are retraced and reformed in the withdrawal. Perhaps the communal binding force that is withdrawn when the performance gives way to the text is preserved at the level of etiquette: a system of imperatives that, mirroring and in a precise sense reversing the force of rational law, bind us to one another at the level of the preliminary, the gestural, the merely preparatory. Perhaps this very opposition between what we are compelled and what we choose to do can be informatively disrupted if we attend to the political logic at work in etiquette.

We are at book 19 of the *Odyssey*. It is Odysseus who speaks. He is in his own home, seated beside his own long-suffering wife, and the man of whom he speaks is Odysseus.

> And so the man is safe,
> as you can see, and he's coming home, soon,
> he's close, close at hand—
> he won't be severed long from kin and country,
> no, not now. I give you my solemn, binding oath.
> (19.345–349)[1]

And yet he lies, of course. Odysseus lies. He lies in order, oddly enough, to invoke a heroic Greek etiquette of hospitality, an ethos ancient even to the pre-Classical Archaic Greeks. It is a heroic etiquette binding—through stunning equivocation—the stranger (*xenos*), who is the guest (*xenos*), to the host (*xenos*), with ties expressed in the currency of gifts (*xenia*), gifts that incur, even as they repay, debts expressed in enduring bonds of friendship, bonds that constitute forms of cohesion at once domestic and political.[2] In their heroic form, as depicted in Homer, these bonds and obligations would have held not between cities but between individual heroes whose guest-friendship obligations could supersede even the imperatives of battle. And yet Odysseus is home from war. So, as I want to show here, Odysseus's Ithaca lies (the lies he tells from the moment of his return) are meant to recall, recollect, and then critically to transform that heroic etiquette into a new form that would make it compatible with the demands of the Archaic Greek city-state. The *Odyssey*, on this view, is a performance whose purpose is to bring about what it describes: the transformation of an etiquette born in representations of piracy and war into an etiquette that could provide the cohesion necessary for the new world of the polis. But even if we locate the *Odyssey* at this transition, and even if we were to adopt, provisionally, the distinction between human bonds that are formal yet equivocal (etiquette) and those that are formally univocal (written law)—a distinction we are working to put into question—why should an archaic political logic located at that transition need to resort to lies?

Repetition

In the first place there is the fact of the return or homecoming—a sort of repetition—and the manner in which this logic of repetition rules out another sort of lie familiar to modern political theory, at least since Locke. Faced with the task of reestablishing order in his own land, Odysseus cannot adopt the naive vocabulary of divine sanction and pristine origins (the preferred lie of, say, Europeans in the New World) precisely because Odysseus's task takes itself to be the reconstitution of a prior order.[3] Or, to put the point polemically, in the archaic political logic at work in Odysseus' return to Ithaca the pernicious self-denying mendacity of appeals to divine or natural origins, of god-given rights and self-evident truths so characteristic of modern political theory, gives way to a different sort of lie.

The modern political theoretical gesture (Rawls, Habermas)[4] is to attribute to the human agents in political discourse a set of rational norms that they "counterfactually" presuppose simply insofar as they plan or plot a political transformation or engage in political discourse. Faced with the need for a radical political/domestic reordering, Odysseus reaches for a lie. And a lie, of course, is not presuppositionless. Indeed this is the critical point. While the lie, too, harbors a logic of presupposition, the logic of the lie does not require the active presupposition of the very same rational norms that it is the purpose of the discourse to discover and test. The logic of the lie does not have to presuppose that the very same rational precepts or rules it is the purpose of political discourse to discover are already actively presupposed to be at work, counterfactually, behind the backs of the participants, who believe that they are debating what counts as a rational precept or rule. Rather, in the logic of the lie, the active presuppositions function not at the same level as the expected outcomes (political norms themselves) but at the level of the preliminaries, let's say at the level of an etiquette of political action. The appeal *of* an etiquette is its appeal *to* a compelling order governing human action, which order is neither merely conventional nor a universal law of nature or human reason.

Representation

The key to employing the notion of an etiquette in the realm of political theory is to note (without embarrassment) that every political affirmation involves an appeal to a prior affirmation. Yet this sort of circularity need not be vicious because it need not presuppose what it claims to justify. The key is to remember that the rationality of human action is not measured in the same way as the rationality of systems (natural or mechanical). This involves not stepping outside of the rationality of systems but supplementing them with the definitive human action: re-presentation. The very idea of human action is that our fundamental political choices might be the result not of a prior and sufficient cause but of our representation of the cause to ourselves as sufficient to warrant action. If the fundamental logic of the political resides not in the cause but in its representation as a compelling and sufficient reason to act, then the rationality of human action rests not on a self-grounding principle but on a self-grounding action: an act of repetition. We repeat or re-present a cause of action to ourselves as a norm or basis for action. In the realm of the human and the political it is always already too late to begin, simply.

Why should this logic of repetition involve an appeal to the logic of the lie? If every originary political moment is a re-presentation, a repetition, it is a repetition in form only since what is being repeated has not yet taken place. What needs to be shown here, in a reading of the Ithaca lies, is that the establishment of political order is a return, a homecoming or repetition; but a homecoming shrouded in the fog of a logic of lies and misrecognition because what the homecoming evokes is not present except in the sense that what has withdrawn leaves an impression. And reading that impression or trace requires a problematic act of re-presentation that borrows not from the logic of rational affirmation, but from the lie.

First Lie

Having been ferried back home by the hospitable Phaeacians—who, by returning strangers home with their swift ships, exemplify the very limit conditions of the etiquette of guest-friendship—Odysseus has been set down, while in a deep sleep, as if in a dream, on the shores of Ithaca. And in the midst of an initial (but on this reading essential) moment of uncertainty in which he cannot recognize his own home, Odysseus begins to lie. He lies first to Athena, who has just lied to him by having disguised herself as "a shepherd boy yet elegant too, with all the gifts that grace the sons of kings" (13.252). In preparation for the important and difficult task ahead, the task of restoring order on Ithaca, Athena has "showered mist over all."[5] A sort of not-knowing is the clear prior condition for the political reordering to be undertaken here. The king will not recognize his home, he will not be recognizable to others and, as if to get the necessary lying underway, he will not recognize Athena. Under these conditions Odysseus first mistakenly curses the hospitable Phaeacians for having dropped him on what he mistakes for foreign soil, then spies the "shepherd boy" and, in the hope of some hospitality, he begins to lie.

The lie Odysseus tells Athena on the beach has important parallels to the later lie—cited above—that Odysseus tells Penelope in their own home. The common elements involve the island of Crete and the Cretan prince Idomeneus.[6] As he will soon repeat twice more, first to Eumaeus, the loyal swineherd, and then to Penelope herself, Odysseus tells the shepherd boy that he is a stranger from Crete.[7] But whereas in the version he relates to the disguised Athena he is a fugitive and a murderer who claims to have killed the son of Idomeneus, in the Penelope version he will claim to be the brother of the same Idomeneus. In fact these complexities multiply, as they do when one lies. In the third version (the lie to Penelope) Odysseus will advance two claims: he will claim to be the brother of Idomeneus, and he will claim that Odysseus is bound in a relation of guest-friendship both to Idomeneus and to the brother of Idomeneus. Yet since it is one and the same Odysseus who claims to be the brother of Idomeneus and who, in speaking the lie, claims that Odysseus is beholden to the brother of Idomeneus then with this lie Odysseus is imposing an obligation of guest-friendship upon himself.[8] Let us briefly examine the course of the three Cretan lies and then return to this odd conclusion.

Why should Odysseus in this first Cretan lie (to Athena disguised as the shepherd boy) claim to have killed the son of the very man, Idomeneus, whose brother he will claim to be in the later version? My suggestion is that when he speaks here to the disguised Athena he is, so far as he knows, not yet home. Or, to be more precise, he cannot be certain that he is safe at home and so his lie appeals, still, to the tribulations and the corresponding virtues of a warrior who has been wronged. This is the etiquette of an imagined Bronze Age warrior in which an act of murder can be the basis of an appeal for hospitality:

> I'm a fugitive now, you see. I killed Idomeneus' son,
> Orsilochus, lightning on his legs, a man who beat
> all runners alive on that long island [Crete]—what a racer!

> He tried to rob me of all the spoil I'd won at Troy,
> the plunder I went to hell and back to capture, true,
> cleaving my way through wars of men and waves at sea—
> and just because I refused to please his father, [Idomeneus]
> serve under *him* at Troy. I led my own command. (13.294–301)

So in this lie he tells while on the beach under Athena's mist of confusion, Odysseus makes himself out to be the murderer of Orsilochus, son of Idomeneus. He claims to have killed Orsilochus in an act of justifiable retribution for an unjust claim made by the boy's father (Idomeneus) over plunder won at Troy. The parallels to the first Book of the *Iliad* are telling.[9] A king with the authority to launch an expedition to join in the sack of Troy and her surrounding cities seems to have made a contestable claim on the spoils of battle won by a courageous and arguably independent prince. All of the questions of authority and of political order raised in Achilles' complaints against Agamemnon are echoed here. Most important, for our purposes, is the fact that insofar as he is not yet home (or fears that he may not be home) Odysseus continues to expect to be welcomed by appealing to an etiquette familiar from the battlefield: the ethos of plunder, murder, and honor depicted in the *Iliad*. Thus he initially appeals to the shepherd boy (Athena) by asserting that he is a legitimate refugee by virtue of being a murderer. Yet as soon as Odysseus learns from Athena that he is in fact home, he will shift the basis of this lie, offering a new Cretan genealogy, one designed to appeal not primarily to the ethos of war and piracy but to recall that ethos precisely in order to modify it in a manner consistent with the demands of homecoming and the requisite restoration of order on Ithaca.

In short, Odysseus's homecoming requires an initial lie, but then in addition and on that established basis, a different lie. These are not simply serial lies, but a layer or structure of mendacity whose aim is to bring about a modification of the etiquette or ethos of war and to address the difficult task of restoring a fractured domestic and political order. Of course to speak of the restoration of order is already to enter into the logic of the lie. If it must be restored then the traditional order cannot be restored since, as a restoration it is already not the original order it might claim to be.[10] The politological claim is that what we are observing here is a restoration that need not pretend to be the mere repetition of, say, the original intent of the founding fathers. Rather, the poet depicts a process that knows itself to be performative precisely to the extent that it takes the form of a re-presentation or restoration. In the *Odyssey* we have the promise of a return to order that takes itself to be a lie. There is something that the lie can accomplish, and that cannot be accomplished simply by the affirmative assertion of a claim to political legitimacy.

After trading lies on the beach, Odysseus and Athena put their cunning minds together to plot this difficult task of a double return: the return of the king must both await and take the form of the return of an order in which he could assume his place as king. This double return replicates the logical aporia that troubles modern political theory: that the justification of a rule requires appealing to a prior, justified, rule.[11] If we resist simply bypassing this problem by invoking natural law or its contemporary cousin, universal normative standards, and if instead we embrace the aporia as constitutive of political rationality, then Odysseus's double return seems somewhat less confounding. Again, he must at one and the same time await and bring about the reordering that would enable him to return as king. He can only return as king if there is an order in which it is possible for him to assume that role, but that role can be reconstituted only if he, the king, first returns and thus restores it. This is the complexity to which the poet first referred when the homecoming was covered in Athena's mists of multiple misrecognition.[12] Their plan is that he must not reveal himself but instead steel himself to undergo further pains and new humiliations; and he will need a new lie.

Second Lie

Halfway between the beach and his home Odysseus takes refuge at the cottage of his loyal swineherd, Eumaeus, to whom he relates the second, newly modified version of the Cretan lie. Despite his lowly circumstances Eumaeus demonstrates a sterling regard for the binding etiquette of hospitality. The clumsy lesson is less domestic than political: even the most humble members of the household can sit and dine alongside kings if they share in the etiquette of kings (and guard their master's property as their own). Odysseus is no less impressed with his loyal

Eumaeus than he had been impressed by the exemplary performance of the Phaeacians. The parallel is important. The Phaeacians are introduced in book 6 as colonists who had fled difficult circumstances to make a new home for themselves at the farthest reaches of the known world. The exquisite quality of their hospitality must be contrasted with the disordered world to which they return Odysseus.[13] The parallel between, on the one hand, the Phaeacians who, as colonists, have preserved the heroic etiquette as the basis for an ideal polis and, on the other hand, the return at the conclusion of the dark ages of certain traditions from the first Ionian colonization is interesting to say the least—even more so since Homer's poetry is Ionian and likely returned to Attic Greece at about the same time as the developing city-states of the mainland were once again facing conflicts over land and were thus in need of new forms of political legitimation that could claim to be venerable and traditional.[14]

If Odysseus represents the re-colonization of a troubled people by their own past—the return of an idea of the heroic to be recast in terms amenable to the economic conditions that brought the mainland out of the dark ages—then it is an important theoretical gesture that Odysseus does not, could not, simply return home. In a place of radical disorder it is necessary to pause and remember the order that would be restored. He pauses for a time at an intermediate point, at the hut of Eumaeus, who, somewhat isolated from the urban disorder, has retained an eye for the obligations and the etiquette of guest-friendship. This suburban setting is critical to the dual purpose of the return. Because the end of the dark age in Greece involved a recovery of agriculture and trade, once fallow lands that had been free for claiming quickly become a source of contention between neighboring cities.[15] The need for political legitimation arose alongside and was in part a direct result of actual disputes over lands claimed by two city-states. At the same time the increase in general wealth and the rise of trade as a new source of wealth in the eighth and seventh centuries produced newly complex contests for power with the traditional landed aristocrats facing opposition from two sides: the newly rich, and a marginalized but landed peasantry.[16] Odysseus's return, then, involves him in the active assertion of a political (not merely a domestic) claim involving disputes with neighboring princes—recall his holdings on the mainland as recounted by Eumaeus—who are now characterized as having forgotten or at least failed in their regard for the traditional etiquette of hospitality and courtship. Eumaeus, again, has not forgotten and thus his hut is the occasion for a transitional lie.

Once Eumaeus's gesture of hospitality had set aside the need for food and drink, it was time for the stranger to give an account of himself. The Eumaeus version of the lie involves a new Cretan genealogy in which, this time, Odysseus would be Castor, the illegitimate son of a wealthy Cretan, who has been deprived of his rightful share of lands by the rich man's "high and mighty sons" (14.238). In the transitional lie Odysseus becomes one of the transitional princes. So, in his lie, he turned his attention to piracy, which he found more agreeable than working land, and became more prosperous than the aristocrats who had shunned him. This newfound prosperity obliged him, when Idomeneus and the people called for it, to help organize the Cretan expedition to Troy. The account of his travails that Odysseus relates to Eumaeus replicates in some important details the story of how Odysseus himself survived shipwreck and was taken in by a hospitable king and then sent home. In the Eumaeus lie, however, what Odysseus had first feared when he awoke on Ithaca is what he claims to have befallen him: that the crew transporting him enslaved him instead, forcing him to escape in rags, only to take refuge here with Eumaeus.

Here at the hut Odysseus meets his son to whom he reveals himself and is from that moment capable of contacting all who will eventually stand beside him in his assault on the suitors. Why then does he continue to lie? An adequate answer to that question would require a politological account of the normative force of the counterfactually asserted "truth" in any lie, an account beyond the scope of this chapter. What can be illustrated here is the critical feature of the normative force of the lie: the fact that with his lies, Odysseus enacts the genesis/restoration of a prior/new political order that takes the form of a self-imposed obligation of etiquette. And it is this seeming contradiction between genesis and restoration that can be pursued directly to the third version of the Cretan lie, the lie he tells Penelope.

Third Lie

To recall, in the third version of the Cretan lie, Odysseus is now the brother of Idomeneus:

> Beside myself Deucalion sired Prince Idomeneus,
> who set sail for Troy in his beaked ships of war,
> escorting Atreus' sons. My own name is Aethon.
> I am the younger-born. (19:205–208)

In the first version of the lie he was the murderer of Idomeneus's son. In the second version he was Castor, the illegitimate son of a wealthy Cretan, who had made his fortune in piracy and joined with Idomeneus as a leader of the Cretan contingent at Troy. In the third version he is the brother of Idomeneus and he is able to make his way into Penelope's heart by proving that he had met Odysseus, a claim made credible by the fact that he is able to describe the cloak and pin that Odysseus was wearing when he left for Troy. Of course to the extent that this identification renders his story credible, it would also seem to prove that he may not have seen Odysseus for twenty years. The stunning accuracy of the cloak and pin description does not support the credibility of his subsequent claim that he had seen Odysseus's treasure, and only just missed seeing the man himself, only days earlier in Thesprotia.[17] What is being achieved in this complex of lies? Why does he continue to lie to Penelope?

The first lie (Athena) had invoked the legendary form of an etiquette depicted as an ethos of war and righteous murder. The second lie (Eumaeus) depicted a transitional passage that mimics Odysseus's own voyage from war to Ithaca. The key to appreciating the politological significance of the third lie (Penelope) is to note what seems to be an unnecessary complication. Given that the critical fact at play here is Odysseus's imminent return, why does he claim to be the brother of Idomeneus and to have met Odysseus, an event that would have occurred twenty years earlier?

As I suggested above, if Odysseus is to reestablish order on Ithaca he must do so without declaring, first, that he is who he is. Rather, he must first establish a minimal order in which it will be possible for him to retake his proper position as king. Only the king can reestablish order (draw the bow), but the king can return, as king, only if there is an order within which he can take that position. The aporia is characteristic of any account of political legitimacy: the original establishment of justice requires a prior idea of justice in terms of which the original act can justify itself. The complication that our man is the brother of Idomeneus is the ideal lie to confront this aporia. When Odysseus had landed on Crete, he had taken refuge from a storm and had, according to this lie, intended to greet the man Idomeneus with whom Odysseus, according to this lie, already had an established relation of guest-friendship:

> He [Odysseus] came into town at once, asking for Idomeneus,
> claiming to be my brother's close, respected friend.
> Too late. Ten or eleven days had already passed since he set sail
>   for Troy in his beaked ships. (19.217–222)[18]

What is established thereby, and what he takes pains to clarify to Penelope, is that as the brother of Idomeneus he had to take Odysseus at his word and treat him as an honored guest:

> So I took Odysseus back to my own house,
> gave him a hero's welcome, treated him in style—
> stores in our palace made for princely entertainment. (19.222–225)

Although the basis of the bond and obligation is a lie, it is only by means of such a lie that Odysseus could manage the task that Athena (and Homer) had set for him: to transform the etiquette of guest-friendship from being the basis of a heroic ethos of warfare into a form that could serve as the basis for political obligations. The legitimacy of political obligations is that they must be both imperative and self-imposed. To say that legitimate political obligations must be imperative simply means that they must carry the weight of legitimate force, they must be binding, enforceable. And yet they must be self-imposed because political legitimacy requires autonomy: the binding force of the law is legitimate political force only if I impose it upon myself.

A law is legitimate when it is an imperative and yet an imperative to which I am able to grant or withhold consent. But if it is truly imperative then how can it be subject to consent? Through what form, the poem is asking, could both of these criteria be met? Its answer is the form of the lie when put to work in an act of political re-presentation. As Odysseus knows better than anyone, if I lie to you what I assert is the truth of my lie. To lie is to assert—as a counterfactually presupposed condition of the lie itself—a minimal prior condition of truth telling. Only if there is a minimal expectation of truth is it then possible to lie. The secret to comprehending the mendacious ground of the archaic political gesture at work in Odysseus's lies is to see that far from imposing upon you (to whom I lie), the fundamental truth of the lie is that through it I impose upon myself.[19] When I lie I am counterfactually asserting a world well ordered enough for there to be trust, because only in such conditions is it possible to lie. A liar as skilled as Odysseus knows that the skillful lie asserts, as a counterfactual transcendental condition, a context of truth within which it is, then, possible to lie. That counterfactually asserted context of truth is the requisite prior order that could make possible the return of an original (king) order. That context is what Odysseus has been developing in the carefully orchestrated series of lies leading from the beach to the hut to his own home. With the three Ithaca lies Odysseus is performing a sophisticated reordering of his world in which, in each successive lie, the counterfactually presupposed level of order is advanced one step. The final lie he tells Penelope completes the cycle of transformation in the moment when, through his lie, he announces, in his own home, that Odysseus owes a debt of hospitality to the man who Odysseus, in the lie, claims to be. Taking advantage of the logic and binding force of an etiquette of hospitality, Odysseus is able to impose a minimal order within his home (oikos/polis) by insisting that he owes an obligation of hospitality to himself and that he must, thus, be received in his own home even if, and precisely because, he is a stranger there. The king must, and cannot, prepare the way for the arrival of the king. In Odysseus's Ithaca lies we are offered an illustration of the establishment of political order that does not evade, but embraces, this defining aporia of political legitimacy.

Notes

1. All *Odyssey* citations are from Homer, *The Odyssey,* trans. Robert Fagles (New York: Viking, 1996); henceforth indicated by book and line number.

2. For a general introduction to the role of guest-friendship in archaic Greece see Oswyn Murray, *Early Greece* (Cambridge, MA: Harvard University Press, 1993), p. 48. A focused study of the practices associated with guest-friendship in Homeric epic poetry is Steve Reece, *The Stranger's Welcome: Oral Theory and the Aesthetics of the Homeric Hospitality Scene* (Ann Arbor: University of Michigan Press, 1993).

3. The Greeks were certainly not averse to inventing and naming founders, men to whom the qualities that personified civic principles could be attributed. If a distinction, then, is to be made between the Archaic Greek and

the modern appeal to political origins it could begin with the difference between naming an individual hero and appealing to a natural or divine origin. The founding hero requires our active devotion to the preservation of his name, whereas the appeal to universal (or divine) laws of nature and reason posits an origin that is, by definition, essentially indifferent to our recognition of it.

4. Equally important from the perspective of contemporary political theory is to resist the facile forms of a postmodernism that set themselves against reason. Those facile postmodernists who declare that all truth is a function of power do more to blunt the real potential of a critical postmodernism than all the neo-Enlightenment critics put together. The politological gesture at work here suggests rather that (contrary to the facile version) there are in fact elements of necessity, transcendental grounds of rational human action, that are not merely arbitrary, but that (contrary to neo-Enlightenment rationalists) these do not take the form of universal, valid, normative principles presumed to govern the very discourse whose task it is to establish those same principles.

5. It is essential to his task, to the reestablishment of a proper and legitimate political and domestic order, that Odysseus not be recognized to be who he is. And this necessity is plainly certified by the poet:

> That very moment
> great Odysseus woke from sleep on native ground at last—
> he'd been away for years—but failed to know the land,
> for the goddess Pallas Athena, Zeus's daughter,
> showered mist over all, so under cover
> she might change his appearance head to foot
> as she told him every peril he'd meet at home—
> keep him from being known by wife, townsmen, friends,
> till the suitors paid the price for all their outrage. (13. 212–220)

6. Idomeneus is the leader of the contingent from Crete, son of Deucalion, who was king of Cnossos and son of Minos (see *Iliad* 2. 735). Furthermore Eumaeus mentions having been taken in by a previous beggar (an Aetolian) peddling a lie that mirrors Odysseus's fabrication: "He'd killed a man, wandered over the face of the earth,/ stumbled onto my hut, and I received him warmly./ He told me he'd seen Odysseus lodged with King Idomeneus down in Crete" (14.430).

7. To Eumaeus (14.228), to Penelope (19.195).

8. In Reece's study of hospitality scenes in the *Odyssey* he notes the objection that these scenes of Odysseus approaching his own home might not be viewed as proper instances of hospitality since "Odysseus is not actually a guest (*xeinos*) in search of a reception at someone else's house but a returning

hero, a master (*'anax*). . . . But while it may be true that Odysseus is in reality the *'anax*, his disguise as a *xeinos* allows a guest-host relationship to develop between him and the suitors." Reece, *Stranger's Welcome*, p. 165. What Reece thereby fails to recognize is the guest-host relationship established between Odysseus and himself, an element of pseudoreflexivity essential to the establishment of political order.

9. "Indeed it is not enough to say that during this period royalty was stripped of its prerogatives in Greece, and that even where it survived it had in fact given way to government by an aristocracy; we must add that the new basileus was no longer the Mycenaean royalty. The kingship had changed not only in name but in character. Neither in mainland Greece nor in Ionia, where a new wave of colonists in flight from the Dorian invasion had begun to settle, is any trace of a royal power of the Mycenaean type to be found. Even if we assume that the independent city-states that joined together in the Ionian League in the sixth century perpetuated an older organization in which local kings acknowledged the overlordship of a dynasty that ruled at Ephesus, its supremacy would be analogous to that exercised by Agamemnon in the *Iliad*, over kings who were his peers and who were subordinated to him only during a campaign conducted jointly under his leadership." Jean-Pierre Vernant, *The Origins of Greek Thought* (Ithaca, NY: Cornell Univeristy Press, 1962), pp. 40–41. More recent scholarship by Snodgrass and Finley, acknowledged and advanced by Polignac, confirms some critical differences between the Homeric descriptions of kingship in the *Odyssey* and what the archaeological record tells us about the political economy of the time. François de Polignac, *Cults, Territory, and the Origins of the Greek City-State*, trans. Janet Lloyd (Chicago: University of Chicago Press, 1995), p. 7. Despite those differences the scholarship also confirms the problematic independence of what Vernant calls the "new" basileus. The problem of reestablishing a political order in the ninth and eighth centuries BC, outlined in Homer's depiction of the homecoming of Odysseus, is not merely a literary invention.

10. Although it is certainly illegitimate to speak in general of "oral cultures" (as if the unity of any culture was its status as not yet literate), it is nonetheless important to note that the transformation of oral traditions into written forms is a material political act. And, if we comprehend the logic of the lie, not its mere intention to deception, we can say that the transformation takes the form of a lie. To preserve the past, unchanged, in a form that we can then appeal to it as a principle of action requires that we change the past (oral to written) while asserting that we have simply preserved it. What constitutional and graphic cultures refer to as freedom doubtless arises at the site of that transformation. Here, randomly almost, is a comment on the politics of the transformation from oral to written form in Icelandic saga: "As sagas were composed from oral tradition I consider them to be formal speech acts. . . . I

believe that the sagas were considered the property of the aristocrats. Only members of the upper stratum would be permitted to write (or dictate) a saga. Their position in society gave them liberty to use traditions in a manner which furthered their own interest. Saga writing was a political act." Knut Odner, "P(th)orguna's testament: A Myth for Moral Contemplation and Social Apathy," in *From Saga to Society: Comparative Approaches to Early Iceland*, ed. Gisli Palsson, (Middlesex, England: Hisarlik Press, 1992); see as well Vernant's classic study of the transition from oral to written logics: Jean-Pierre Vernant, "The Reason of Myth," trans. Janet Lloyd, in *Myth and Society in Ancient Greece* (New York: Zone Books, 1988).

11. Is the establishment of justice just? It must and yet it cannot be; for to claim that the establishment is just is to presuppose a principle of justice at the very moment when it is the determination of that principle that is in question. The solution being traced out here is that every originary political moment must take the form of a repetition or re-presentation of a prior state, albeit one that probably never existed. Convincing contemporary political theorists that this gesture is not vacuous is the task of a forthcoming work.

12. And Odysseus understood the need for duplicity. When he hears of the disorder at his palace (the suitors consuming his wealth and dishonoring the etiquette of courtship), when Athena informs him of the suitors who have abused his home and gone so far as to have plotted to murder his son, the poet has Odysseus reveal the degree of the danger and disorder: "Clearly I might have died the same ignoble death/ as Agamemnon, bled white in my own house too,/ if you had never revealed this to me now, goddess" (13.336–440).

13. The Phaeacians represent, on this reading, the role of the first Ionian colonists who had fled Attica at the onset of the dark ages and who had, arguably, preserved in their songs memories of an age that comes to be re-presented as Heroic. This is just one reason why Odysseus must return in a sleep. For he cannot be who he is when he arrives. He is traveling across time, across epochs. He travels from the ethos of Troy, a time of late Mycenaean Bronze Age heroes, to a new political order characterized by trade, renewed prosperity, and the rise of the polis. The poem is, on this reading, a commentary on the political circumstances at about the time of the Homeric composition in the late eighth century. So the logic of the temporal sequence is not linear. It is a dream logic. Odysseus's return (he is delivered, as if in a dream) invokes what Freud would call a dream work or dream logic in which the recounting or repetition of the content of the dream becomes, itself, a formative document in the dreamer's life, quite apart from its validity as a report of an actual dream. See Sigmund Freud, *Die Traumdeutung*, in *Gesammelte Werke*, vol. 2 (Frankfurt am Main: Fischer, 1999). Finally, back on Ithaca, it is the Phaeacian culture that seems to have been a dream, or a colony that had escaped the disorder of the collapsing Mycenaean palace centers, and that can now contribute to the

reordering of its own prior homeland, a reverse colonization that mimics precisely the return from Ionia of preserved prearchaic traditions, not the least of which would have been these songs about the Trojan war and about the homecomings themselves.

14. For a beautifully argued summary of the view that Homer was Ionian see Paolo Vivante, *Homer* (New Haven: Yale University Press, 1985). On the reestablishment of once severed contacts between mainland and islands (some of which were colonies from the earliest Ionian colonization) see A. M. Snodgrass, *The Dark Age of Greece* (New York: Routledge, 2000). On the question of appeals to traditional or ancient foundations as a basis for new claims to political legitimacy in the eighth and seventh centuries see the introductory essay by Jean-Pierre Vernant to the collection he edited, *La mort, les morts dans les sociétés anciennes* (Cambridge: Cambridge University Press, 1988), and in the same collection, A. M. Snodgrass, "The Archaeology of the Hero."

15. François de Polignac, *Cults, Territory, and the Origins of the Greek City-State*, trans. Janet Lloyd (Chicago: University of Chicago Press, 1995), p. 38.

16. Snodgrass, *The Dark Age of Greece*, pp. 390–394. Oswyn Murray, *Early Greece* (Cambridge, MA: Harvard University Press, 1993).

17. Odysseus recycles here several details from the Eumaeus lie, details involving Thesprotia, and a near meeting with Odysseus, who happened to have left just a day before to go from Thesprotia to Dodona for the purpose of consulting Zeus as to how best to make the final stage of his journey; compare 19.340 and 14.370.

18. This being one of three times when, were Odysseus all the people he claims to be in his lies, he would have just missed bumping into himself. Imagine the meeting on Crete between Castor (Odysseus in the Eumaeus lie), Idomeneus, Idomeneus's brother Aethon (Odysseus in the Penelope lie), Idomeneus's son Orsilochus, and the unnamed stranger who killed Orsilochus (Odysseus in the Athena lie) had Odysseus only arrived in Crete ten days earlier.

19. Kant is the first and perhaps the last philosopher to comprehend this fundamental quality of the lie. He sets it forth in the *Groundwork of the Metaphysics of Morals* in preparation for a discussion of autonomy. See Immanuel Kant, *Grundlegung zur Metaphysik der Sitten* (Hamburg: Felix Meiner Verlag, 1994).

CHAPTER TWENTY

Take Clothes, For Example

Hazel E. Barnes

William James believed that we have the genesis of ethics if there are two loving souls together on a rock. Etiquette can even dispense with the loving; all that it requires is coexistence. Can you imagine a time when etiquette had not yet been invented? It seems always to have been there. Yet etiquette cannot be reduced to a description of how things are done at given times and places, for it carries an imperative of sorts. Granted, its imperatives are hypothetical, not categorical, though frequently the stakes are so high as to be virtually compelling. Some people might claim that etiquette is concerned primarily with the superficial forms of daily life. I should say rather that it gives form to life. The work of etiquette is to socialize the self. As such it is often inextricably tied to other socializers—laws, ethics, and aesthetics. Like the others, it reveals the values, beliefs, and presuppositions of the particular society from which it springs. But it has its own distinguishing characteristics; it is not purely ancillary. To start with, etiquette makes overt display of what, at least traditionally, proponents of ethical systems, natural law, and aesthetics have mostly sought to hide: its rules are not universal, its mutability, both as to place and to time, is flagrant; its sole foundation is prevalent public opinion. So how does it work, since it offers no rational justification and is not supported by a police force?

Etymologically, English "etiquette" and "ticket" are related. Cognates in other Indo-European languages bring the connection still closer. French *étiquette* and Spanish *etiqueta* can both be used to refer not only to conventional rules for approved behavior, but to a ticket or a label. "Ticket" suggests the idea of admission, the privilege of joining a particular collection of persons. Indeed, etiquette is inseparably linked with conformity. "Label" is more ambivalent. Its purpose is to separate one thing or type of things from others. And part of the function of etiquette is precisely to distinguish—as in the protocol for seating at state dinners. In all areas of etiquette we find this interplay between sameness and difference. Etiquette provides for the individual's need to belong to a group, but to this group rather than to that group; also it allows for limited self-expression within a group. There may be cases of wholesale rejection of all etiquette, though these, if not pathological, are likely to be temporary, most often indicating a revolt against the requirements of a particular code in favor of a new one. Etiquette seems to stand midway between ethics (and laws) and aesthetics—restraint on the one side, creativity on the other. We can more clearly see its connection with both, and its distinctive way of socializing the self, if we look at one specific area. Take clothes, for example.

My reasons for choosing clothes? They are the most universal and the most particularized. They exhibit the extreme of mutability. To coopt an ancient Greek poet, "Quick as the flick of a butterfly's wing / Is the change that fashion brings."[1] Clothes proclaim loudly the given society's values and prejudices—both overt and hidden. They demonstrate the paradoxical quality of etiquette. Clothes are designed to conceal and to reveal. They are a means of self-display—but display to others. Sometimes clothes are determined by the most serious of deeply held beliefs. But they are allied also to the artistic impulse and to the spirit of play.

Most basically, I suppose, clothes have been worn to give warmth, to protect the skin, and to indicate sex differentiation—or to conceal it, which is in itself an indication. Only this last enters into the Adam and Eve story; significantly, it appears in tandem with the need to make distinction between right and wrong. The first couple adopted a unisex solution with the fig leaf. One wonders how long it took them to discover more colorful and varied coverings, and whether Adam insisted that Eve's be different from his. And on those first cold nights outside the Garden, did they so much as glimpse the ethical implications of putting on furs and feathers? Enough of that. The biblical tale is not universal. But the link between clothes and morality is significant. Sex differentiation has continued to transform the etiquette of clothes into legal and political issues. Out of the host of available examples, I select two of the most glaring.

First, I point to the dress code imposed upon women in Moslem countries.[2] In its extreme form this requires the all-covering capelike *abaya*, or chador, and burka (a facial mask). In Iran, where I encountered the legally enforced code, which applied also to foreigners, a head scarf and covering for the arms and legs were essential. Iranian women wore an ankle-length shapeless coat. We Western women (I was attending an international philosophy conference) skirted the edge of the law with long sleeves and slacks. There was no escaping the head scarf, which we had to wear everywhere outside our hotel rooms. Supposedly the dress code was founded on the religious teaching of Mohammed and the Koran, and I am sure that many men and women believed that this custom was in accordance with God's will. In truth, of course, it was based on the belief that sexual relations were unacceptable outside of marriage and that every precaution must be taken to guard against any temptation on the part of men to desire them. That all of this was motivated by the male wish to possess one woman (or more in earlier times) exclusively and to dominate all women does not alter the situation. Religions are human inventions, and for centuries it has been primarily men who have defined the human. This is not to say that all Moslem women resent the dress restrictions. One Iranian woman whom I met told me that in a country where sexual permissiveness was not allowed, the code protected them. At universities in Turkey, some women adopted the head scarf, against regulations, in order to affirm their rights as Moslems. Someone might object that here I have abandoned etiquette and put myself on another level, but my point is to show how all but inextricable etiquette and religion and ethics are, even in the apparently most superficial matter of clothing.

Returning to my stay in Iran, I noticed a particularly interesting phenomenon. Conformity was law, and I observed that especially at formal and official events, when the women wore chiefly black, it was difficult to recognize immediately even those with whom I was personally acquainted. At other times the desire of each one to distinguish herself was manifest. Head scarves showed amazing variety in colors and patterns. The long garments worn on everyday occasions varied widely in materials (ranging from coarse synthetic to silk and velvet) and were of different colors, though always darker ones. It was etiquette, not religion or law, which dictated black for special occasions and allowed some degree of personal choice the rest of the time. Ethical considerations and regard for the demands of etiquette were mixed in my own reactions and those of others in our small minority of women scholars. It was fear of the law that kept our head scarves on our heads in public situations. A few of us debated whether we ought not to remove the scarves during the conference meetings when we gave our papers—as a feminist protest. What deterred us was the feeling that to do so would create a problem for our hosts, who were showing us the utmost in hospitality, and that we would be guilty of an embarrassing breach of good taste as guests. We were uncomfortable, psychologically as well as physically, but etiquette won out over ethics.

My second example is familiar: the never articulated presumptions underlying the history of fashion in Europe and America from the medieval period till sometime in the last century. Whatever the prevailing style may have been for men and for women, one rule remained steadfast. The sharp differentiation between their apparel was directly related to society's view of their respective role and function. Men, whether they displayed a well-shaped leg or confined it in trousers, wore clothing suited for ease of movement and action, for doing things. Women, especially among the upper classes, wore all that would keep them on the pedestal on which they were perched, adorned and adored, though not necessarily comfortable. Eventually an active, independent woman who had achieved celebrity status (a George Sand) dared to wear pants, evoking scandal but not legal prosecution. As Simone de Beauvoir remarked, it is not easy to determine whether the choice of early feminists to dress like men was to claim equal rights or simply because masculine clothing allowed greater freedom and convenience. Today's adoption of unisex styles is an obvious reaction against clothes as a proclamation of sexual difference—if not a denial of it, then at least a rejection of it as primary. Today's feminists have made so much of the connection between clothes and women's status that I need not belabor the point.

Clothes are linked to religion and law in instances where sex is not the issue. One example comes from Jewish history. Henry Claman has described how the adoption of distinctive clothing was sometimes a gesture of pride and sometimes a degrading label.[3] From biblical times on, Jewish men were expected to wear certain fringed garments, and this was an affirmation of their faith. In the eighth century some Moslem countries required both Jews and Christians to wear a special kind of garment and a badge. Illustrations in a Jewish book of ritual (about 1300) picture Jews wearing conical hats of a kind that appears elsewhere in Christian art representing Jews. Apparently the hat was originally adopted by the Jews themselves, but when the Fourth Lateran Council (1216) demanded that Jews and Saracens of both sexes wear clothing to prevent their ever being mistaken as Christians, there was considerable resentment on the part of Jews, who rightly regarded the law as a humiliation. We all know the ultimate outcome—the infamous yellow star that the Nazis imposed on Jews.

I turn to the brighter aspects of clothes etiquette as related to ticketing and labeling. There is no reason, for instance, to view negatively the nuns' habits and priestly robes prescribed by the Catholic Church—though it is significant that in twentieth-century United States, the rules for nuns' dress were greatly modified as the church began to lay more stress on service to the world rather than retreat from it. In the secular sphere, dress etiquette serves primarily to indicate function or to mark occasions. More than anything else it makes for convenience. How much needless bother there would be if you could not at quick glance distinguish a waiter from a customer, an airline attendant from a passenger, a policeman from a bystander! Such formal designations are so necessary that they almost fall outside the realm of etiquette, which comes into play more obviously apropos of occasions. The hostess at a formal dinner would not expect a hospital nurse to arrive in her uniform, nor a football player (even a famous one) in his. The notion that clothing must be appropriate to a specific social situation, even when no special activity is involved, is not immediately apparent. I can think of many psychological factors that might be operative in the example I chose. Our hostess might feel that an offender was trying to become the focus of attention. Or that it was an intrusion of the workplace into a private situation. Or that the guest did not find the dinner important enough to take the trouble of changing. But beneath all this is the assumption that social relations can function effectively only when all agree to conform to their established patterns and that the imposition of some sort of rules is intrinsically good. To fail to do so is to challenge the presuppositions we have tacitly agreed to live by and to suggest, disturbingly, that they might be questioned.

It is noteworthy that rebels against a particular society use clothes to express their rejection of the old and their embrace of the new. Conformity is still required but has changed its style. The gray uniform put on the Chinese by the Maoists is an extreme example. A more interesting and longer lasting one is our own social revolution in the middle of the last century, which came about without authoritarian decree. The Beats, the civil rights marchers, the anti-Vietnam protesters, the hippies, and so on all adopted hair styles and clothes quite different from the usual. Contempt for the established etiquette was shown by the fact that jeans, chosen for their association with manual workers, were often worn dirty, patched, or deliberately torn. Paradoxically, there were two quite different consequences. Among some young people conformity to one fashion in dress was replaced by another, and difference was accentuated. I remember one impecunious graduate student refusing the gift of a tailored suit for her teenage daughter because the girl would not wear "straight clothes." You can still find shops which offer only countercultural apparel. More significantly, just as the new generation's movement succeeded in improving the rights of minorities, of women, of people with disabilities, so its fashions gradually came to be close to worldwide, adapted and modified but still recognizable. Charles Reich, in *The Greening of America*, took denim jeans as a symbol of the liberating force that he thought was opening the way for a new and improved way of life. Reich's optimistic hopes are far from having been fully realized. He was right in foreseeing that change in prevailing fashions reflected the higher value placed on comfort and the blurring of class distinctions.

Aesthetics and the etiquette of clothes are so closely connected that they considerably overlap, without conflicting. Both are concerned with the creation and the imposition of form, texture, and color for their own sake. In terms of survival, they are not among our prime necessities; both contribute to making life worth the struggle to survive. Creativity and the spirit of play are dominant. Admittedly, there are graver connections between clothes and economics—not to mention such things as consumerism, conspicuous consumption, and snobbishness. But the designing, making, and wearing of particular clothing can be a legitimate source of aesthetic delight, both for the wearer and for the beholder. Under special circumstances, it represents, in fact, a conscious artistic production, whether in a film or at a wedding. Even on the everyday level, clothes may be a minor but enriching pleasure, just as one may experience a genuine joy facing a natural sunset, one that is on a lesser scale but still commensurable to the response evoked by a Turner.

Clothes are a self-presentation, and it is in this aspect that we find their imbrication with the rules of etiquette to be most evident. Here also we see, quintessentially, the interaction of the duo, conformity and distinction. My choice of dress is decided by the kind of image I want to be mirrored in the appraising looks of others—of particular others or of any others I may happen to meet. (*Which* others is one of the factors involved in my choice.) Unless my intention is to defy convention, I will move freely between certain limits of expectation. I will not wear a bikini to a funeral or a clown costume at an academic meeting. Nor anywhere, outside a costume party, the dress an ancestress wore in the 1920s. But beyond this minimum, the acceptable possibilities are infinite. One person may seek conformity to prevailing style so ardently as to try to be mirrored solely as one of the crowd, taking to the absurd the counsel of Alexander Pope, "Be not the first by whom the new are tried, / Nor yet the last to lay the old aside."[4] Someone else will try to excel by ushering in what is expected to become standard. Some want above all to find clothes that set off advantageously their particular figures and coloring; others are content that the garment looks good on the rack. There are those who prefer clothes that clearly proclaim what they cost. And so on forever.

The vagaries of fashion stand at the opposite extreme from ethics. The latter traditionally is required to ground itself on what is taken to be unshakable principles. The ethical person acts and judges by what the person authentically—that is, inwardly—believes to be true or right objectively, or as close to objectively as is humanly possible. The etiquette of clothes embraces transience and is based squarely on the importance of eliciting a desired response in others. But before dismissing it as trivial, unnecessary, as something we would be better off without, we should look more closely. As one form of socializing the self, the etiquette of clothes is more than a restriction and regulation of our spontaneous impulses. It is, to be sure, a means by which the collective inscribes its beliefs and values. It provides, too, a way by which individuals may choose how they wish to project themselves into the group that receives them. Dressing for others is also self-expression. It is even a self-definition. Nonhuman animals cannot change their guise so as to reflect outwardly what they want others to see in them. True, we are dealing only with appearance. But Hegel reminded us that the appearance is real as an appearance. And it is meaningful. It is a communication. "You can't be vulgar alone," said Sartre. You can't be attractive alone either, or seductive or threatening. You can't even be yourself all by yourself.

Ritual, I suppose, is where the etiquette of clothes is most closely connected with aesthetics. I often hear people explain that while they don't accept all of the doctrine of the Catholic Church, they feel spiritually moved by its ceremonies—by the music, the impressive cathedral setting, the very form of what is said and done. Surely another factor is the robes of the clergy. Beautiful in themselves, they suggest a different world from the one outside. Here, paradoxically, clothes represent not mutability but continuity. The same is true of a college commencement, though the academic regalia seem to be more obviously a ticket of admission for the undergraduates and a label of achievement for the faculty and the administration.

Since clothes are revelatory of a zeitgeist, I may remark briefly on what the etiquette of fashion reveals about our own. I am thinking particularly of the scene in the United States now—although increasing globalization is a characteristic of style in our time. I could understand it if someone were to say that we might describe the present situation as either one of total freedom or sheer chaos and that perhaps these are two sides of a coin. I myself would point to greater emphasis on permissiveness, individualism, and the spirit of play. The permissiveness is seen first of all in allowance for physical comfort. Corsets and celluloid collars have been forgotten. Stilt heels are visible but no longer de rigueur. Running shoes go everywhere, regardless of what is worn above them. The difference between formal and informal wear remains, but the informal has won out for most occasions. An amusing innovation is dress-down Fridays. This custom was adopted in the name of allowing one day a week for greater ease and individualism. Reportedly, however, the problem of just what constitutes dress down complicates things to the point that some men long for the security of suits and ties. The tyranny of fashion has not disappeared. Even jeans must be skintight or baggy according to what the particular season calls for. At the same time self-expression has been given greater scope. The most obvious instance is T-shirts with slogans that may express loyalty to someone or something, or the wearer's personal opinion, or exhortations ranging from "Save the Whales" to something obscene.

Especially interesting is the matter of sex differentiation. Though dresses on men are limited mostly to transvestites, women wear not only clothes that resemble men's styles, but apparel designed for men—if it fits. Yet, paradoxically, we have the miniskirt—not, by the way, a style notable for its convenience. Brief skirts are designed to reveal. The charge has been made that they make women into sex objects in an age when liberated women have revolted against being considered as such. Of course, we could look at them another way. One of the demands of feminists is that women should enjoy sexual freedom, including the right to make overtures instead of just responding to them. Perhaps the scant skirt is an acknowledgment that the privilege has been won. In any case, women who reject them, whether out of modesty or for personal aesthetic reasons, are free to wear their dresses ankle length, with or without a revealing split in the material.

The relation between sex and the etiquette of clothes is not often a source of serious conflict here and now. Ethical problems arise in other contexts. I think of two examples. The most obvious is the issue of furs. If animal rights activists have their way, the desirability of laws prohibiting the wearing of fur may soon become the subject of public dispute. I cannot even imagine the consequences of the next logical step, the proscribing of leather. Even now a person might weigh carefully, and for several reasons, the etiquette of putting on a fur coat to go to a meeting of conservationists. A different sort of debate is the one concerning school uniforms. Proponents urge that it would support democracy among the students; those opposed hold such insistence on conformity to be one more example of the growing suppression of individualism. Both sides claim that the adoption of uniforms would diminish (or increase) the expense and be more convenient for parents.

The spirit of play in clothes etiquette is not new, of course. We have only to think of the macaronis, the dandies, the followers of Oscar Wilde. Still, I think that the idea of having fun with clothes has taken on more appeal. It is shown by the simple absurdity of some designs and by the calculated juxtaposition of colors and patterns that conventional aesthetics has usually forbidden. We see it in the deliberate reversal of the original utilitarian purpose of an item of clothing; for example, in the youthful habit of wearing baseball hats backward. Our unparalleled affluent and leisured society has made more room for play in many areas. With respect to clothes even the poor can join in the game.

When two of King Lear's daughters threatened to take away his honor guard of retainers, arguing that he did not need them, the King exclaimed, "O. Reason not the need!"

> Allow not nature more than nature needs,
> Man's life is cheap as beast's. Thou art a lady:
> If only to go warm were gorgeous,
> Why, nature needs not what thou gorgeous wear'st,
> Which scarcely keeps thee warm. (act 2, scene 4)

In the changing fashions of clothes we see especially clearly the blend of pure gratuity and the ongoing definition of what we want human life to look like that is the hallmark of any and all etiquettes.

Notes

1. Freely adapted from Simonides (556–478 BCE.), who wrote of change as such (metastasis).

2. Iranian regulations called for modest clothing for males also, but they were noticeably not enforced.

3. For this paragraph I am indebted to Henry N. Claman, *Jewish Images in the Christian Church: Art as the Mirror of the Jewish-Christian Conflict 200–1250 C.E.* (Macon, GA: Mercer University Press, 2000), pp. 121–126.

4. Alexander Pope, "An Essay on Criticism," lines 335–336.

Contributors

Hazel E. Barnes is distinguished professor emerita of philosophy at the University of Colorado and the author of works in philosophy and classics. Her books include a translation of Sartre's *Being and Nothingness*; *An Existentialist Ethics*; *Sartre and Flaubert*; *Sartre*; *The Meddling Gods: Four Essays on Classical Themes*; and an autobiography, *The Story I Tell Myself: A Venture in Existentialist Autobiography.*

Alison Leigh Brown is professor of philosophy in the Humanities, Arts, and Religion Department at Northern Arizona University. Her most recent book is *On Foucault: A Critical Introduction* (Wadsworth).

Tina Chanter is professor of philosophy at DePaul University. She is the author of *Ethics of Eros: Irigaray's Rereading of the Philosophers* (Routledge, 1995); *Time, Death, and the Feminine: Levinas with Heidegger* (Stanford University Press, 2001); and *Abjection: Film and the Constitutive Nature of Difference* (Indiana University Press, forthcoming). She is the editor of *Feminist Interpretations of Emmanuel Levinas* (Penn State Press, 2001), and of the Gender Theory series published by State University of New York Press.

Michael D. Colberg is a practicing attorney and clinical social worker involved with adoption rights issues for same-sex parents. He lives in New York with his daughter and his partner.

Robin Truth Goodman is assistant professor of English at Florida State University. She is author of *Infertilities: Exploring Fictions of Barren Bodies* and coauthor, with Kenneth J. Saltman, of *Strangelove: Or How We Learn to Stop Worrying and Love the Market.*

Trent H. Hamann is an assistant professor in the Department of Philosophy and Honors Program at St. John's University in Queens, New York. He has written and published essays on a range of topics, including the politics of ethical comportment, subjectivity as a heterotopic site, philosophy and the postmodern city, and film. He is currently working on a book called *Foucault and the Art of Impolitics.*

Hildegard Hoeller is associate professor of English at the College of Staten Island, CUNY. She is the author of *Edith Wharton's Dialogue with Realism and Sentimental Fiction* (University of Florida Press, 2000) and coauthor, with Rebecca Brittenham, of *Key Words for Academic Writers* (Longman, 2004). She specializes in nineteenth- and twentieth-century American literature. Her articles have appeared in journals such as *American Literary Realism, American Transcendental Quarterly, Dreiser Studies, South Caroline Quarterly, Edith Wharton Review, Research in African Literatures,* and others.

bell hooks is the author of more than twenty books for adults and children, including *Ain't I a Woman* and *Teaching Community: A Pedagogy of Hope.* She is currently distinguished professor at Berea College in Berea, Kentucky.

Don Hanlon Johnson is director of the somatics graduate program at the California Institute of Integral Studies and a former Rolf practitioner. He is the author of *Body, Spirit, and Democracy* and *Bone, Breath, and Gesture.*

Lynne d Johnson is a writer, cultural critic, and educator. She was most recently published in *Da Capo Best Music Writing 2004.* Her core teaching currently focuses on racial and ethnic relations in a course entitled The Sociology of Group Behavior at the Metropolitan College of New York.

David Farrell Krell is a professor of philosophy at DePaul University. He is the author of eight scholarly books and two works of fiction—*Nietzsche: A Novel* and *Son of Spirit: A Novel.*

Kevin MacDonald teaches philosophy at the Fashion Institute of Technology in New York City.

Karmen MacKendrick is associate professor of philosophy at LeMoyne College in Syracuse, New York. She is the author of books on the body and aesthetics.

Nickolas Pappas is associate professor of philosophy at City College and the Graduate Center, City University of New York. He is the author of *The Routledge Guidebook to Plato and* The Republic, now in its second edition; *The Nietzsche Disappointment*; and articles on topics in ancient philosophy, nineteenth-century philosophy, and aesthetics.

Mark S. Roberts teaches in the Philosophy Department at the University at Stony Brook. He is coeditor of *High Culture: Reflections on Addiction and Modernity.*

Kenneth J. Saltman is associate professor of social and cultural studies in education at DePaul University. He is author of *Collateral Damage: Corporatizing Public Schools—A Threat to Democracy.* He is also coauthor, with Robin Truth Goodman, of *Strangelove: Or How We Learn to Stop Worrying and Love the Market* and *Education as Enforcement.*

Ron Scapp is professor of humanities and teacher education at the College of Mount Saint Vincent in the Bronx, where he is also chair of the Philosophy Department. His books include *Teaching Values: Critical Perspectives on Education, Politics, and Culture*, and he is coeditor, with Brian Seitz, of the series *Hot Topics: Contemporary Philosophy and Culture*, published by State University of New York Press.

Brian Schroeder is associate professor of philosophy and coordinator of Religious Studies at the Rochester Institute of Technology. He is the author of *Altered Ground: Levinas, History, and Violence*; coauthor, with Sylvia Benso, of *Pensare ambientalista: Tra filosofia e ecologia*; coeditor, with Lissa McCullough, of *Thinking Through the Death of God: A Critical Companion to Altizer* (State University of New York Press, forthcoming); and *Contemporary Italian Philosophy: At the Threshold of Ethics, Politics and Religion* (forthcoming).

Brian Seitz is associate professor of philosophy at Babson College. He is the author of *The Trace of Representation*, coauthor of *Politology: The Athenians* *and the Iroquois*, and coeditor of the series *Hot Topics: Contemporary Philosophy and Culture*, published by State University of New York Press.

Thomas Thorp is associate professor of philosophy at Saint Xavier University in Chicago. He is coauthor of *Politology: The Athenians and the Iroquois.* His published essays attempt to draw Continental political theory (Habermas, Derrida) into conversation with ancient Greek sources.

Jeff Weinstein was an arts and popular culture critic and editor at the *Village Voice* for more than seventeen years, was fine arts editor and staff writer at the *Philadelphia Inquirer* and is currently arts and culture editor at *Bloomberg News*. He is author of *Life in San Diego* (a novella) and *Learning to Eat*, both published by Sun & Moon Press. He has written for the *New Yorker, Artforum, Art in America*, and many other publications. His short story "A Jean-Marie Cookbook," reprinted in *Contemporary American Fiction*, was awarded a Pushcart Prize.

Shannon Winnubst is associate professor of philosophy and a member of the feminist studies program at Southwestern University in Georgetown, Texas. Writing about subjects such as vampires and drugs, she works in the intersections of twentieth-century French philosophy and feminist, race, and queer theory.

Index